To date the study of T. S. Eliot's development has traditionally posed one major obstacle: the problem of connecting the periods before and after his religious conversion. What does the young aesthetic revolutionary and author of *The Waste Land* have to do with the later champion of Christian orthodoxy? Faced with this problem, scholarly inquiry has for the most part agreed that a radical rupture took place in 1927, as Eliot's skepticism was overcome in one leap of faith. Such a view, however, obscures the history of Eliot's political commitment – which was in fact of longer standing and more deeply seated than has previously been acknowledged. In *T. S. Eliot and Ideology*, Kenneth Asher argues instead for a strongly continuous Eliot, an Eliot whose work from beginning to end was shaped by a vision inherited from a French reactionary tradition that culminated with Charles Maurras. Asher demonstrates how this ideology provides the intellectual framework for Eliot's literary essays, for his writing on culture and society, for his poetry and drama. Inviting fresh readings of such works as *The Waste Land, Four Quartets, Murder in the Cathedral,* and *The Cocktail Party,* Asher's approach portrays in a new light not only Eliot's version of literary history and literary theory, but also his plans for social reorganization. He further demonstrates the influence of Eliot's ideology on the New Critics, through whose agency Eliot's impact on the study of literature extended well into the middle decades of the twentieth century.

CAMBRIDGE STUDIES IN AMERICAN LITERATURE AND CULTURE 86

T. S. ELIOT AND IDEOLOGY

CAMBRIDGE STUDIES IN AMERICAN LITERATURE AND CULTURE

Editor

ERIC SUNDQUIST, *University of California, Los Angeles*

Founding Editor

ALBERT GELPI, *Stanford University*

Advisory Board

NINA BAYM, *University of Illinois, Champaign-Urbana*
SACVAN BERCOVITCH, *Harvard University*
ALBERT GELPI, *Stanford University*
MYRA JEHLEN, *University of Pennsylvania*
CAROLYN PORTER, *University of California, Berkeley*
ROBERT STEPTO, *Yale University*
TONY TANNER, *King's College, Cambridge University*

Books in the series

85. Robert Milder, *Reimagining Thoreau*
84. Blanche H. Gelfant, *Literary Reckonings: A Cross-Cultural Triptych*
83. Robert Tilton, *The Pocahontas Narrative in Antebellum America*
82. Joan Burbick, *The Language of Health and the Culture of Nationalism in Nineteenth-Century America*
81. Rena Fraden, *Blueprints for a Black Federal Theatre, 1935–1939*
80. Ed Folsom, *Walt Whitman's Native Representations*
79. Alan Filreis, *Modernism from Right to Left*
78. Michael E. Staub, *Voices of Persuasion: The Politics of Representation in 1930s America*
77. Katherine Kearns, *Robert Frost and a Poetics of Appetite*
76. Peter Halter, *The Revolution in the Visual Arts and the Poetry of William Carlos Williams*
75. Barry Ahearn, *William Carlos Williams and Alterity: The Early Poetry*
74. Linda A. Kinnahan, *Poetics of the Feminine: Authority and Literary Tradition in William Carlos Williams, Mina Loy, Denise Levertov, and Kathleen Fraser*
73. Bernard Rosenthal, *Salem Story: Reading the Witch Trials of 1692*
72. Jon Lance Bacon, *Flannery O'Connor and Cold War Culture*
71. Nathaniel Mackey, *Discrepant Engagement: Dissonance, Cross-Culturality and Experimental Writing*
70. David M. Robinson, *Emerson and the Conduct of Life*
69. Cary Wolfe, *The Limits of American Literary Ideology in Pound and Emerson*
68. Andrew Levy, *The Culture and Commerce of the American Short Story*
67. Stephen Fredman, *The Grounding of American Poetry: Charles Olson and the Emersonian Tradition*
66. David Wyatt, *Out of the Sixties: Storytelling and the Vietnam Generation*

Continued on pages following the Index

T. S. ELIOT AND IDEOLOGY

KENNETH ASHER

State University of New York
Geneseo

CAMBRIDGE
UNIVERSITY PRESS

PUBLISHED BY THE PRESS SYNDICATE OF THE UNIVERSITY OF CAMBRIDGE
The Pitt Building, Trumpington Street, Cambridge CB2 1RP

CAMBRIDGE UNIVERSITY PRESS
The Edinburgh Building, Cambridge CB2 2RU, United Kingdom
40 West 20th Street, New York, NY 10011-4211, USA
10 Stamford Road, Oakleigh, Melbourne 3166, Australia

First published 1995
First paperback edition 1998

Printed in the United States of America

Library of Congress Cataloging-in-Publication Data is available.

A catalog record for this book is available from the British Library.

ISBN 0-521-45284-8 hardback
ISBN 0-521-62760-5 paperback

For Evelyn

CONTENTS

═══════

Acknowledgments *page* ix

Introduction 1
1 Historical Background 11
2 The French Connection 35
3 Orthodoxy and Heresy 60
4 Architect of a Christian Order 84
5 Visions and Revisions 109
6 Eliot and the New Criticism 133
Conclusion 160

Notes 167
Index 191

ACKNOWLEDGMENTS

I would like especially to thank Francesco Binni for his encouragement and advice on this project from its inception. It would not have been possible without him. I owe an enormous debt of gratitude also to James Longenbach for his scrupulous reading of the manuscript and generous help throughout. Kenneth Deutsch led me to sharpen my conception of ideology. And finally, I owe a particular debt to Eugene Stelzig, who in this, as in so many other instances, has been a supporter and invaluable critic. Permission to quote from the following works of Eliot has been granted by Faber and Faber Limited and by Harcourt, Brace, and Company: *Collected Poems 1909–1962*, *Four Quartets*, *Murder in the Cathedral*, and *The Cocktail Party*. Parts of this book have appeared in altered form in the journals *ELH* and *Essays in Literature*. I would like to thank the editors for their permission to reprint this material.

INTRODUCTION

The past decade has seen Eliot's reputation recede to its lowest ebb of the century. The postmodern attack on the pillars of modernism has managed at times to spare Virginia Woolf for her blurring of traditional gender roles, Joyce for his delight in sheer wordplay, and even, in critical tours de force, the unlikely pair of Pound and Lewis on the shaky basis of their disruptive styles.[1] Eliot, however, as the primary spokesman and symbol of that against which literary postmodernism has defined itself – modernist high culture – has been refused almost all amnesty. His claim to establish enduring criteria of value was, to pose the complaint in the language of these antagonists, a futile attempt to legitimate his narrative by reference to a metadiscourse.[2] Further, as one of the progenitors of the New Criticism, the primary theoretical whipping boy of deconstruction, he has been systematically indicted on the related charge of being a particularly unabashed advocate of "logocentrism." Indeed, he seems at times to have been doubly annoying to such critics precisely because he is so obviously self-indicting. Deconstructive techniques are hardly necessary to lay bare the implications of lines such as these:

> And the light shone in darkness and
>   Against the Word the unstilled world still whirled
>   About the centre of the silent Word.
> ("Ash-Wednesday," V)

Superbly confident in his blindness, he lacked even the glimmer of insight that might have led him to encode his epistemological bad faith.

The case against an elitist, absolutist Eliot has been carried on most recently in the name of a multiculturalism that takes issue sharply with him as the chief modern apologist for a hereditary canon of Western literary classics. A growing cultural diversity in England and even

more obviously in the United States, coupled with the perceived
need to amplify the voices of long-standing marginalized groups,
made Eliot's insistence on the tradition seem an obvious exercise in
oppression. No one seemed to remember or, if they remembered,
to care that Eliot had immersed himself in Buddhist literature and
philosophy during his Harvard years: he learned Sanscrit, read the
sacred writings of the Buddhists, worked his way through the philosophy with James Haughton Woods, and took a final year-long
course from Masaharu Anesaki. As it turned out, it was a cultural
diffidence rather than a cultural disdain that caused him in the end
to leave Buddhism for less exotic studies: he came to realize that as
an outsider he could never know in his bones what it felt like to be
a Buddhist. Moreover, even the most cursory glance at Eliot's appraisal of the English canon reveals that he was aggressively revisionary. The Romantics were radically devalued; Dryden was advanced
at the expense of Milton; Donne and the Metaphysicals were given
a sudden centrality; *Hamlet,* arguably the most indisputable of canonized texts in the English tradition, was criticized for failing to provide an "objective correlative" of Hamlet's grief: Shakespeare,
unable to cope with his material, had overreached himself. While it
is true that Eliot pushed this version of the canon with insistence –
at his worst with an arrogant high-handedness – the complaint that
he was the provincial and rigid champion of a received body of wisdom is essentially groundless.

   The one merit of these cases against Eliot, misguided and over-
stated as they often are, is that they at least are open to the idea that
extraliterary concerns might have shaped his work in ways generally
unacknowledged previously. Typically, almost all attempts to place
the work of Eliot in a larger intellectual context have looked to the
poetic tradition. In his immediate past, affinities are found with La-
forgue, Baudelaire, and various other French symbolists; earlier, with
the Metaphysicals, whom he revived, or with Dante, whom he regarded as Christian Europe's culmination. His critical writings are
taken to be epiphenomenal of the poetry (Eliot himself, late in life,
said they were no more than this), colored perhaps by his ambivalent
relationship to Matthew Arnold's essays on poetry and culture. But
such studies, even when valuable, as they often are, tend to obscure
what I perceive to be the thoroughgoing nature of Eliot's political
commitment.

   Simply put, it seems to me that from beginning to end, Eliot's
work, including both the poetry and the prose, was shaped by a

political vision inherited from French reactionary thinkers, especially from Charles Maurras. Even in the few excellent studies that deal with the political dimension of Eliot, his profound indebtedness to this larger tradition is given little more than passing notice, and certainly not presented as the major force in his intellectual life.[3] The failure of most other scholarship to acknowledge the centrality of Eliot's political agenda is not surprising since Eliot himself tended to camouflage it prior to his famous pronouncement of 1928 in which he declared himself to be a "classicist in literature, royalist in politics, and anglo-catholic in religion" (if we substitute Catholic for Anglo-Catholic, this is a verbatim echo, *fifteen* years later, of the *Nouvelle Revue Française*'s accurate description of Maurras's beliefs) and even afterward was less than straightforward about its dominating influence on his thought. Before 1928 he tended to portray himself as one dedicated to a poetic revolution; after 1928, as one dedicated to a religious restoration.

The cultural engineering implied by all this moves us toward the "ideology" of my title. Dauntingly, the term itself has been used in such a wide variety of frequently incompatible ways over its nearly two-century history that one of the most valuable recent studies of the subject has despairingly described the dissensus as "a dialogue of the deaf."[4] While it would seem therefore to be virtually impossible to establish any definition that could pretend to encompass this range of usage, it should nonetheless be possible to at least identify the major axes of the debate and with care to locate a position in relation to them.

Let me then try to establish one such axis by contrasting the classic account of Marx with that of Karl Mannheim. According to Marx's well-known conception, ideology consists of mutually supporting ideas and beliefs that, though derived from a contingent set of economic conditions, nonetheless present themselves "as the only rational, universally valid ones."[5] Ideology in this sense serves as the tool of the ruling class to legitimize the arrangements from which it derives its privilege, and thus for Marx is an instrument of power in the interest of the oppressor. So powerful, in fact, is the seductive nature of ideology that according to an 1893 letter of Engels to Mehring, it takes in even its creators:

Ideology is a process accomplished by the so-called thinker consciously, it is true, but with false consciousness. The real motive forces impelling him remain unknown to him; otherwise it

would simply not be an ideological process. Hence he imagines
false or seeming motive forces. Because it is a process of thought
he derives its form as well as its content from pure thought,
either his own or that of his predecessors.[6]

This false consciousness involves self-delusion in a double sense: in
addition to being unaware of their own motivations, the ideologues
are ultimately deluded about the march of history, that essential
truth that Marx and Engels claimed to know with certainty. On this
view, then, ideology is a collective mystification that Marx's scientific
analysis seeks to expose.

The Marxist historicizing of ideas provided a starting point for
Mannheim in his landmark contribution to the literature of ideology, *Ideology and Utopia* (1929). While openly acknowledging his
debt, Mannheim nevertheless took issue with Marx's notion of ideology at what had always been its most vulnerable point: the difficulty
in demonstrating how Marx's own theory had attained an Olympian
status above the march of history. Pointing to the undeniable fact
that Marxism itself had evolved since the master's death, Mannheim
– in a move perhaps itself inevitable – historicized the historicizer in
claiming that Marx's insights were themselves as much a product of
social conditions as those he criticized. Mannheim concludes, consistent with this observation, that there are *no* objective values,
merely norms accepted and abandoned by succeeding societies:
"There is, then, no norm which can lay claim to formal validity and
which can be abstracted as a constant universal formal element from
its historically changing content."[7] The resultant study of ideology,
which Mannheim refers to as "the sociology of knowledge," endeavors "to understand the narrowness of each individual point of
view and the interplay between these distinctive attitudes in the
whole social process."[8] Mannheim thus abandons the Marxist criterion of truth; instead he speaks of ideas in terms of their congruity
with the existing social order.[9]

Although Mannheim's position avoids both the logical problem
that shadowed Marx's account and also the Manichaean rigidity that
often characterized its practical application, he cannot free himself
from the thoroughgoing relativism implicit in his absorption of philosophy in sociology. He finds himself ultimately trapped in what
Clifford Geertz has called "Mannheim's Paradox": he would speak
from the objective perspective of the scientist while denying that
such a perspective is available.[10] Aware of the problem, Mannheim

tried to rescue his stance by labeling it "relationism," but this was essentially a distinction without a difference.

In the wake of poststructuralism with its fundamental aversion to referential theories of truth, the bulk of recent ideological readings of literature have adopted versions of Mannheim's sociology of knowledge – and have been burdened with the attendant "paradox." It is difficult to see, for example, how one can simultaneously subscribe to an ethical and epistemological relativism and still vent moral outrage on those who have discriminated on the basis of race, gender, or class. And, of course, the converse – moral approbation – is equally inappropriate. In this regard even as scrupulous and fairminded a critic of literature in terms of its ideology as Sacvan Bercovitch cannot completely disentangle himself from Mannheim's dilemma. On the one hand, he acknowledges the necessary partiality of his own view:

> And lest I seem to have exempted myself from that [ideological] process, I would like to declare the principles of my own ideological dependence. I hold these truths to be self-evident: that there is no escape from ideology; that so long as human beings remain political animals they will always be bounded in some degree by consensus; and that so long as they are symbol-making animals they will always seek in some way to persuade themselves (and others) that *their* symbology is the last, best hope of mankind.[11]

But, on the other hand, a few pages later he invokes transhistorical values in praising Whitman and Emerson: "What they did see, when they plumbed the emotional and conceptual ground of the rhetoric, was profound, humane, and exhilarating, a set of beliefs and promises which may rank among the most liberating, most energizing ideas produced by any culture, past or present."[12] In the end, though, to label the problem "Mannheim's Paradox" is to suggest a false novelty, for it is really just an instance of the age-old problem of maintaining a coherent relativism, something revealed at least as early as Plato's dismantling of the Protagorean doctrine in the *Theaetetus*.

But even if one is to move toward a middle ground, away from the extreme positions of Marx and Mannheim, and hold open the possibility of attaining to significant truths without insisting that one is irrefragably in possession of them, the situation does not substantially improve. It requires only the reflection of an instant to ascertain that anything that might tentatively qualify as ideology must be made up of assertions some of which are true, some of which are false. We might reasonably enough claim that the more false claims an ideology makes, the more likely it is to be pernicious, but this does not help us with a basic definition. This being the case, it seems best to abandon the criterion of truth as something that will offer much help in identifying ideology. When I speak, then, of Eliot's ideology, I am making no claim about the truth or falsity of the positions he holds nor am I claiming that he was deluded because he might have considered them true.

Mention of delusion returns us to the notion of "false consciousness," which entailed, besides a misreading of historical reality, a blindness to personal motivation on the part of those who profited from and propagated an ideology. Marx and Engels, however, don't always faithfully adhere to this view of "false consciousness." At times they imply something more like a conscious conspiracy on the part of the ruling class, and this confusion in their own position about the degree of awareness in the ideologues themselves establishes the points along which stretch the second major axis in the debate over ideology.[13] The line of debate here may appear partly obliterated since it seems safe to say that among contemporary sophisticated Marxists, few feel comfortable with the starkness of the position that Engels enunciates.[14] Born in the attempt to sort out historical materialism from the *freischwebend* consciousness of German idealism, an idealism that according to Marx and Engels legitimated in turn the false bourgeois glorification of autonomous individualism, their case is driven toward the opposite extreme: an automatism in which ideas are "reflexes" of the material conditions of life.[15]

Yet a variety of this position enjoys much currency in the less rigid form of Foucault's theory of discourse. Owing as much to a reading of Nietzsche as to Marx, Foucault posits, as is widely known, a web of cultural practices that enmesh all who live within it as it empowers or marginalizes behavior and shapes consciousness accordingly. So helpless is the individual in the toils of discourse that Foucault – how rhetorically is not always easy to determine – announces "the death of man," the demise of the self. But the problem that bedeviled Mannheim returns to haunt Foucault. How can an "archaeologist" of culture as Foucault fashions himself pretend to the scientific analysis this term would suggest while simultaneously relativizing all knowledge. Further, his work is shot through with a tone of moral disapproval, but if there are no freely choosing selves, who are the objects of his implied censure or the moral agents who might bring about change? Neither Foucault nor those who adopted his concept of discourse have provided satisfactory answers.

At the opposite extreme we can place Lenin, who regarded ideology as a weapon of manipulation in class warfare, the more consciously used the better. And because he was willing to consider the proletarian agenda an ideology (albeit in the service of historical truth), he openly admitted to wielding it to advantage himself. With this in mind, he labeled the Communist Party "the conscious avant-garde."

Now although one would certainly not want to link Eliot with Lenin in almost any other regard, they do both share this belief in the ability of a highly conscious elite to shape a culture for the masses. Moreover, they have a common source in Georges Sorel, who, much like Ernst Jünger in Germany, showed the strange ability to appeal to both the left and right.[16] Equally impatient with the decadence of modern society and timeserving politicians who did no more than pander and tinker, Sorel called for a cleansing revolution that would bring about a new "way of life." In his most influential work, *Reflections on Violence* (1908), a book read by both Lenin and Eliot, Sorel insisted that this apocalyptic vision could be realized only if the masses could be galvanized with "myths." These myths are symbolic representations of deeply felt needs to change the world: "The myths are not descriptions of things, but expressions of a determination to act."[17] Emotionally self-referential, they are thus impervious to external falsification. This characteristic in combination with a myth's profound – and primarily irrational – ability to unite and mobilize a community of believers allows Sorel to compare modern revolutionary myths with religion.

Eliot's attention was directed to Sorel, most likely by T. E. Hulme, who translated *Reflections* in 1916 and provided an introductory essay in which he lauded Sorel's distaste for liberal optimism as evidence in support of his own obsession with Original Sin, the metaphysical basis for his – and with his help, Eliot's – classicism.[18] Eliot reviewed Hulme's translation, and ten years later when he supplied the readers of the *Criterion* with six essential texts of the modern classical mind, he listed, along with works by Maurras and others, Sorel's *Reflections* and the posthumously gathered writings of Hulme, *Speculations*, which includes the essay on Sorel.[19]

While rejecting Sorel's call to violence (and here is where Eliot and Lenin part company radically), Eliot is obviously much impressed with Sorel's conception of myth as an indispensable tool for the renewal of a society. Following Sorel's lead, he typically refers to communism in the pages of the *Criterion* as a masterfully crafted naturalistic myth and underlines the need for those on the right to create a powerful countermyth.[20] And it is in these terms that Eliot thinks of his own project: a classical, later Christian, revival. Where he differs importantly from Sorel, however, showing in this respect a greater debt to the French reactionary tradition, is in the conviction that his myth is based on the natural order of things. The dimly articulate feelings of the mass respond to the myth, but for Eliot and the right they cannot be its source or justification. Not only, then, will the myth be shaped from above, but as he learns from Maurras especially, this inevitably entails certain concealments and displacements. It is, then, as a conscious manipulator of myth taken in its politicized Sorelian sense that I consider Eliot an ideologue, a working definition that has at the very least the advantage of growing out of Eliot's own understanding of what he was doing.

With this definition in mind, a brief overview of Eliot's ideological commitment would run as follows. As a young man he adopts from Charles Maurras and the long tradition of French reactionary thought an advocacy of "classicism." This term, in France, embraced the whole range of antagonisms to the Revolution of 1789 and was commonly understood to do so. It aligned one against romanticism (believed to be the spiritual sickness that spawned the Revolution), democracy, and Protestantism. This opposition was organized in behalf of the Latin tradition in literature, as well as royalism, Catholicism, and a rigidly hierarchical social organization culminating in hereditary aristocracy. In Maurras's version this was colored by suspicion of the Teuton and hostility toward the Jew, the first only marginally participating in Latin culture, the second parasitic upon it. Maurras articulated this position eloquently and ushered it into the new century in a copious outpouring of books, articles, and pamphlets on a range of topics: literary criticism, political theory, religion, economics, and comparative culture. What I propose to argue is that the Maurrasien inheritance provided Eliot with a dominant intellectual framework that he retained throughout his life. This is not to say that no change occurred over a career that spanned half a century; after Maurras's condemnation by the Vatican in 1926, Eliot worked feverishly to realign the component parts of this ideology, subordinating everything to religion. But as he wrote to Paul Elmer More in 1936, "I am very happy you like the essay on Religion and Literature . . . I think that what appears to another person to be a change of attitude and even a recantation of former views must often appear to the author himself rather as part of a continuous and more or less consistent development."[21] It is this continuity in Eliot's thought that I will be stressing.

What is constant, too, is that the political dimension that was the focal point of the Maurrasien compound is advanced almost always sub rosa in Eliot. Early in his career Eliot presented classicism to an English audience as nearly exclusively a literary preference, something easy enough to do given general ignorance of the term's full implication in France. His unwillingness to be more open was due in large part to the fact that he himself – a more scrupulous thinker than Maurras in general – was unsure exactly how the politics, religion, and literature necessarily entailed one another. This difficulty was exacerbated by the fact that he was trying to impose classicism on a traditionally Protestant country (a problem registered in his later reference to Anglicanism as Anglo-Catholicism). Immediately upon the Vatican's condemnation of Maurras for valuing Catholicism primarily for its political function, Eliot began taking religious instruction in the Anglican faith and was accepted into the communion the following year. Thereafter, though he fought the same antagonists, he engaged them in the name of the Christian commonwealth. Politics led Eliot to religion but he rarely acknowledged the political element that constituted a central part of what he understood – and in his writings intended – by his religion.

The main purpose of my book is not, however, to indict Eliot on the charge of being an ideologue, but to show how that ideology shaped his literary essays, his writing on culture and society, and his poetry and drama. With regard to the poetry and drama this will yield readings that shift the focal point of works such as *The Waste Land, Four Quartets, Murder in the Cathedral,* and *The Cocktail Party.* Because the connecting link among his various works, both prose and poetry, is ideological – hence obscured – this unity, extending over time and subject matter, has gone almost totally unremarked. The problem of detecting this ideology in the generations he so deeply influenced is even greater, for typically his admirers embraced his work in the terms offered. It is an awfully long jump, for example, from Wimsatt's essay "The Affective Fallacy" back to the French counterrevolutionary animus against the Romantic cult of personality personified in the individualism and emotionalism of the demonized Rousseau. Yet it is this sort of connection that I believe to be essential and will be endeavoring to draw in discussing Eliot's impress on the twentieth century.

Thus, although I have learned a great deal from such excellent recent studies of Eliot and modernism as Michael Levenson's *A Genealogy of Modernism,* Sanford Schwartz's *The Matrix of Modernism,* Louis Menand's *Discovering Modernism,* and James Longenbach's *Modernist Poetics of History,* it is with the more specifically political treatment of Eliot that I would place my own work. The line of such scholarship begins with John Harrison's roughly sketched *The Reactionaries* (1967), reaches a much higher level of sophistication in William Chace's *The Political Identities of Ezra Pound and T. S. Eliot,* and builds successfully on Chace's work in Michael North's *The Political Aesthetic of Yeats, Eliot, and Pound.* This last especially, in its placing of Eliot in a broader European perspective, I have found most congenial to what I have attempted to do. Profitable, too, have been Jeffrey Herf's *Reactionary Modernism* (1984) and Russell Berman's *The Rise of the Modern German Novel* (1986), both of which, though they deal with German modernism, have taught me to see ways in which politics intersects with literary culture.

Chapter 1 of my book traces the evolution of French reactionary thought from Joseph de Maistre up to Charles Maurras. Chapter 2 follows Eliot from his contact with these ideas up through the early years of his editorship of the *Criterion* and the writing of *The Waste Land* to the time of Maurras's condemnation and his own conversion. The attempt to recast the classicism–romanticism debate in religious terms – orthodoxy versus heresy – is the subject of Chapter 3. Chapter 4 deals with Eliot's attempt to project a new society based on his ideology, seen most clearly in *The Idea of a Christian Society* and *Notes Towards the Definition of Culture.* The *Four Quartets* I treat as a companion piece, the poetic expression of Eliot's highly politicized religious vision. In Chapter 5 I move to the end of Eliot's career, first dealing with the chilling play *The Cocktail Party,* Eliot's major attempt to reach a mass audience with his notion of a Christian order; I then look at the late essays, reading them as attempts to downplay any evidence of a political element in his corpus as he fashions a view of himself for posterity as poet and man of God. Chapter 6 is devoted to the emergence of the New Criticism and what it owes to Eliot's ideology in terms of literary history and theory.

1

HISTORICAL BACKGROUND

In his justly admired work *Interpreting the French Revolution* (1978), François Furet claimed that the Revolution had at last passed into history: it had finally settled into the French past as an event, still endlessly discussable, but no longer a galvanizing political issue. His judgment was amply borne out by the innocuous pageantry of the recent bicentennial celebration and the fact that the French government did not think it at all odd to invite Margaret Thatcher and George Bush, nor did the two leading conservatives of the Western world think it inappropriate to attend. Yet some of those in attendance would have remembered a time when the Revolution still had the power to organize European politics in radically divisive ways. Mussolini had spoken openly of the Fascist revolution as an attempt to undo the damage of the French one, an analysis that was absorbed by Franco and Hitler, for whom the immediate threat of Marxism was merely the logical extension of what had been unleashed in 1789. In France, the Vichy government portrayed itself not as collaborationist, but as representative of traditional French values overturned by the Revolution. The homely virtues inscribed on Petain's banner "Travail, famille, patrie" were clearly intended as a rebuttal to the promiscuously flamboyant "Liberté, égalité, fraternité" of the revolutionaries. In turn, the *épuration* that followed Vichy's collapse found historical precedent in the bloody purge of royalists more than 150 years before.[1] The most compelling of modern French counterrevolutionary thinkers, Charles Maurras, spent his last years imprisoned as a traitor, in somber imitation of those he had spent his life trying to resurrect.

Nor were these twentieth-century events merely a sudden recrudescence of old passions. For more than a century and a half after the National Assembly of 1789 first organized itself into left wing and right wing, the French Revolution served as Europe's most accurate ideological litmus test. When Hippolyte Taine insisted that "the essential thing is the idea we hold of the principles of 1789,"[2] all of the politically conscious nineteenth century would have quickly agreed. To take a stand on these principles was to take a stand on modern, liberal society itself, for the Revolution declared on behalf of liberty in place of feudal ties, on behalf of equality in place of hierarchy and inherited social status, and on behalf of civic fraternity in place of the narrower bonds of religion or privilege. Of course, liberals were generally embarrassed by the excesses after 1791 and preferred to speak of two (or more) revolutions or concede that practice betrayed principle, but they thereby kept their allegiance to the informing ideas of the Revolution intact.[3] Mankind's shackles were being shed even if this regrettably had caused the amputation of some limbs. Thus assured, they saw the Revolution as caused by the human spirit's steady progress toward the telos of enlightenment. The conservative reaction, on the other hand, was from the beginning a more complicated one. Unlike the liberals, conservatives had no difficulty explaining the Reign of Terror – repugnant principles bred repugnant results – but because they saw the Revolution as a *disruption* in history, they rendered the question of causation extremely problematic. Why had natural law been temporarily abrogated? The issue was a burdensome one and nowhere more so than in France, where the conservatives could maintain with most plausibility that all the modern ills of their country were directly traceable to the Revolution. In fact, it would be no exaggeration to say that the French Right defines itself essentially by its explanations for the Revolution.

The most compelling of the early responses and one that, in its apocalyptic vision, set the tone for much of what followed was that of the Catholic apologist Joseph de Maistre. In sharp reaction to the rationalistic optimism of the revolutionaries, Maistre begins by positing a much bleaker view of man as a creature indelibly and deeply tainted with Original Sin. Far more than just a nod in the direction of Catholic orthodoxy, Maistre's insistence on man's fallen nature is the cornerstone of all his political and ethical speculations. Indeed, so deeply does this awareness of man's corruption color Maistre's imagination that it will occasionally bubble over in ghoulish, Bosch-like passages. Maistre portrays the savage, almost completely devoid of nobility, as a murderous yahoo:

> While the son kills his father to preserve him from the bothers of old age, his wife destroys in her womb the fruit of their brutal

lust to escape the fatigues of suckling it. He tears out the bloody hair of his living enemy; he slits him open and roasts him and eats him while singing; if he comes across strong liquor, he drinks it to drunkenness, to fever, to death, equally deprived of the reason which rules men through fear and the instinct which saves animals through aversion.[4]

That "civilized" man does not follow the daily habits of his moral ancestor is due almost exclusively to the vast network of institutional restraints erected over time. Obedience is guaranteed by the fear of reprisal as represented by the executioner, whom Maistre honors in his most notorious passage:

> A dismal signal is given; a minor judicial official comes to his house to warn him that he is needed; he leaves; he arrives at some public place packed with a dense and throbbing crowd. A poisoner, a parricide, or a blasphemer is thrown to him; he seizes him, he stretches him on the ground, he ties him to a horizontal cross, he raises it up: then a dreadful silence falls, and nothing can be heard except the crack of bones breaking under the crossbar and the howls of the victim. He unfastens him; he carries him to a wheel: the shattered limbs interweave with the spokes; the head falls; the hair stands on end, and the mouth, open like a furnace, gives out spasmodically only a few blood-spattered words calling for death to come. He is finished: his heart flutters, but it is with joy; he congratulates himself, he says sincerely, *No one can break men on the wheel better than I.* He steps down; he stretches out his blood-stained hand, and justice throws into it from a distance a few pieces of gold . . . God receives him in his temples and permits him to pray.[5]

Essentially a voluntarist, Maistre regarded reason as an ancillary faculty incapable of effecting any lasting change for the better in our situation. Our failure was one of faith and obedience, not understanding – we were never meant to understand. Much as Nietzsche and Dostoevsky would argue later in the century, reason served merely as the agent of our desires, desires that for Maistre were almost uniformly perverse. Thus, it should be obvious that the benevolent clear-sightedness presupposed by the architects of radical change is simply not available to us nor, even if it were, would the mass of men be able to make the necessary quantum leap forward in moral compliance. Enlightenment meliorists whose speculations were taken up by the Revolution were thus blind to the fact of both our necessarily tenebrous intelligence and our incorrigible will. It would be hard to imagine hubris with any less justification. Yet according to Maistre, even more serious than the revolutionaries' misreading of the future was their misreading of the past. It is precisely because of our inherent frailty that God has interceded in human affairs to ordain institutions; history reflects, then, not just the continuous will of humankind, but that of God himself.[6] Granted, man being an imperfect agent of the divine will, revelation may manifest itself stutteringly, yet nine hundred years of throne and altar in France make the general plan clear enough. For the Revolution to sever this tradition is, therefore, not merely political folly, but sacrilege, and it is as such that Maistre denounces it to his receptive audience of fellow émigrés: "There is a *satanic* element in the French Revolution which distinguishes it from any other revolution known or perhaps that will be known."[7]

Beyond just serving a psychological need in his audience, Maistre's underscoring of the malevolent *singularity* of the Revolution is intended to defend the conservative case at its weakest point. Because the conservatives ratify their position by pointing to history, an obvious ally when it slow-footedly bore along medieval institutions, what happens when history turns against them? Specifically, if history is the unfolding of God's will, why isn't the Revolution to be included? To find an answer, Maistre is pushed in a direction where he was perhaps heading in any event: toward a mythic reading of events. The temptation to revolution is regarded as a divine test and one that the French have failed miserably. Thus, the Revolution comes to be treated as something akin to the Fall. It *changes* history but in its uniqueness stands *outside* history. It is nothing less than the explosion of pure Evil in time: "What distinguishes the French Revolution and what makes it an event unique in history is that it is radically *evil;* no element of good relieves the picture it presents; it reaches the highest point of corruption ever known; it is pure impurity."[8] The biblical analogy can be pressed further, for to Maistre the easy euphoria promised Adam and Eve through knowledge is recapitulated in the meretricious appeal of the Enlightenment. The French forfeited the Eden of authoritarian institutions in grasping for a rule of Reason. And the author of the mischief, the intruder into the Garden – the serpent – is the Swiss Jean-Jacques Rousseau from Protestant Geneva. Through the cunning of his specious logic,

Rousseau caused the French to forget that human community was the result of obedience of the will and not a matter of individual *contract,* rationally assented to. For Maistre, Rousseau's notion of a pure democracy, much like evil for Augustine, cannot exist; it is merely the negation of the good: "I can define democracy as *an association of men without sovereignty*"[9] – a psychological, and hence political, impossibility.

This identification of Rousseau as the source of the Revolution became a staple of French conservative thought, both because there was some justification for the theory and because it allowed conservatives to show that if the Revolution wasn't, strictly speaking, unnatural, it was at least un-French. And insofar as counterrevolutionary thought identified the alien element as arid rationality, it was able to borrow ideas and momentum from the simultaneously developing Romantic movement, which shared its anti-Enlightenment animus, if not always its political orientation. Beyond the distrust of the Goddess Reason, common to both were the emphasis on organicism, mystical adulation of the national genius, and nostalgia for a lost medieval unity. Thus, Maistre's analysis of the Revolution, flowing into the more general Romantic reaction to the eighteenth century, remained virtually unchanged as the position of the Right well into mid-century.

Included within Maistre's organicist speculations was a theory of language that was to profoundly influence Eliot's classicism as he learned it from Maurras. Words, Maistre argues, are not ad hoc creations of mankind invented as the need arises to communicate, but are rather repositories of divine wisdom accreting connotation through human experience.[10] And because God has revealed himself most fully through the Roman Catholic Church, Latin and the Romance languages that evolved naturally from it enjoy a special status. The Latin inheritance constitutes, then, the grand linguistic tradition that takes its place alongside the institutions of church and throne as divinely sanctioned. To jettison a word and substitute a neologism is to break a bond with God and mirrors in its own sphere other more obvious forms of rebellion. Thus, Maistre's own beautifully crafted French, far from being a mere indulgence in rhetorical embellishment, was nothing less than an act of faith. In this regard he saw himself in stark opposition to the revolutionaries. It was perfectly consistent, he believed, that those who toppled kings, scoffed at the church, and marked their ascension as *L'An un,* would enjoy basking in months with names like *Thermidor.* Degenerate language

signals a degenerate age: an observation that makes possible the po-
liticizing of aesthetics, the aestheticizing of politics.

The counterrevolutionary position remained almost wholly the
creation of Maistre until a surprising ally appeared in the person of
the inveterate liberal Ernest Renan. As a young man, Renan had
been among the most gifted seminarians at St. Sulpice, destined for
what promised to be an illustrious ecclesiastical career. Yet just before taking holy orders, he confides to his sister, "Je ne crois pas
assez," and surprises everyone by turning away from the church.
Under the influence of the new German exegesis of the Bible –
perhaps the cause of his own waning faith – he produces the naturalistic *Vie de Jésus* (1862), in which he presents Jesus as the most
gifted in a long line of prophets, but, like the Old Testament figures
who preceded him, purely mortal. The book raced through numerous printings and, needless to say, immediately became anathema to
traditional French Catholics. (Renan's account of Jesus as "un
homme incomparable" ended up costing him his academic position.) Moreover, Renan's questioning of church doctrine was mirrored in both the larger political and cultural spheres, where he had
been a supporter of the revolution of 1848 and, more generally –
rejecting the pessimism of Original Sin – a firm believer in human
salvation through science. By the 1860s his writings, taken as a whole
by an unsympathetic observer, might have confirmed beyond the
slightest doubt Maistre's description of the hydra-like aspect of liberalism.

However, in a volte-face nearly as shocking as his refusal of holy
orders, Renan, badly shaken by the humiliating French defeat in the
Franco–Prussian war of 1870, the appearance of the Paris Commune, and the subsequent loss of Alsace-Lorraine, abandoned his
republican stance and threw his weight behind the conservative explanation for France's maladies.[11] In words that could have been
spoken by Maistre, Renan discovered in the execution of Louis XVI
a national self-mutilation from which the French still suffered: "The
day when France cut off the head of her king, she committed a
suicide."[12] Only because republicans are obsessed with the power
wielded by authority do they fail to recognize that "originally civilization was an aristocratic creation, the creation of a very small number."[13] Even supposedly democratic Athens was, in effect, controlled
by a handful of nobles, Renan now contends. Unfortunately, these
truths have been lost on the French, in marked contrast to the recently victorious Prussians whose success was made possible because

they were well aware of the necessity of hierarchy and discipline. Their "quasi-feudal" society thus showed itself the true heir to the ancien régime, Renan believed, and should stand as a model for French regeneration.

Up to this point, apart from the Germanophilia, Renan's Tacitean admonition to the flaccid Latins broke little new ground. Yet tucked away within the staple arguments were two additions that were to become salient features in Maurras's vigorous counterrevolutionary polemics. First, in addition to the by now familiar charge against Rousseau of inspiring the revolutionaries to create a constitution a priori, Renan sees Jean-Jacques's rampant individualism as preparation for the gross materialism of the bourgeoisie, whose orgy of self-indulgence allowed the more civic-minded and duty-bound Prussians to prevail. Collective greatness has been bartered for petty pleasures through the introduction of a toxic foreign element. While Renan does not offer anything even vaguely approaching a sophisticated economic analysis, he is sure that this alien money-making spirit has eroded the French's traditional loyalties. Almost inevitably this suggestion of economic parasitism and absence of ancestral allegiances would attract the strong French undercurrent of anti-Semitism, culminating in the Dreyfus affair, though nothing could have been further from the intention of the man who held the chair of Semitic languages at the Collège de France.

Renan's attack on the Revolution's implication with bourgeois liberalism resembles – minus the detailed analysis of capitalism – Marx's, though, of course, Renan's communitarian desires cause him to look backward to feudalism, Marx's forward to communism. Further, because Renan and Marx owe a common debt to Feuerbach's "unmasking" of religion's supernatural assumptions, they are similarly aware of the use of otherworldly doctrine to justify the political and social status quo. Again, though, their reactions differ: Marx calls for a cleansing atheism; Renan insists that faith must be maintained in order that people accept "their duties as children of God."[14] Christianity is necessary, though not necessarily true: "One may be a royalist without accepting divine right, just as one may be a Catholic without believing in the infallibility of the Pope, Christian without believing in the supernatural and the divinity of Jesus Christ."[15]

And this essentially Machiavellian regard for religion introduces the second new, and in this case subversive, element into the reactionary store of ideas. Maistre had insisted that "every conceivable institution either rests on a religous idea or it is ephemeral" and

quite clearly believed that the truth of the ideas was precisely what
guaranteed the endurance of the institutions. In contrast, what Renan's hard-headed appraisal of religion's usefulness does is to create
for the first time a space in the conservative camp for nonbelievers.
A politically motivated Catholicism, with minimum coloration, could
now swell the ranks of militant true believers not strong enough to
be more scrupulous. Yet this skeptical importation from the left, the
faithless faith of the erstwhile liberal, would later come close to de-
stroying the French Right under the leadership of Charles Maurras.

The defeat of 1870 and the specter of the Commune made another surprising convert from liberalism in Hippolyte Taine, who
had been an unwavering enthusiast of the popular cause ever since
the 1848 revolution.[16] More deeply disillusioned than Renan because formerly more committed, the man who had once defended
the *sans-culottes* against Carlyle's attack responded to the recent turn
of events with a mammoth multivolume indictment of the French
Revolution as the source of the recent debacle: *Les Origines de la
France contemporaine* (1876–93). Those who liberated the Bastille, ancestors of the Communards, now appeared to Taine as "the dregs
of society," mere "bandits." But Taine reserves the bulk of his opprobrium for those who set the masses in motion, the Jacobins.
While the *Origines* demonstrated the scrupulous scholarship for
which Taine was justly renowned, it is jarringly interspersed with a
series of outraged blasts against the Jacobins – "born out of social
decomposition like mushrooms out of compost"[17] – unmatched
since Maistre. The biological metaphors of romanticism have now
been completely absorbed in Taine and are played off against the
inflexible, rectilinear social planning of the Revolution:

> Nothing could be more adverse to the interest of the oak than
> to be tortured into bearing the apples of the apple-tree; nothing
> could be more adverse to the interest of the apple-tree than to
> be tortured into bearing acorns; nothing could be more op-
> posed to the interests of both oak and apple-tree, also of other
> trees, than to be pruned, shaped and twisted so as all to grow
> after a forced model, delineated on paper, according to the
> rigid and limited imagination of a geometrician.[18]

And behind the whole misguided enterprise is, of course, once again
Rousseau, the guilty Euclid who concocts these universalizing theo-
rems about man and society which the obsessed Jacobins try to put
into practice.

In their hypertrophied confidence in Reason, ignorant of the particular history of nations, Rousseau and the architects of revolution suffer from what Taine calls the *esprit classique:*

> To pursue in every research, with the utmost confidence, without either reserve or precaution, the mathematical method; to derive, limit and isolate a few of the simplest generalized notions; and then, setting experience aside, comparing them, combining them, and, from the artificial compound thus obtained, deducing all the consequences they involve by pure reasoning, is the natural process of the classic spirit.[19]

This spirit had its origins, argues Taine not unpersuasively, in the drawing rooms of the seventeenth century, where the rarefied and abstract intelligence of a La Rochefoucauld yields gemlike generalities about human nature in a limited language devoid of all local color. It is likewise observable in the philosophy of Descartes and the plays of Racine, and ultimately inspires the creation of the Académie française, with its project of limiting and purifying the French language. It relies on a language into which "neither the Bible, nor Homer, nor Dante, nor Shakespeare could be translated."[20] It is with this language that Rousseau felt confident in deducing "the constitution, government and laws of every system of social equity."[21] Thus, although no true French conservative would have dared suggest that the century of Louis XIV laid the ground for Rousseau, Taine did supply them with fresh evidence that new modes of consciousness must create new vocabularies to accommodate themselves, and ultimately this new language enables political change.

This identification of Rousseau with classicism reflects Taine's belief in the unfolding of historical epochs, each with its own regnant "spirit," something he learned from Hegel and, more immediately, from Comte, whose positivism dominated French intellectual life during the Second Empire. By amassing reams of "scientific" data, Comte had endeavored to demonstrate the intimate connection between ideas and institutions in each of history's three stages: the religious, the metaphysical, and the dawning positive age. Whereas the evolutionary claim of progress in all this – and a progress that led away from religion – was antithetical to conservatives, the evidence that an age could be thoroughly permeated with a spirit lent sociological credence to their view of the Revolution as a widespread contagion. And it was in support of this belief in a scientifically ascertainable zeitgeist that Taine made a second large, though indirect, contribution to the conservative cause. In the famous introduction to his *Histoire de la littérature anglaise* (1863–4), Taine sorted himself out from previous historians who "did not know that the moral constitution of a people or an age is as particular and distinct as the physical structure of a family of plants or an order of animals."[22] Moreover, like these subjects of scientific inquiry, the moral constitution of an age could be identified and, as it turns out, the best way to do so is through the literature, for "it resembles that admirable apparatus of extraordinary sensibility, by which physicians disentangle and measure the most recondite and delicate changes of a body."[23] Ultimately, what stands revealed upon examination of particular works of literature is the formative pressures of "la race, le milieu, le moment," that is, race, geographical and sociopolitical environment, and the precise point along the larger historical continuum. Thus baldly stated, Taine's method was too starkly deterministic to survive the change in century, but absorbed by Maurras, Lasserre, and finally Eliot himself, it enjoyed a surprisingly lengthy half-life.

The final significant element of nineteenth-century French conservative thought, and one that played a growing role as the century drew to a close, was anti-Semitism. Never far below the surface of French thought even in the best of times, anti-Semitism became particulary virulent after 1870 when shaken national self-esteem gave rise to speculations of parasitism, culminating, in the Dreyfus case, with accusations of outright *Dolchstoß*. As has been mentioned, the groundwork for such thinking had been laid when Renan detected behind the ignominious defeat at the hands of Prussia the emergence of a capitalistic bourgeoisie more interested in *le franc* than *la France*. From there it was left to Edouard Drumont in his widely read *La France juive* (1886) to point to the Jews as the motor behind capitalism: "France, thanks to the principles of 1789 which the Jews had cleverly exploited, was disintegrating. Jews had taken control of the public purse, and invaded all sectors except the army."[24] This opinion was seconded by the marquis de la Tour du Pin who was confident that Jewish capitalists were responsible for the internal tensions that continued to debilitate France: "It is the Jewish idea which has led the rich to exploit the poor by means of the modern form of usury, capitalism; the poor to hate the rich by means of the proletariat."[25] And finally when Dreyfus was convicted of treason as an officer of the French army, Drumont's last inviolate sanctuary,

Maurice Barrès added his suave voice to the attack. Whether or not Dreyfus was guilty must be determined, Barrès maintained, not according to a "Kantian" notion of absolute justice, but according to "French" justice, which had as its sole criterion the welfare of the nation – and arraigned before this tribunal, Dreyfus most certainly must be condemned.[26] It would be difficult to get much further from the Rights of Man.

At the end of the nineteenth century, then, the conservative position is made up of a loosely related series of fears: of the revolutionary spirit, liberalism, progress, democracy, Rousseau, capitalism, the Enlightenment, foreigners in general, and Jews in particular. Against this is poised the rather shaky counterweight of a Catholicism that may be ardent (as in Maistre) or merely practical (as in Renan) and a monarchism out of date since the Restoration. That such a congeries of attitudes could pass viably into the new century and become a real political force is due primarily to the genius of one man, Charles Maurras, who managed to mold the conservative case into a coherent, or almost coherent, whole.

Like Renan and Taine, Maurras, too, was originally galvanized by the French defeat in 1870. Although only a child at the time, he seemed to feel the aftershock of humiliation with nearly the same force as his mentors experienced the actual insult. Maurras, however, was not moved to admire the victors as had Renan, who held up the model of the Prussian state, or Taine, who, echoing Madame de Staël, called on the French to learn from the literature produced by the passionate, poetic northern soul. But it was not until 1894, at the age of twenty-six, that he was able to make any advance on their analyses. In that year he came across Fichte's *Reden an die deutsche Nation* (1808), a reveille to Germans' slumbering national consciousness in the face of the Napoleonic threat, and call to his countrymen to fulfill Germany's historical mission. Suddenly it was all clear to Maurras. Germany had indeed found its appropriate herald in Fichte, the philosopher who had spun a world out of the transcendental Ego. This prophet of the unbridled *Ich* was quintessentially German, an anarchist who could trace his roots to Luther and, even further back, to the Teutonic forests of Tacitus. It remained only for Maurras to give a name to this spirit of chaos: *romanticism*. Half symbol, half analytic tool, this term allowed Maurras to look freely and indiscriminately across the realms of politics, religion, and literature, as well as backward and forward in time beyond the boundaries of what had traditionally constituted the

Romantic period. With this pantoscopic lens he was able to bring into focus the whole range of nineteenth-century conservative phobias and, in sharpening the picture, sharpen the response.

The daring of Maurras's maneuver consists not only in the breadth of his vision, but also in his complete volte-face on the conservative stance toward the Enlightenment. There is no question in his mind that the Revolution was every bit as pernicious as his predecessors claimed and that Rousseau had caused it almost single-handedly, but Maurras could detect little evidence of reason in Rousseau and less in his handiwork. Wasn't it much rather the case, Maurras argued, that in Rousseau one might observe the eccentric, the man who heeded only the peculiar rhythm of his own untutored sensibility, in short, the proto-Romantic. Self-entranced (and what a self, lamented Maurras), Rousseau set out to entrance the masses:

> Virtue, incarnate in a "me" of dingy quality, was declared the right and proper judge of the human race. His outraged and plaintive sensibility, set up as the law, was in last resort the court of appeal against the universe. The more sincerely abject, the more naturally slavelike he became, the more he claimed that men should accept all he said, should obey him, should worship him.[27]

Thus, as Maurras saw it, his conservative forebears had indicted the right parties, but on the wrong charges: "Taine's error [in identifying the Rousseauian revolution as the product of reason] astonishes us."[28] Discursive argument, rhetorical decorum, and study of the slave-based classical world where these flourished could only support the other side. Revolution, he concluded, is purely a Romantic phenomenon, for "the Greco-Roman tradition is as innocent [of revolution] as the spirit of the medieval Roman Catholic Church." So intent was Maurras to divorce this classical tradition from any taint of romanticism that, faced with obvious counterevidence in the person of the ardently Romantic and equally Catholic Chateaubriand, he promptly reclassifies him, on the basis of his penchant for rhapsodizing in solitude, as a Protestant in the guise of a Catholic.[29] What Maurras failed to see, or could not conveniently admit, was the extent to which the counterrevolutionary thinkers had themselves run parallel to, and even borrowed from, Romantic thought, evident all the way from the irrational nature of Maistre's faith to the mystical nationalism of Barrès (Rousseau's individualism writ large). As a result, Maurras's antiromanticism, though often brilliantly elaborated, will show marked signs of the ingenuity of contortion.

Having organized the adversarial position under the rubric of romanticism, Maurras rallies the Right to the banner of *classicism.* While there was nothing original in the term as used in opposition to romanticism, never had it been made to bear the freight Maurras placed on it. Like his use of the term *romanticism,* it had a meaning far beyond the mere designation of an artistic mode. In fact, for Maurras, it was synonymous with nothing less than the great tradition of Western culture itself that, originating in Greece, passed to ancient Rome and hence, via the Roman Catholic Church, to Latin Europe, especially to France. The hallmark of this tradition was the courage to discriminate, resulting in political and religious hierarchy as well as artistic decorum, itself the elegance that comes from a recognition of the gradation of styles. Only cultured elites could guarantee social stability, artistic beauty. But Maurras, like all philosophically rigorous conservatives, was not content to rest here with a case based on sheer longevity or empirical survey of comparative excellences. To be fully persuasive there must be appeal to the nature of things, and this he produced by invoking the principle of Order, hypostatized as an ontological category: "It remains for us to delineate what we envision as the normal form of the kingdom. We conceive of it as the regime of Order. By that we mean an Order conforming to the nature of the French nation and the laws of universal reason."[30] Maurras is not naive enough to believe that the best always rise to the top, but because of the primacy of Order any random injustice in the treatment of individuals must be willingly borne. Order serves, then, in Maurras's cosmos with something of the same force as the form of the Good in Plato's; and, as in Plato, it is reason – liberated by Maurras from complicity with Rousseau – that ratifies the whole.

With a compelling Manichean neatness, Maurras has thus organized the world into a conflict between, on the one side, the forces of order: reason, hierarchy, community, and tradition; and, on the other, the forces of chaos: unbridled emotion, equality, individualism, and revolution. It remained only to show how the pattern of history recorded the battleline between these forces, and this Maurras does in a few deft strokes. Simply put, the classical tradition maintained a virtually unbroken dominance in the Greco–Roman world (democratic Athens and republican Rome are considered – insofar as they are considered at all – as brief, failed experiments, visited by corrective purging).[31] Yet all the while outside the gates could be heard the howl of chaos, emanating from Hebrew prophets who claimed to have personal access to God, to be His spokesmen on earth called to chastise sinful authority.[32] Of these the most potentially dangerous was Jesus himself, who actually managed to breach the barricades of Rome with his message. But the tradition proved stronger, and the radical anarchism of Jesus was neutralized by the creation of the Catholic Church:

> The merit and honor of Catholicism was to *organize* the idea of God and to remove from it this venom. On the path which leads to God, the Catholic finds legions of intermediaries: these may be terrestrial or supernatural but the chain from one to the other is continuous. Heaven and earth are populated with them just as formerly they were with gods.[33]

And thus things remained for over a millennium until once again the spirit of chaos broke loose in Wittenberg when Luther placed the Bible in the hands of individuals and, in substituting conscience for authority, waged religious revolution: "une sédition de l'individu contre l'espèce."[34] Yet, as before, the tradition held firm in Latin Europe, and the creative reaction to Luther's challenge culminated in the glories of Louis XIV. For a second time the forces of destruction were ironically condemned by history to create only the greater good. The barbarians had, however, set up camp in Protestant Geneva, and it was from there two centuries later that Rousseau slipped across the border to gain a measure of success denied to both Jesus and Luther; he smuggled within the walls the Trojan horse of revolution out of which sprang democracy, capitalism, socialism, and a host of other modern evils.

While the lack of distinctions evident in this disparate final catalog may seem especially inappropriate in one who took such pride in intellectual finesse, Maurras believes himself justified in hurriedly lumping these various disruptions together, for given the enormity of the offense – an attack on cosmos – any more finely tuned discrimination would be idle. Linked by the shared subversiveness of anarchic individualism, then, the terms of reproach, *romanticism, democracy, Protestantism,* and the like, are treated as though virtually synonymous. Thus, Maurras, in his indictment of Rousseau, can slide easily, without explanation, from one term to another:

> In Rousseau then (and it is the one point we can clearly distinguish in this disordered individual) is to be found the break in

France with certain habits of the spirit, certain standards of taste, certain customs and traditions of the state: his *Héloïse,* his *Confessions,* his attitude and way of life lead us back (and it is a real retrogression) to that reign of "nature" the affectation of which produces romantic sensibility; his profession of faith reduces religious life to the god within oneself, without ritual or priest, that is the culmination of Protestant logic; his political ideas are soon to subject France to the doctrine which destroys monarchies and which dreams up republics.[35]

As with Marx, there is an attempt here to demonstrate connection between nominally discrete realms of activity. But whereas Marx posited primary causation in the economic substructure of a society, Maurras never establishes any pattern of causation. He is content to base his arguments on analogy rather than the specifics of influence:

> The vocabularies of literary criticism and of politics come together and complement one another: the sacred freedom of the word, the sovereign liberty of the citizen, equality in literary subject matter, equality of all elements of society, a vague fraternity which creates the "rights of all" and their right to all.[36]

Such a mode of argumentation presupposes a static, ordered universe where we might expect similar proportion in different phenomena, so that the whole can be folded in on itself like a carpenter's rule. However, if one rejects the existence of the fundamental principle – Order, on Maurras's view – the case becomes almost impossible to defend at any secondary level of discourse. Consequently, Maurras's unified field theory of politics, religion, and literature will be enormously persuasive to those who share his premise, but sheer legerdemain to those who do not.

The seductiveness of Maurras's position is greatly enhanced by his own indisputably keen sense of beauty, whether he is responding to the landscape of Athens and Florence or the poetry of Dante. In this regard – brushed by turn of the century aestheticism – he lends an appeal to the stark doctrine of Maistre, obsessed with corruption. Impossible for his precursor would have been Maurras's delight in the sensuous surface of the *Commedia:* "Elle [Béatrice] ne monte au ciel que formée de la terre, vêtue et colorée de tous les charmes de la vie. C'est pourquoi soyons sages et gardons-nous bien d'oublier la surface brillante, l'odorant et suave épiderme de la chanson."[37]

Maurras, of course, later reminds us that sensibility must be subordinated to the rule of Order, yet he is equally insistent that we see a continuity between the beauty of Beatrice the woman and the beauty of Beatrice the saint. Even less orthodox readers than Maistre might not have felt entirely comfortable with Maurras's observation that the poem's energy was a manifestation of sublimated physicality:

> Mais premièrement le poète commença par l'aimer, par la perdre et par la pleurer. Heureux et bienheureux le lecteur, le critique d'assez jugement pour avoir compris que voilá bien la chair et le sang du poème, sa matière et sa vie ardente, ce qui vibre de fort et de chaleureux dans sa voix.[38]

It is Dante's remarkable ability to incorporate this passion without loss in his larger theological architectonics that causes Maurras to see in him the prime instance of what Eliot would later fashion the unified sensibility: "The most intellectual of all the poets is at the same time the most moving."[39]

Maurras's almost pagan delight in the sensuality of the physical and his untroubled incorporation of it into Christianity reflect more than just the exuberance of a well-developed aesthetic sense, however. They register as well a view of history that recognizes no perceptible rupture between the Roman Empire and the Roman Catholic Church. Because Maurras values Catholicism chiefly for its imposition of order and its preservation of hierarchy, he has no difficulty seeing it as continuous with the institutions and informing spirit of classical Rome. Perhaps nowhere is the eccentricity of this view more apparent than when he asks his readers to consider Dante "a Catholic Lucretius," insofar as both authors delved into "hidden points of the system of nature." The obvious implication here is that they were looking at the same thing, though it would be hard to imagine a system more unlike Dante's divinely organized cosmos, complete with scrupulously adjudicated afterlife, than the random atomism of *De rerum natura,* indifferent to the gods and rejecting any personal continuance after dissolution of the body.[40] Unperturbed by any such discrepancy, however, Maurras finds a Dante as little exercised as he himself is by the task of linking pagan philosophy and Christian theology: "The difficulty between the Christian supernatural and the pagan supernatural which troubled Chateaubriand are reconciled here [in Dante] *without trouble"* (italics added).[41]

Maurras's lack of concern with the religious essence of Dante's Christianity was licensed by his teacher Renan's disregard of dogma. But whereas Renan used the freedom he created for himself in this way to concentrate on Jesus the man and his ethic, Maurras seems steadily embarrassed by Christianity's namesake, to say nothing of the low-born Jews who surrounded him. Maurras's Christianity tends instead to take on the flavor of the civic religion of the Romans: it ratifies the political status quo without examining it very closely or providing even the implicit criticism of an alternative axis of evaluation. Thus, Maurras is much impressed with Dante's ability to conduct a fiercely partisan political life unhampered by his religious duties, to combine "a Florentine patriotism *le plus ombrageux* with a universal Catholicism *le plus dégagé*."[42] When the two aspects of Dante's life interact as they do in the *Inferno*, Dante has no compunction in consigning political opponents – for what occasionally look like essentially political reasons – to an eternity of divinely sanctioned anguish. All this Maurras admires and is in keeping with what he takes to be the ultimate lesson of Dante's work and life. Toward the end of his eighty-page commemoration of the sixth centenary of Dante's death, Maurras describes his value for the ages: "To the useful lesson of antiromantic truth, this Florentine in mourning for his *bel San Giovanni*, this energetic *cittadin della citta partita* added a serious lesson in civic duty (*civisme*)."[43] We are left with an account of Dante as essentially a political being, a patriot, described in terms virtually indistinguishable from those appropriate to his fellow Florentine and exile, Machiavelli. The *Commedia* yields not beatific vision but "antiromantic truth."

The passing on of this truth from generation to generation constitutes the tradition according to Maurras, and even the greatest must listen humbly and attentively to those who came before, as Dante did to Aristotle, Virgil, Latini, and others.[44] In light of this, it would be tempting to say that political institutions are valuable primarily because they guarantee the continuance of high culture and that in a broad sense Maurras's doctrine is primarily aesthetic. But this would be misleading, for the very artifacts of high culture that Maurras singles out are those – like the rigidly hierarchical *Commedia* or the imperial *Aeneid* – that reflect and support the existing institutions (though, of course, not every functionary within them). Maurras is never troubled by a problem that, throughout his life, will vex Eliot in his defense of this tradition: can there be a great work of art whose political or religious principles are less than correct? For Maurras, supremely confident in the permanence of "antiromantic truth," the answer is simply no. Moreover, this is not just a metaphysical certainty but a psychological one as well: degenerate ideas *must* assume degenerate shape because they are likewise the product of disordered minds. Formal beauty is always a faithful reflection of immutable truth, and as Nolte correctly points out, this holds for states and religions every bit as much as for works of art.[45] The substance of the truth – order and rank – are equally political, artistic, and religious virtues.

The numbers of those attracted to Maurras's version of an ordered universe under serious attack grew markedly in the first decade of the twentieth century. In 1899 a small group of radical anti-Dreyfusards had gathered in Paris's Café de Flore for the express purpose of recalling France to the grandeur of the ancien régime.[46] Their militant vigor and intense nationalism yielded the fledgling movement's name: l'Action française. What distinguished this circle from the dozens of other youthful café cliques that bloom and die in a season was the driving energy and intellectual rigor of its most compelling member, Charles Maurras. The radical robustness of his message appealed to youth, disenchanted with the effete parliamentary debate of the elder generation; for older conservatives, he miraculously made the nearly dead hope of royalism seem vibrant once again; and for Catholics of both generations, dismayed at the Republic's campaign to separate church and state, he provided an aggressive champion. His solution was readily comprehensible: a restoration of France to "nationalisme intégral," a France purged of all traces of the principles of 1789 and their corollaries, in effect, a call for the eradication of the Republic, foreign influence, and the sway of capital. In *Enquête sur la monarchie* (1901), Maurras plangently lamented the disappearance of old bonds of family, town, province, and church, formerly gathered up in the person of the monarch. And in *L'Avenir de l'intelligence* (1905) (a book Eliot would read shortly and as editor of the *Criterion* recommend to his readers as one of the six great bulwarks of the new classicism), Maurras called on Frenchmen to choose between gold and blood.[47] Either one could have a France dominated by largely foreign finance, which manipulates the opinion of the unwitting democratic masses through newspapers, or one could return to native hereditary hierarchies born of the soil, passed on through the blood. But for those who desired the latter, time was growing short. It was up to a small intellectual elite to free itself immediately from the constraints of the marketplace and speak on behalf of the old tradition, and not just speak, for unless words led to institutions no victory could be more than personal, ephemeral: "If one wants to avoid an individualism appropriate only for Protestants, *the moral question must become a social question:* there are no morals without institutions."[48]

By 1908 such sentiments had attracted enough financial support for the Action française to publish a daily newspaper, which, proclaiming its platform in an inaugural manifesto entitled "Reaction d'abord," promptly staked out a position on the extreme right. And there it vociferously remained until its final issue two world wars later in 1944. The committed ardor of the editors was matched by that of their distributors, a group of royalist students who called themselves Camelots du Roi (street vendors of the king). Before the end of the year, these young enthusiasts, discontent with their minor role, had evolved into something between fraternity pranksters and street thugs, making as much news as they hawked. They habitually disrupted Sorbonne lectures and in the spring term of 1909 thrashed Professor François Thalamas for his negative opinion of Joan of Arc. Carried along on the tide of ensuing notoriety, one of their members was emboldened to publicly slap Premier Briand, the Republic's most prestigious advocate of the separation of church and state. Clearly it was becoming harder and harder to ignore this aggressive movement. While only a minority of French youth actually followed Maurras all the way to royalism, the thrust of his arguments and the tone of his polemics captured the imagination of the new generation. In a survey of educated Parisian youth from the ages of 18 to 25 conducted by Henri Massis and Alfred de Tarde in 1912 and published in 1913 as *Les Jeunes gens d'aujourd'hui*, Maurrasien attitudes were everywhere apparent. Impatient with what seemed to them the decadent relativism and endless introspection of the late nineteenth century, the new French desired certitudes from which could follow vigorous action.[49] Looking back forty years later, Massis summed up his subjects:

Criticism of the parliamentary regime, reaction against those who disturbed the social order, against Germanism, against romantic excesses . . . Their very vocabulary seemed to have been affected by it [Maurras's doctrine], and the word *French* on their lips sounded more rigorous, more offensive, almost warlike, a sound whose Maurrasien accent was easy to recognize.[50]

It was into this febrile environment that another young man in search of certitudes entered in the autumn of 1910, the 22-year-old Harvard graduate student T. S. Eliot.

This was not, however, Eliot's first encounter with Maurras's agenda, for oddly, this call for a classicism long outmoded in France found some resonance in the United States, where it had never been in mode. In the late nineteenth century, lacking any viable native philosophy to counter the crassness of post–Civil War industrial capitalism (republican virtue, like the Republic, had died in the war), American intellectuals turned desperately to Europe for elevating principles.[51] What evolved disappointingly, but perhaps predictably, was the Genteel Tradition, a studied refinement consisting largely of well-to-do Bostonians aping English manners while averting their glance from the ugliness that sustained their leisure. Of art they asked nothing more than adornment or, at its most sublime, a repository of sensibility. At the turn of the century, however, justified dismay at the moral slackness of this cosmetic propriety was voiced most eloquently – and stridently – by Irving Babbitt, professor of French and comparative literature at Harvard, who, like his student Eliot, was a skeptical midwesterner still hungry for first principles. In 1908 Babbitt believed he found what he had been looking for in Paris. There he was initiated into the world of nostalgic French classicism in Maurrasien salons and at the lectures of various disciples, the most influential of whom was Pierre Lasserre, literary critic of the Action française's newspaper.[52] In the previous year Lasserre had burst on the Parisian literary scene with the publication of his *Le Romantisme français*, a wholesale attack on the French Romantic canon from a Maurrasien perspective. One by one, Hugo, Lamartine, Chateaubriand, Senancour, Constant, and the ubiquitous Madame de Staël are reduced to misguided epigones of Rousseau, the *fons et origo* of romanticism. Maurras's stance on Rousseau, always doctrinaire, has in Lasserre hardened to dogma: "There is nothing in Romanticism which is not from Rousseau. Nothing in Rousseau which is not romantic."[53] To demonstrate the derangement of the Rousseauian soul Lasserre invokes Aristotle and "avec lui tous les philosophes classiques," all of whom uniformly teach that hierarchy is as necessary to our internal disposition as it is to external society. Specifically, the soul, to count as human, must "subordinate sensibility to intelligence, imagination to reason, the affective and spontaneous forces to the reflective force."[54] Clearly, then, the romantic man is a complete inversion of the good man. The best that can be said for Rousseau is that in championing primitivism he is at least consistent, for he has, by definition, forfeited his own claim to full, civilized humanness.[55]

Babbitt, himself an enthusiastic student of Greek and Latin who had ended up teaching French only because there was no opening in classics at Harvard, responded strongly to the attack on romanticism, couched as it was by Lasserre in Aristotelian terms. Having turned his back on Andrew Carnegie's gospel of wealth as well as the Genteel Tradition's gospel of taste, Babbitt had derived sustenance for his lonely crusade from what he called the humanist's bible, Aristotle's *Nichomachean Ethics*. But until he encountered the French reactionaries, he had only a hazy notion of how Aristotle might be translated into an American idiom. As his colleague at Harvard George Santayana expressed the problem with typically mordant insight, "[Gifted Americans] found it uphill work . . . to live in familiar friendship with the Greeks and Indians."[56] This difficulty of finding a common denominator for classical culture and American history could be resolved, of course, by reducing one to the terms of the other, and essentially this is what Babbitt learned from the French telescoping of their own recent past. Following the lead of Maurras and Lasserre, Babbitt detected a fatal lack of restraint in the American character, which led both to sloppy emotionalism in letters and to sprawling industrialism on the larger landscape; the vice could be conveniently summed up in one word – romanticism. Like his French mentors, Babbitt saw democracy merely as the political aspect of romanticism, the pathetic attempt to place the right to discriminate in the hands of the masses, whose combined ignorance supposedly would refine itself into a benevolent general will. The evident abrogation of enlightened authority had, moreover, permeated all facets of American life, even the confines of Harvard, whose innovative system of electives, snorted Babbitt, allowed "the wisdom of the ages to be as naught compared to the inclination of a sophomore."[57] Behind these woes, large and small, Babbitt, too, detected the ominous figure of Rousseau:

At bottom the French are right in perceiving how much in modern life is involved in one's attitude toward Rousseau; they are right in centering their attack and defense on the great father of radicalism, instead of fixing attention on some contemporary radical, who is usually only his remote and degenerate offspring.[58]

Babbitt was even less concerned, if possible, than his French sources with precisely how Rousseau gave birth to "the degenerate posterity" of the modern world, but he never for a moment doubted his paternity and relentlessly drummed antiromanticism into the admiring Eliot and his succesors at Harvard over the next quarter century.

The most dangerous of Rousseau's recent offspring appeared to Babbitt to be Henri Bergson, whose philosophy drew on all the worst in the Romantic tradition. An unsympathetic reading revealed to Babbitt that Bergson's much touted notion of *temps durée* was merely "the latest form of Rousseau's transcendental idling"[59] and that the *élan vital* was one more "glorification of impulse"[60] in fancy philosophic dress. It was in opposition to the latter that Babbitt conceived a counterterm, the *frein vital,* or vital check, upon which he hoped to erect his version of classical humanism. This vital check was to be the regulation of impulse by the disciplined will that, following Aristotle, Babbitt saw as the function of a proper education. For us moderns, this meant a thorough grounding in the ancients, whose wisdom, if absorbed, would make the vital check second nature, something akin to the habitualness of true virtue as Aristotle described it. Of course, Babbitt was not naive enough to believe that the rigors of a classical education would be feasible on a large scale, but then he never posed as a democrat. He willingly concedes that the classical model he proposes is a breeding for aristocracy: "Ancient humanism is as a whole intensely aristocratic in temper; its sympathies run in what would seem to us narrow channels; it is naturally disdainful of the humble and lowly who have not been indoctrinated and disciplined."[61] Although the United States would remain nominally a democracy, power would be exercised from above by the *aristoi.* To this ideal, more through force of personality than rigor of argument, Babbitt managed to gather a small group of the like-minded, in whose number the young Eliot must be counted. Eventually, in part because of Babbitt's unwillingness to tolerate any deviation, even this small group gradually dwindled, until by the time of his death in 1933 Babbitt's *aristoi* was a class of scarcely more than one. Yet in 1910, as Eliot departed Harvard for his year abroad, the tonic stringency of Babbitt's classicism seemed almost the only viable alternative to the fuzzy impressionism of a played out romanticism and the related social doctrine of popular progress.

This classicism that provided Eliot with a critical orientation was not without serious problems of its own, however. In the case of Babbitt's American version, there was the obvious difficulty of expanding beyond coterie status. Jokingly, Harvard students claimed that Babbitt was achieving worldwide recognition as evidenced by the fact that his reputation had just left Cambridge.[62] Yet despite a prolific outpouring of both scholarly works and publications in more popular journals such as the *Nation* and the *Atlantic Monthly*, Babbitt, in fact, made few extramural converts. Perhaps it was doubly fitting that his chief acknowledgment came when, several decades after his death, his old department of comparative literature established the Irving Babbitt Chair, whose first occupant was Harry Levin, a former student. Nor was the lack of enthusiasm for Babbitt's French import sheerly the result of an underbred populace as he liked to console himself. The almost universally chilly response Babbitt received from his countrymen could have been, it seems, anticipated from the beginning, for the absence of a classical tradition in the United States that might be played off against romanticism left him perpetually in the rather strained position of having to urge self-discipline on individuals so that they might revolt against individualism. Eliot's subsequent removal to England and obsession with a tradition, half discovered, half created, is clearly a response to Babbitt's American dilemma.

The difficulties posed by Maurras's classicism were every bit as vexing and much more difficult to run away from. (In all fairness, it is to Eliot's credit that he never tried to do so, though he ended up defending positions that fell more and more into disrepute.) In his early career, Eliot was increasingly haunted with the problem of demonstrating, rather than merely asserting, the intimate connection between politics, literature, and religion that he derives from Maurras. Only for so long can force of character and assertiveness of expression silence the suspicion that the nodal point of confluence may reside in the mind of the author rather than in the historical matrix. And, of course, the suspicion is exacerbated when the particular terms grow out of a foreign historical matrix in the first place. Beyond the fact that classicism is susceptible to the charge of being nothing more than a series of preferences distinguished from a series of animosities called romanticism, it is also vulnerable to an implication with that very romanticism from which it recoils. Maurras's invocation of *déesse France* and the organic medieval unity over which she presided is clearly much more deeply indebted to Romantic notions of the *Volk* than to the urbane cosmopolitanism of the Age of Reason. As Julien Benda correctly pointed out in *La Trahison des clercs,* and he had primarily Barrès and Maurras in mind, modern proponents of the culture-state must trace their ancestry to the Romantic period, for before that Europe had scarcely any notion of international rivalries based on national genius.[63] But ultimately even more painful for Eliot than either of these two inherited problems of classicism was the nature of its commitment to the church it championed. Already in 1911, the year in which Eliot encountered the Action française first-hand in Paris, objections were being raised to Maurras's insistence on Catholicism as a bastion of civic order and tradition, regardless of the truth of doctrine.[64] Whereas there could be little doubt that Maistre had valued the throne primarily because it supported the altar, Maurras, without much effort to disguise his move, reverses these priorities. Thus, it was only a matter of time until the Vatican was forced to condemn this dubious ally, a blow that left Maurras belligerent, but Eliot in disarray. The last half of Eliot's career, given over largely to religious and cultural speculation, was spent rearranging the pieces of the shattered Maurrasien legacy.

2

THE FRENCH CONNECTION

Although he began addressing Babbitt as "Dear Master," the recently graduated Eliot, in retracing his mentor's pilgrimage to Paris in 1910–11, seemed determined to put the older man's judgments to a rigorous test. Within a few months of his arrival he started attending regularly the lectures of Bergson, Babbitt's current bête noire, at the Collège de France. Bergson, in the aftermath of his most popular work, *L'Évolution créatrice*, was then enjoying the dizzying celebrity that only fashionable Paris can bestow on its intellectuals. But if Eliot came to mock, he stayed to worship; carried along on the general wave of enthusiasm in the packed hall – Bergson's popularity was such that he had to issue his own students reservations to ensure them a seat – he experienced a "temporary conversion."[1] We learn little from Eliot, then or later, about the precise nature of the philosopher's appeal, but he does confess that the infatuation lasted long enough for him to have written "The Love Song of J. Alfred Prufrock" as a Bergsonian, and a quick glance at this early poem confirms the assessment.[2] Prufrock's social encounter places him right on the fault line of a rapidly moving chronological time and the slower, almost infinitely expandable, internal world of *durée réelle*. As Prufrock moves at Proustian speed in his private world, the clock has inexorably changed the hope of "There will be time" into the missed opportunity of "And would it have been worth it," leaving him in frustrated impotence. According to Bergson, we must applaud Prufrock's attempt to tap into his alienated inner life but lament the fact that he was not then able to act spontaneously on the insight. To have done so would have been, for Bergson, the only guarantee of freedom of the will: the successful introjection of felt time into the materialistic public world that, for better or worse, is our habitat.[3] It is this attempt by Bergson to establish a realm superior to the smug parade of everyday events, the caravan of "progress," that must surely have been attractive to the like-minded Eliot.

Yet, almost as predictably, the attraction gives way to rejection, for Bergson, in valorizing inner as opposed to outer flux, still fails to provide the static moment of being that Eliot sought: "The Bergsonian time-doctrine [is] wholly destructive" for "there is no external standard"; thus, "Everything may be admired because nothing is permanent."[4]

At the same time, a more slowly developing but much longer lasting impression, indeed, a permanent one, was being made by the thought of Charles Maurras. Eliot had, of course, already heard of Maurras from Babbitt but seems to have had little firsthand knowledge of Maurras's work until his time in Paris. There Eliot experienced both the contemplative and the active sides of Maurras as he read *L'Avenir de l'intelligence* and found himself simultaneously in the midst of the *Camelots'* street theater.[5] Many years later in a testimonial to the enduring influence of Maurras, he would try to capture the excitement aroused in him and the like-minded by this initial encounter: "Maurras, for certain among us, was a kind of Virgil who led us to the gates of the temples."[6] With heightened interest he returned to Harvard and followed Maurras's career in the pages of the *Nouvelle Revue Française* which in 1913 succinctly described the Maurrasien position as "classique, catholique, monarchique," a constellation Eliot would later adopt as his own ideological coat of arms.[7] But given Babbitt's impasse, Eliot had to wait until he arrived in England to discover what relevance any of this might have outside France. There in 1915–16 he was introduced, probably by Pound, to the thought of the young T. E. Hulme, who spent his short career expounding the French reactionaries to British literati. And what Hulme taught them was that the irreducible element in the reactionary compound was a belief in Original Sin:

> What is the root of the contrasted [to the Romantic] system of ideas you find in Sorel, the classical, pessimistic, or, as its opponents would have it, the reactionary ideology? This system springs from the exactly contrary conception of man; the conviction that man is by nature bad or limited, and can consequently only accomplish anything of value by disciplines, ethical, heroic, or political. In other words, it believes in Original Sin. We may define Romantics, then, as all who do not believe in the Fall of Man. It is this opposition which in reality lies at the root of most of the other divisions in social and political thought.[8]

Human nature itself, then – regardless of nationality – requires steady external constraint. This being so, Hulme can freely admit that the classical–romantic distinction, as popularized by "Maurras, Lasserre, and all the group connected with *L'Action Française*," is essentially a product of the French political scene but not be troubled by the foreign origin.[9] Even in countries where the classical tradition had been weak, it could be argued that it *ought* to have been stronger. This universalizing tendency of Hulme's observations on Original Sin makes the counterrevolution exportable for the first time, and Hulme has no trouble ferrying Maurras's classicism across the channel: "It is my aim . . . to explain why I believe in Original Sin, why I can't stand romanticism, and why I am a certain kind of Tory."[10]

That Hulme never did more than simply assert the connection between Original Sin and authoritarian institutions scarcely seemed to matter – Eliot had what he needed. In 1916 he was confident enough to conduct an extension course in Yorkshire in which, armed with Hulme's insight and relying on a syllabus heavy with Rousseau, Maurras, Lasserre, and Babbitt, he set forth the French antiromantic position.[11] The outlines of the first two lectures from Eliot's *Syllabus of a Course of Six Lectures on Modern French Literature* make clear the extent to which he had thoroughly imbibed the French reactionary orientation and, especially since these outlines are rarely published, are worth quoting at length:

LECTURE I

The Origins: What Is Romanticism?

Contemporary intellectual movements in France must be understood as in large measure a reaction against the "romanticist" attitude of the nineteenth century. During the nineteenth century several conflicting tendencies were manifested, but they may all be traced to a common source. The germs of all these tendencies are found in Rousseau.

Short sketch of Rousseau's life.
   His public career consisted in a struggle against
   1) *Authority* in matters of religion.
   2) *Aristocracy* and *privilege* in government.
His main tendencies were
   1) Exaltation of the *personal* and *individual* above the *typical*.

2) Emphasis upon *feeling* rather than *thought*.

3) Humanitarianism: belief in the fundamental goodness of human nature.

4) Depreciation of *form* in art, and glorification of *spontaneity*.

His great faults were 1) Intense egotism. 2) Insincerity.

Romanticism stands for *excess* in any direction. It splits up into two directions: escape from the world of fact, and devotion to brute fact. The two great currents of the nineteenth century – vague emotionality and the apotheosis of science (realism) alike spring from Rousseau.

LECTURE II

The Reaction Against Romanticism

The beginning of the twentieth century has witnessed a return to the ideals of classicism. These may roughly be characterized as *form* and *restraint* in art, *discipline* and *authority* in religion, *centralization* in government (either as socialism or monarchy). The classicist point of view has been defined as essentially a belief in Original Sin – the necessity for austere discipline.

It must be remembered that the French mind is highly theoretic – directed by theories – and that no theory ever remains merely a theory of art, or a theory of religion, or a theory of politics. Any theory which commences in one of these spheres inevitably extends to the others. It is therefore difficult to separate these various threads for purposes of exposition.

The present-day movement is partly a return to the ideals of the seventeenth century. A classicist in art and literature will therefore be likely to adhere to a monarchical form of government, and to the Catholic Church. But there are many cross-currents. Our best procedure is to sketch briefly the relation of politics, literature, and religion, and then consider the work of a few representatives of these three interests . . . We shall consider men of letters only as they represent political, religious, or philosophical tendencies.[12]

As these lecture notes make evident, Eliot is fully aware that the classic–Romantic distinction is code for a debate which ranges far beyond the literary. (Indeed, the last sentence quoted suggests that literature has become something of a handmaiden to these other concerns.) And though in the course of time he would express the classic–Romantic dichotomy differently, the political and cultural biases encoded in the privileged term *classicism* were to remain Eliot's for the rest of his life.

From 1916 to 1919 Eliot published dozens of book reviews and essays in a variety of journals, ranging from the politically oriented *New Statesman* to the more literary *Egoist* and *Athenaeum* to the purely philosophical *International Journal of Ethics* and the *Monist*. But in all of these, when he felt the need to place his remarks in a wider intellectual context, he invariably employed the French framework. It is in these very early efforts that we can see his attempt to apply the Maurrasien doctrine to non-French subject matter for the first time. Occasionally, especially early on, the effect will be forced, as in the rather gratuitous reference to Rousseau in an otherwise excellent essay on Leibniz:

> No philosopher is more fantastic than Leibniz in presentation, few have been less intelligently interpreted. At first sight, none is less satisfactory. Yet Leibniz remains to the end disquieting and dangerous. He represents no one tradition, no one civilization; he is allied to no social or literary tendency; his thought cannot be summed up or placed. Spinoza represents a definite emotional attitude; suggestive as he is, his value can be rated. Descartes is a classic, and is dead. "Candide" is a classic: Voltaire was a wise man, and not dangerous. Rousseau is not a classic, nor was he a wise man; he has proved an eternal source of mischief and inspiration.[13]

More often, however, Eliot will gain a trenchancy from his convictions, all the more impressive when considered against the backdrop of gauzy "appreciations" that had until then passed for criticism in England. In praising a book by the American Leacock, who "upholds the classical, the Oxford education," he crisply notes:

> His attitude is austere, pessimistic, almost mediaevalist. He believes in discipline, form, restraint; in a real contrast of good and evil not to be obscured by talk about "social evolution" . . . And he sees in the chaos of American life only an advanced stage of the disease which menaces Europe; the philosophy of comfort without ideals, the cheap and easy utilitarianism of popular education and the dead level. There are a few writers in America who share Mr. Leacock's views.[14]

This concern for upholding the classical tradition (though Eliot is not yet prepared to say precisely what that entails) and the suspicion of those (like Leibniz) who don't fully participate in it is likewise evident in the poetry of these years. In "Burbank with a Baedeker: Bleistein with a Cigar," the Jew Bleistein, as alien, can only stare in uncomprehending vulgarity at the lines of classic beauty:

> But this or such was Bleistein's way:
>   A saggy bending of the knees
> And elbows, with the palms turned out,
>   Chicago Semite Viennese.
>
> A lustreless protrusive eye
>   Stares from the protozoic slime
> At a perspective of Canaletto.

Similarly in the two Sweeney poems, "Sweeney Erect" and "Sweeney Among the Nightingales," "apeneck" Sweeney, lower class and Irish, is played off against Homeric parallels – minus any trace of the affection with which Joyce treated his modern Ulysses, Bloom:

> Paint me a cavernous waste shore
>   Cast in the unstilled Cyclades,
> Paint me the bold anfractuous rocks
>   Faced by the snarling and yelping seas.
>
> Display me Aeolus above
>   Reviewing the insurgent gales
> Which tangled Ariadne's hair
>   And swell with haste the perjured sails.
>
> Morning stirs the feet and hands
>   (Nausicaa and Polypheme).
> Gesture of orang-outang
>   Rises from the sheets in steam.
>
> This withered root of knots of hair
>   Slitted below and gashed with eyes,
> This oval O cropped out with teeth:
>   The sickle motion of the thighs

Jackknifes upward at the knees
　　Then straightens out from heel to hip
Pushing the framework of the bed
　　And clawing at the pillow slip.

The prejudicial nature of these (and other of Eliot's) verses is not an unfortunate lapse of taste with no integral connection to his overall vision as Christopher Ricks suggests in his otherwise evenhanded study *T. S. Eliot and Prejudice,* but something quite close to the center of his brand of classicism.[15] The Jew lies outside the tradition, Sweeney beneath it. Only in a democracy could they arrogantly parade their vulgarity. But Eliot exposes them for the subhuman specimens they are: "Rachael *née* Rabinovitch / Tears at the grapes with murderous paws," her kind "spawned in some estaminet of Antwerp"; Sweeney has an "apeneck" and the sexual appetites of an "orang outang" to match. Moreover, in the case of Sweeney we can plainly see what both of Eliot's most recent biographers have noted, namely, that at some level his insistence on classical order is motivated by a loathing of the sexual impulse.[16] If for Matthew Arnold the lower class, bereft of Sophocles, is a threat to break down the railings of Hyde Park, Eliot goes much further and imagines that their time off from anarchy is spent in animalistic copulation. In thus translating emotion into passion and then portraying that passion in the most sordid way possible, Eliot has placed Sweeney at the farthest remove from the new, classical poet who seeks "an escape from emotion."[17]

By the time of *The Waste Land,* Eliot is fully convinced that one either sustains the tradition or is perversely parasitic upon it. Worst of all is to be perversely parasitic through indifference, for this argues a disdain of the tradition far more unregenerate than that demonstrated by those who court damnation. The latter at least acknowledge history's authority though they rebel against it; the former, more completely self-absorbed, do not feel obliged to take any stand at all. As Eliot was to write some years later in an essay on Baudelaire: "Genuine blasphemy, genuine in spirit and not purely verbal, is the product of partial belief and is as impossible to the complete atheist as to the perfect Christian. It is a way of affirming belief."[18] The indifferent, in contrast, Eliot regards as the living dead, and it is they who make up the vast majority of *The Waste Land*'s population and will roam through Eliot's poetry for the rest of his career. Surprised at their vast number, the protagonist echoes Dante as the pilgrim newly arrived in Hell: "I had not thought death had undone so many." The original of this line, so often quoted in commentary of Eliot's poem, is *not*, however, from the Limbo section of the *Inferno*, a mistake begun by Matthieson, taken up by Brooks, and now commonly repeated. Limbo, the first circle of the *Inferno*, is reserved for virtuous pagans, a group far too distinguished to bear any relevance to London's lackluster hordes. Eliot's quotation is actually from the preceding canto that describes the vestibule of Hell, a place inhabited by those who in life took no sides. Intensely committed both religiously and politically, Dante has Virgil dryly observe: "even Hell would not receive them, / For fear the damned might glory over them." And in a touch that bears the distinct signature of his temperament, Dante visits on them a loathsome punishment, not matched until much lower in the spiral of sin. Thus, if Eliot is using allusion here with the care typical of him, we should regard the inhabitants of the Waste Land, not as being in a state of torpor as is generally done, but in a state of anguish. The rawness this implies is far more consistent with the tone of lines such as the following, spoken by the well-to-do woman in "A Game of Chess":

> "My nerves are bad to-night. Yes, bad. Stay with me.
> "Speak to me. Why do you never speak. Speak.
> "What are you thinking of? What thinking? What?
> "I never know what we are thinking. Think."

For Eliot, as for Dante, no one can exist in spiritual comfort outside the tradition.

Yet while Eliot, throughout his life, will stress his debt to Dante, Eliot's notion of tradition is much thinner, inspired as it is more by fear of vulgar energy than any positive passionate devotion. As a result, there is a formalism in Eliot that one does not detect in Dante. Tradition is conceived of as a series of interlocking rituals designed to contain the manifestations of Original Sin rather than as an edifice suspended from above. It is certainly no accident that Eliot organizes the chaotic material of *The Waste Land* essentially with Weston's *From Ritual to Romance* and Frazer's comparative study of religious custom. As Stephen Spender correctly notes, "Instead of a basis of accepted belief, the whole structure of Eliot's poem is based on certain primitive rituals and myths, which he seems to feel must be psychological certainties."[19] These patterned folkways provide a means of defusing individual passions and torments and accommodating them to group life. Ritual and myth are, then, essentially *func-*

tional for Eliot. They are guarantors of civic order. And this position will place him far closer to Maurras and Machiavelli than to Dante.

Thus I. A. Richards was not much wide of the mark when he claimed that *The Waste Land* demonstrated "a severance between his [Eliot's] poetry and *all* beliefs," for the poem is not really about the decay of belief as has often been assumed, but rather the decay of ritual. Even if it be argued that ritual requires belief to sustain it – certainly Eliot's understanding of myth – the belief seems to exist for the sake of the ritual rather than vice versa. Indeed, the welter of mythologies contained in *The Waste Land* presupposes their common sufficiency to answer a constant human need: the ritualistic regulation of impulse.

For Eliot, as for Freud, this primal energy, at its most basic, is sexual. The difference is that according to Eliot it is the *failure* to restrain this energy that has caused the discontent of modern civilization. The curse of *The Waste Land* is brought about by an amorphous – hence unhealthy – sexuality. (This was even more apparent in the original draft, which began with a drunken visit to a brothel.) Once again it is the low-born Sweeney and his women, responding only to the rhythms of their hormones, who stand completely outside the grace of any ritual:

> But at my back from time to time I hear
> The sound of horns and motors, which shall bring
> Sweeney to Mrs. Porter in the spring.

Though we might have arrived there via almost any set of lines, the allusion to Marvell takes us immediately to the most difficult aspect of the poem, the relationship between the present and the past. Most critics are now agreed that Eliot is relying on both continuity and contrast in telescoping time, but what this means in any very precise way has been harder to pin down. Let me suggest that the continuity of the poem is based on the constant brute fact of Original Sin, the contrast on modern culture's failure to deal with it or even to acknowledge it. In terms of Marvell and Sweeney, there is the obvious commonality of the urgings of desire, but Marvell has sublimated the desire in an aesthetic object. (It makes no difference whether the desire was his or a generalized desire conventionally rendered.) His carpe diem poem relies, of course, on Latin models – lost on Sweeney – and in this way engages tradition to transmute libidinal energy. Similarly, to take just one more example, the brusque couplings of the Thames daughters are juxtaposed to Leicester's flirtation with Elizabeth. As the explanatory footnote points out, Leicester seized the moment to make a light-hearted proposal of marriage. While there is a frivolous element to the scene (Eliot is far from suggesting the past was ideal), nonetheless it does culminate in an offer of *marriage* and is carried out with a stylized grace. Eliot, I believe, is content that the ritual of courtship is being performed; to probe more deeply into the internal state of those performing the ritual would have taken him where he certainly did not want to go, in the direction of Protestantism with its emphasis on the individual conscience of the participant.

It does not seem to be overstating the case, then, to claim that cultural history for Eliot is really the evolution of barriers built to cope with Original Sin, the most obvious manifestation of which is raw sexuality. The tainted universality of human nature is what allows him to claim, as explanation for his dreamlike condensation of figures, "so all the women are one woman." If Original Sin is the most interesting thing we can posit of human beings, then they are. Consistent with this, Eliot can employ Tiresias, the man with experience of the sexuality of both genders as a kind of transhistorical consciousness. We should recall, however, that in the passage Eliot quotes from Ovid, Tiresias' unique knowledge enables him to inform the inquisitive gods that women derive more pleasure from sex than men. This legendary anecdote authorizes Eliot to indulge in a patristic detestation of the female body as the primary locus of corruption. The lascivious Mrs. Porter and her daughter may wash their *feet* in soda water in the poem, but Eliot's note directs us to the vulgar Australian original which had "cunts" in place of feet. This was preceded in Eliot's original draft of the "Fire Sermon" by the mercifully deleted Fresca episode which follows her to the toilet and then to the application of French perfumes "To disguise the good old [emended to "hearty"] female stench." The draft ended as does the final version with St. Augustine praying for the gift of asceticism in the face of so much female temptation. And behind Augustine in Carthage we are meant to recall both Aeneas in the toils of Carthaginian Dido and, as Virgil's Roman audience would have, Antony similarly and more thoroughly entranced in Africa by Cleopatra. Here, as it would always be for Eliot, the Roman world is smoothly continuous with the medieval Christian world, united in their suppression of the passions as inimical to internal and external order.

Because the French reactionary matrix of Eliot's thought has rarely been given the attention it deserves, those who trace his development have generally posited a marked change in focus in the mid-1920s when he *overtly* declared his allegiances.[20] Prior to that time, it is argued, Eliot, bearing the impress of nineteenth-century aestheticism and having nurtured his own emergent talent in the rarefied atmosphere of coterie journals, waged a purely poetic revolution. His critical essays of this period were intended to reappraise the poetic tradition in order to justify his own seemingly novel verse – nothing more. But, so the argument runs, as first communism, then fascism emerged to threaten lackluster postwar liberalism, Eliot was compelled to turn his attention rather abruptly to politics, religion, and culture, now more broadly conceived. Evidence for this disjuncture can be quickly adduced by juxtaposing selections from Eliot's editorial commentary in the *Criterion* just before and just after the "change":

There has been a growing and alarming tendency in our time for literary criticism to be something else; to be the expression of an attitude "toward life" or of an attitude toward religion or of an attitude toward society, or of various humanitarian emotions.

(July 1924)

The man of letters today is interested in a great many subjects – not because he has many interests, but because he finds that the study of his own subject leads him irresistibly to the study of the others; and he must study the others if only to disentangle his own, to find out what he is really doing himself. Three events in the last ten years may be instanced: the Russian revolution (which has directed our attention to the East), the transformation of Italy (which has directed our attention to our own forms of government), and the condemnation of the Action Française by the Vatican. All of these events compel us to consider the problem of Liberty and Authority, both in politics and in the organization of speculative thought. Politics has become too serious a matter to be left to politicians.

(November 1927)

Now certainly, Eliot did become more aggressively and systematically concerned with political and cultural issues as the twenties wore on, a preoccupation that was later to culminate in *After Strange Gods* (1934), *The Idea of a Christian Society* (1939), and *Notes Towards the Definition of Culture* (1948). What is misleading, though, about this notion of an aesthetic Eliot grudgingly metamorphosing into arbiter of the larger affairs of his society is that it belies the extent to which his literary judgments had from the beginning been influenced by ideological considerations. If we look at his essays from the early twenties, it is apparent that his version of literary history conforms to the contours of political history, though exactly how politics influences poetry is not yet worked out. The most striking example of this occurs in his later anthologized review essay "The Metaphysical Poets," which first appeared as the lead article in the *Times Literary Supplement* for October 20, 1921. In the book under discussion, Grierson's *Metaphysical Poetry*, Grierson had characterized the Metaphysicals by "the peculiar blend of passion and thought, feeling and ratiocination which is their greatest achievement," but rested content with this recording of the phenomenon. Eliot, with his extraordinary gift of creative assimilation, seizes on Grierson's formula for the excellence of the Metaphysicals and turns it to much greater use. For Eliot, the passing of the Metaphysicals registers something much more than the decay of a literary mode. In contrasting Herbert with Tennyson, he asserts that "the difference is not a simple difference of degree between poets. It is something which happened to the mind of England between the time of Donne or Lord Herbert of Cherbury and the time of Tennyson and Browning," which he identifies as the "dissociation of sensibility ... from which we have never recovered."[21] But gingerly Eliot wants to claim more, for the dissociation of sensibility, we learn, runs parallel to the dissolution of the old monarchy, with the final poetic and political ruptures occurring simultaneously: "The poets of the seventeenth century (up to the Revolution) were the direct and normal development of the precedent age."[22] Eliot's tentativeness here is visible in the use of parentheses, as what he gives us is something less than causality, but more than coincidence.

Similarly, extraliterary pressure – though never directly acknowledged – seems to have shaped the small canon of examples Eliot holds up for approval as instances of a prelapsarian sensibility, still unified. According to Eliot, what characterizes the poets whose work he cites is that they were "engaged in the task of trying to find verbal equivalents for states of mind and feeling."[23] Yet no matter where one chooses to accent this statement, it constitutes a criterion so flexible that nearly any preference might be smuggled in under its aegis.[24] Somewhat more exclusive perhaps is the suggestion that the ideal poet is "constantly amalgamating disparate experiences," but why this sensibility should have flourished during one age and faded during the next becomes clear only upon examination of the touchstone passages of metaphysical poetry Eliot quotes at length. In every case the conjunction of dissimilar elements is the result of gearing up or down the hierarchy of the Great Chain of Being: eyes are like stars, globes are like tears, tears are like the opening of the heavens, and so on. The growing suspicion that it is not so much the metaphoric mind that appeals to Eliot as the classical–medieval worldview which supports it is strengthened by the final selection, a poem of Chapman's, which, metaphorically unremarkable, is little more than a bald statement of this view:

> in this one thing, all the discipline
> Of manners and of manhood is contained;
> A man to join himself with th' Universe
> In his main sway, and make in all things fit
> One with that All, and go on, round as it;
> Not plucking from the whole his wretched part,
> And into straits, or into nought revert,
> Wishing the complete Universe might be
> Subject to such a rag of it as he;
> But to consider great Necessity.[25]

This submerged connection between the healthy poetic imagination and the sustaining tradition of religiopolitical hierarchy recurs in the 1921 essay on Andrew Marvell, where Eliot wonders whether the dissenting, leveling Puritan mentality does not by nature corrode the easy civility evident in the best verse. Though again Eliot coyly sidesteps a definitive statement, his sympathies are clear enough as he examines the intriguing case of Marvell, an acknowledged Puritan, yet at the same time a poet whom he generally admires. He begins by trying to assimilate Marvell to the larger tradition by making him, in a series of quick, if dubious, moves, a spokesman for his age:

The fact that of all Marvell's verse, which is itself not a great quantity, the really valuable part consists of a very few poems indicates that the unknown quality of which we speak is probably a literary rather than a personal quality; or, more truly, that it is a quality of a civilization, of a traditional habit of life . . . Marvell's best verse is the product of European, that is to say Latin, culture.

Of course, Eliot admits that Marvell was exposed to, even tainted with, Puritanism, but – and here parallels to Eliot's own case emerge – he was saved from the worst ravages of the contagion by an inoculation of "the French spirit of the age . . . quite opposed to the tendencies latent or the forces active in Puritanism." Milton, on the other hand, is less lucky. Undoubtedly because ever since Johnson, Milton had come to stand for the quintessential republican in the literary canon, his almost total immersion in the Latin tradition – far exceeding Marvell's – cannot save him. As a result, Eliot ruefully concludes that the revolutionary Puritan influence "does great damage to the poetry of Milton."[26]

Thus, with profound effect on literary criticism for the next half century, English literary history comes to be written after a French model in which 1688 corresponds to 1789 as the date of ejection from the Eden of authoritarian institutions. Shakespeare, writing before the Fall, qualifies as "classical," though the Romantics had championed him against neoclassical charges of unruliness; neoclassicists such as Pope, who would seem to be Eliot's natural allies, are viewed with suspicion and rarely mentioned, falling as they do on the Romantic side of the great watershed. Swift has "a diseased character."[27] And needless to say, the Puritan tradition from Milton (the English Rousseau) through Blake to Lawrence is viewed as eccentric, and subversive in whatever delight it might convey. But lest this seem like slavish acceptance of cultural colonialism, Eliot assures his readers early in the *Criterion*'s career that the grand tradition need not be imported from France, for – though not many had noticed – England is itself a Latin country.[28] The English burden in the twentieth century is therefore to reject the previous age's error and return to native, classical ways, the direction pointed out by Hulme:

> He [Hulme] appears as the forerunner of a new attitude of mind, which should be the twentieth century mind, if the twentieth century is to have a mind of its own. Hulme is classical, reactionary, and revolutionary; he is the antipodes of the eclectic, tolerant, and democratic mind of the end of the last century.[29]

And ideally, the reactionary sociopolitics and the new artistic classicism will be mutually nourishing, so that neither appears to be the epiphenomenon of the other: "A new classical age will be reached when the dogma, or *ideology*, of the critics is so modified by contact with creative writing, and when the creative writers are so permeated by the new dogma, that a state of equilibrium is reached."[30]

Before going on to consider the specifics of "this new classical age," we should pause to examine the evaluative apparatus that Eliot has brought to bear on the literary past. What is especially worth stressing, because almost universally downplayed, is the severity of Eliot's employment of the classic–romantic opposition. On the surface, the distinction does, indeed, seem muddied because Eliot is willing to grant that those poets who suffer from romanticism nevertheless may have very real poetic talent. Thus, even in his treatment of the English Romantics themselves, we have no difficulty finding passages of genuine praise. (The estimation of Shelley would be a glaring exception, for his combination of romanticism, atheism, and sympathy for political revolution makes him virtually the embodiment of the Maurrasien nightmare. About Shelley almost nothing good can be said.)[31] In the case of Blake, for example, Eliot notes that his peculiarity is due to an excess of honesty and goes on to remark the following virtues: "Blake was endowed with a capacity for considerable understanding of human nature, with a remarkable and original sense of language and the music of language, and a gift of hallucinated vision."[32] In Byron, too, Eliot detects a great gift, that of narrative, and does not hesitate to rank him among the best of English poets in that regard: "As a *tale-teller* we must rate Byron very high indeed: I can think of none other than Chaucer who has a greater readability, with the exception of Coleridge."[33] And such laudatory remarks can be found as well in discussions of Keats, Wordsworth, and as the comparison in the preceding passage makes clear, Coleridge. In virtually every instance, however, the admirable quality is portrayed against a larger background of profound error and is thereby revealed as just a local excellence, the existence of which is actually lamentable for having been put to use in the wrong cause. The passage on Blake already quoted goes on:

> Had these [virtues] been controlled by a respect for impersonal reason, for common sense, for the objectivity of science, it would have been better for him. What his genius required, and what it sadly lacked, was a framework of accepted and traditional ideas which would have prevented him from indulging in a philosophy of his own.[34]

The cause of this waywardness is that Blake, like a sort of renegade asteroid, has careened outside the Latin orbit following the precedent of Milton:

> Milton's celestial and infernal regions are large but insufficiently furnished apartments filled by heavy conversation; and one remarks about the Puritan mythology an historical thinness. And about Blake's supernatural territories, as about the supposed ideas that dwell there, we cannot help commenting on a certain meanness of culture. They illustrate the crankiness, the eccentricity, which frequently affects writers outside the Latin tradition, and which such a critic as Arnold should have certainly rebuked.[35]

Likewise, Byron, highly susceptible because of his Scottish Calvinist upbringing, carries the Miltonic taint, which vitiates his entire corpus. In his case, it appears as a fascination with rebellious pride – a wearing of the mark of Cain as a badge of distinction, and a desperate attempt to merit it:

> But there is a very important part of the Byronic make-up which may appropriately be mentioned before considering his poetry, for which I think his Scottish antecedence provided the material. That is his particular diabolism, his delight in posing as a damned creature – and in providing evidence for his damnation in a rather horrifying way. Now, the diabolism of Byron is very different from anything that the Romantic Agony (as Mr. Praz calls it) produced in Catholic countries . . . It could only come from the religious background of a people steeped in Calvinistic theology.
>
> Byron's diabolism, if indeed it deserves the name, was of a mixed type. He shared, to some extent, Shelley's Promethean attitude, and the Romantic passion for Liberty; and this passion, which inspired his more political outbursts, combined with the image of himself as a man of action to bring about the Greek adventure. And his Promethean attitude merges into a Satanic (Miltonic) attitude. This romantic conception of Milton's Satan is semi-Promethean, and also contemplates Pride as a *virtue*.[36]

This delight in the role of damned outsider, regrettable as an ideal and clumsily achieved in practice, passes over to the poetry, according to Eliot, in frequent stanzas of pure bravado, giving the whole an air of tinny theatricality.

If all Eliot were doing in these evaluations based on his particular extension of the term "Romantic" were attempting to expand the chronological boundaries of a standard literary province, then his enterprise would resemble in its circumscribed ambition those studies that argue, say, that the English Renaissance should be regarded as ending much later in the seventeenth century than is commonly thought. If all he were doing in his importation of the classic–Romantic dichotomy from France were akin to the case of a critic who believed that the term "baroque" might be used in English literary studies with the same vigor as it is in continental studies, then, again, his contribution, though provocative, would be limited in subject and period. But Eliot is doing far more than either of these. He is imposing an *ideology* on English literature: a systematic worldview focusing on religion, politics, and literature, along with corollary explanations for historical evolution and economics – in short, an interpretation of culture in general. To say this is to claim far more than that Eliot was an unwitting "carrier" of ideology, a critic whose formulations might be said to support a certain societal power structure merely because he didn't question it; rather, consciously and with increasing urgency, Eliot is pushing an all-encompassing interpretation of society that has as its goal the ultimate revamping of relations along the lines of a French reactionary model. To be sure, Eliot uses the model before he is prepared to defend it in all its parts or elaborate convincingly the details of interrelationship, but this should not blind us to the fact that judgments that purport to be literary are in reality motivated by concerns that are in essence those of, to borrow René Wellek's term, "cultural politics."[37]

That this is so has been difficult to detect, both at the time and later, for at least three reasons. The first is that Eliot is typically read through the lens of the New Criticism, which in large part was derived from him. The New Critics kept the anti-Romantic animus insofar as they severed the work from its author, thereby eliminating the suspect cult of personality and its attendant ideal of poetry as "the spontaneous overflow of powerful feelings." They also valorized irony and paradox, the virtues Eliot detected in Metaphysical poetry, as opposed to the more direct address of Wordsworth's "man speaking to men" or the musicality of Burns.[38] But in going on to sever the work from *any* extraliterary connection, they suspended Eliot's tastes in a historical vacuum. The question that arises is whether they did not see the derivation of his judgments, or whether they were indeed aware of their origin yet believed that by uncoupling them from history and treating them as purely aesthetic, they might more successfully defend his agenda on an exclusively literary front. As Terry Eagleton has recently noted, the extremely conservative tilt of the Southern Agrarians who formed the American vanguard of the New Criticism might lead us to believe the latter.[39] And certainly, after Eliot's Page-Barbour lectures at the University of Virginia in 1933, which later were published as *After Strange Gods*, there could be no mistaking his larger intentions. In the case of the New Critics, then, perhaps we should speak of a strategic disregard born of complicity. (Eliot's complex relationship to the New Critics will be discussed at length in Chapter 6.)

The second reason for the failure to identify Eliot's ideology is a related one: the incredible insularity of English studies for most of its history. Foreign thought, especially when it showed up in nonliterary form, was, until recently, virtually taboo in the professional study of modern English. Who then would have bothered to read Maurras and see Eliot's point of departure?

The third reason is the counterreputation of Eliot's poetry as avant-garde, on the cutting edge of "progress." The daring rhythms and jarring juxtapositions of *The Waste Land* made it seem akin in tone and spirit to the new jazz or cubistic experimentation in painting. The designation "modernist" served to confirm the appraisal. What no one bothered to do was to relate the poem's underlying hunger for an order made possible by mythology and ritual to Maurras's reactionary call for the same thing, already echoed in Eliot's critical writings. Those who felt surprised, even betrayed, by Eliot's 1927 conversion weren't paying close enough attention.

But if Eliot escaped a frontal attack on his larger ideological concerns in the twenties, he still had to struggle with the problem of internal consistency. His clarion call for "a new classical age" nurtured by a symbiotic equilibrium between "ideology" and "creative writing" was easy enough to make, much harder to exemplify. This sort of claim that politics and aesthetics entail one another is, of course, the linchpin of the French reactionary case and brings Eliot squarely up against the weakness of the French argument. The cautious use of his French sources in the early essays and the frequent arrogance of tone that marks his subsequent commentary as emergent cultural czar both mask his legitimate unease on this point. Eliot's inherited difficulty in demonstrating cross-fertilization is underlined in his statement of purpose inaugurating the new *Criterion* (January 1926). He describes the "tendency" of his journal as classical, and after clarifying this term as a call for "a more severe and serene control of the emotions by Reason," he lists recent works that exemplify the new classical bent: "*Réflexions sur la violence,* by Georges Sorel; *L'Avenir de l'intelligence,* by Charles Maurras; *Belphégor,* by Julien Benda; *Speculations,* by T. E. Hulme; *Réflexions sur l'intelligence,* by Jacques Maritain; *Democracy and Leadership,* by Irving Babbitt."[40] Yet none of these volumes is poetry; none of the authors, despite an occasional off-hand verse, a poet.[41] Nor is it at all obvious how Eliot's then most recent poem, "The Hollow Men" (1925), could be seen as classical rather than Romantic. (Stephen Spender goes so far as to compare the poem to the work of Shelley, of all Romantics the one most abhorred by Eliot.)[42] Indeed, when the unsympathetic editor of the liberal journal the *Calendar* pointed out just this rift between classical "dogma" and poetic practice, Eliot could only respond lamely that such criticisms were all too easy to make.[43] And a number of critics have continued to make the case for Eliot as a crypto-Romantic, in both his poetry and his theory of poetic creation.[44]

The classical cause received a blow much more difficult to sidestep when in December 1926 the Vatican condemned the Action française for, in effect, valuing the Catholic Church primarily as an organ of political stability while minimizing the spiritual reality of the church, the faith itself. The charge was inevitable, having been adumbrated, as has been mentioned, as far back as 1910. And there had been more than a few hints of official displeasure in the years following. Perhaps not without reason had Julien Benda said of the leader of the Action française, deaf since his teenage years, "Maurras est sourd à force de ne pas écouter."[45] Of course, the church might have spoken a bit louder sooner. If there is fault to be found with the condemnation, it is insofar as it was so long delayed for political reasons. For the first quarter of the century, Maurras made a valuable, if unorthodox, ally in the campaign against liberalism and anticlericism; ironically it was when his influence grew too vast, in the enthusiastic nationalism that followed World War I, that it no longer could be tolerated. (The incident that set off the immediate chain of events leading to the condemnation was a poll of the Belgian Catholic Youth Association, which named Maurras overwhelmingly as their doctrinal inspiration.) As to the case itself against Maurras, it was manifestly just, for he never made any secret of the fact that he regarded Christ as little more than a dangerous Jewish upstart, drained of his anarchic poison only by the sedulous ministrations of the Catholic Church. Unabashedly, Maurras championed Catholicism as antidote to the gospels, all in the name of the only transcendental he did recognize: Order. Moreover, if there were any doubt about Maurras's priorities before the condemnation, there could be little after. In response to the call to recant, he claimed that to do so would necessitate a betrayal of France and defiantly concluded, "Non Possumus," at least the Latin equivalent of Luther's "Hier stehe Ich. Ich kann kein anders."

Eliot, for his part, despite his subsequently developed keen eye for heresy, had invested too much in this one to be willing to identify it as such. In 1927 he underwent his secret religious conversion to the Church of England and simultaneously offered a covert defense of Maurras in the essay "Machiavelli." There he argues that Machiavelli had been grossly misunderstood because his detractors had failed to realize that he was essentially a patriot who valued the good of the commonwealth above all else. Eliot is willing to concede that, according to Machiavelli, the general welfare may entail the repression and coercion of the citizenry, but insists that this is an unavoidable consequence of Original Sin, which Machiavelli, unlike modern liberals, is honest enough to acknowledge. Approvingly, Eliot confirms "liberty is good; but more important is order and the maintenance of order justifies every means."[46] Just prior to Maurras's condemnation, the brilliant young French neo-Thomist philosopher Jacques Maritain, a contributor to the *Criterion* and a writer whose works Eliot read carefully, had put to use his study of casuistry in attempting a last-minute rescue of Maurras. In September 1926 he published *Une opinion sur Charles Maurras et le devoir des catholiques* in which he pleaded that Maurras had only meant to consider the church in its *political* aspect, reserving commentary on its spiritual nature for those whose vocation it was to address such things. Apparently impressed with this line of argument, Eliot imports it into his defense of Machiavelli:

> Machiavelli's attitude toward religion and toward the religion of his country has often been the subject of misunderstanding. His attitude is that of a statesman, and is as noble as that of any statesman, *qua* statesman. In fact, it could be no other than it is. He is opposed neither to religion nor to the Catholic Church.[47]

To those nonetheless appalled by Machiavelli's apparent indifference to religion, Eliot counters by reminding that he "maintained steadily that an established Church was of the greatest value to a State"[48] and, on the basis of this, concludes that Machiavelli might have been quite happy as a member of the Church of England.[49] By this stage, though, Eliot's defense of Machiavelli merely repeats the very accusation against Maurras, and if his intention is to suggest that Maurras is no less orthodox than Machiavelli, the point undoubtedly would be granted eagerly.

Simultaneously, in the pages of the *Criterion*, Eliot is waging a further defense of the harried Maurras, again, though, obliquely. In the June 1927 issue (the month of his conversion), Eliot's editorial commentary has the subheading "Politique d'abord." While the full significance of this French phrase may have been lost on the bulk of his readers, it certainly would not have been in France, where it was widely recognized as the most notorious of Maurras's rallying cries, a slogan intended to stress the radical importance of political change (and endlessly quoted in the case against him to indicate the misguided primacy of politics in his system, at the expense of religion). Eliot begins boldly:

> It is a trait of the present time that every "literary" review worth its salt has a political interest; indeed that *only* in the literary reviews, which are not conscientious organs of superannuated political creeds, are there any living political ideas. We have just received the first number of *Les Derniers Jours,* a bi-monthly pamphlet edited and at present written by two very intelligent young men of letters, Drieu La Rochelle [soon to become one of France's foremost literary fascists] and Emmanuel Berl. Their interests and methods are right.[50]

Eliot then goes on to sort out his own stance as an English "neo-classicist," but it is not until the book review section of the same issue that we see the profound effect recent events in France have had on his thinking. In a lengthy review of five works on politics and economics, all with a conservative bent, he singles out Anthony Ludovici's *A Defence of Conservatism* as the most valuable. Yet he has a major reservation about Ludovici's urging English Tories to turn from the Church of England to the more stringently hierarchical Catholic Church:

> In this I believe – apart from the fact that he will offend the sentiments of many Conservatives who might have much to learn from him – that he is wrong in principle and betrays some

ignorance of history. Toryism is essentially Anglican; *Roman Catholicism, which in our time draws its greatest support from America, is most in harmony with Republicanism. Mr. Ludovici is deceived in appearance . . . if he followed contemporary French politics and the relations of the Vatican with Royalism and Republicanism in France, he might come to different conclusions.* (italics added)[51]

This petulant association of the Catholic Church with republicanism because it censured Maurras shows evidence of the polemical crudity of his French master at his worst – as well as the inherent clumsiness of tying oneself irrevocably to a set of perpetually paired opposites. But even more stunning is his decision to place the Catholic Church essentially outside the tradition rather than Maurras. Well, indeed, might Eliot describe his position as "politique d'abord."

Thus, by the time Eliot, at Babbitt's urging, announces himself openly in the preface to *For Lancelot Andrewes* (1928) as "classicist in literature, royalist in politics, and anglo-catholic in religion," this trinity of enthusiasms is a disintegrating compound. But having at long last made an overt stand with the French reactionary position, Eliot spends 1928 valiantly trying to defend it. The *Criterion* begins the new year with the first installment of a two-part essay by Maurras translated by Eliot, and in the March issue, along with the second part, Eliot takes on the Catholic polemicist Leo Ward in an article entitled "The Action Française, M. Maurras, and Mr. Ward." Ward had just published the first book in English on the condemnation of the Action française and, in arguing that this "pagan" movement was eminently deserving of its fate, piled quotation on quotation to demonstrate the "anti-Christian" message of Maurras. Eliot, in response, is forced to maneuver in shallow water but tries to make the best of it. From the beginning, unable to completely deny the charge, he is reduced to justifying Maurras's lack of faith as a moving example of personal integrity that ought not to subvert his followers' Christianity. (Did the grotesque irony of defending Maurras on the basis of individual conscience, the dreaded inner voice of Protestantism, not occur to Eliot?) Indeed, Eliot attests, "I have been a reader of the work of Maurras for eighteen years; upon me he has had exactly the opposite effect."[52] This testimonial is heartfelt and true, for reactionary politics and classicism clearly entail the Christian church for Eliot. And this connection explains the otherwise bizarrely irrelevant argument that Maurras's impeachers have overlooked "the fact that he is also an important [classical] literary critic, and has written as fine [classical] prose as any French author living."[53] As evidence, apparently, the second part of Maurras's essay on criticism is positioned immediately after Eliot's article, and perhaps expecting it to have the same effect on his readership that it did on him, Eliot claims "his influence in England is not yet begun."[54]

The debate carries on to the June 1928 issue, where Ward continues to bombard Eliot with less than orthodox quotations by Maurras and pushes home the point that if these heterodox statements have become much less frequent as Maurras has grown older (an observation Eliot had made), it is only because he has become more devious. However, the most stinging remark of all comes at the end of his piece, where he expresses amazement that Eliot would sculpt England's future out of the debris of France's past:

> Finally, in regard to Mr. Eliot's belief that some inspiration for the solution of English problems may yet be found in the study of Maurras, I can only express my extreme astonishment. Maurras has himself often stated that his theories were framed to meet a peculiarly French state of things ... and in France itself, according to a recent French critic (M. André Billy) "son influence va en décroissant." Most of M. Maurras' political ideas were already to be found in Joseph de Maistre and his more rhetorical nationalist outbursts are easily outdone by Mussolini ... As a sincere friend of the *Monthly Criterion* I can only hope that it is in no danger of becoming a refuge where French philosophies go to when they die.[55]

Undoubtedly, even more galling than the association of Maurras with Mussolini (Eliot would soon be prepared to acknowledge these fascist similarities himself), or the estimation that Maurras's influence was on the wane in France (hard to dispute since Catholics would have to imperil their soul now to follow him) was the assertion that Maurras never intended his theories to be exported. For the previous twelve years Eliot had struggled against all odds, and almost all evidence, to show that they were. Now, near the height of his authority, the foundation of his whole critical edifice was being called into question. In disarray, Eliot could only counter by trying to present Maurras as a neo-Thomist since (one supposes) Maritain, who had defended him, was. As his final word he reasserts the old position: "I say only that if anyone is attracted by Maurras' political theory, and if that person has as well any tendency towards *interior* Christianity, that tendency will be quickened by finding that a political and religious view can be harmonious."[56]

Yet Eliot was too clever a controversialist not to see the flimsiness of his own rebuttal. The reactionary case had been built on the *necessary* connection of a particular religion, politics, and art, whereas Eliot is reduced to arguing that they aren't by nature incompatible ("*can be* harmonious"), and even this claim, given Maurras's transmogrification of Christianity, is dubious. In light of this, Eliot's immediate reaction is first to shift the debate onto purely political grounds: "I confess to a preference for fascism [as opposed to communism] in practice, which I dare say most of my readers share; and I will not admit that this preference is itself wholly irrational,"[57] while arguing for Maurras's politics as salvation from the excesses of fascism: "Most of the concepts which might have attracted me in fascism I seem already to have found, in a more digestible form, in the work of Charles Maurras."[58] But Eliot is merely regrouping in such statements, struggling to recast the reactionary formula in more workable form. (That he chose to catch his breath in the shadow of fascism's ramparts, while not totally forgivable, should not be taken to represent his steady, considered opinion.) Indeed, what finally emerges from the reassessment of 1928–9 marks the only real rerouting of Eliot's thought, a much more significant alteration than that represented by the supposedly new Eliot of *For Lancelot Andrewes,* where he had merely enunciated a position nearly two decades in the making. Simply put, over the next few years, Eliot comes to posit religion as the generating substructure that his congeries of values had always lacked; reactionary politics and classical art, the primary focus of his original concern, are reduced to epiphenomena.

This restructuring is harbinged in "Second Thoughts About Humanism," a criticism of Babbitt published during the summer of 1929. In this essay, Eliot delicately takes his former mentor to task for espousing humanism while remaining skeptical about the Christian religion upon which Western humanism is parasitic. In one sense the charge is unfair: Eliot, from this point on in his life, simply cannot conceive of a serious thinker being indifferent to religion. Agnosticism and atheism, he imagines, must be maintained vigorously against the urge to believe; a *dubito* requires the same daily renewal as a *credo.* Nonbelief thus operates, according to Eliot, as a shadow religion. In another sense, of course, the charge is quite just, for Babbitt's "inner check" does look suspiciously more like Christian conscience minus a belief in Christ than anything the Harvard professor can point to in the classical world. More importantly, Eliot's insistence that Babbitt's classicism confess its reliance on Christianity mirrors his own reevaluation. No longer will he be content with a classical–Romantic dichotomy; the telling line of demarcation is now horizontal: "Either everything in man can be traced as a development from below, or something must come from above. There is no avoiding that dilemma: you must be either a naturalist or a supernaturalist."[59]

This is not to say that Eliot by any means abandons his old allegiances in rearranging them. He dedicates his 1929 essay on Dante, the supernatural poet par excellence, to Maurras, the recently exposed naturalist. But Eliot, again showing his genius for assimilation, has quietly adopted the essence of the Catholic case against Maurras: politics (and art), properly understood, must be ultimately in the service of Christianity. The religiously based communitarianism that Eliot evolves in the thirties and forties represents his attempt to relocate Maurras's conservative revolution on this firmer ground.

3

ORTHODOXY AND HERESY

Having rejected Babbitt's humanism, which at best was available only to the few, and having overhauled Maurras's classicism, which was arbitrary at crucial points, Eliot emerges in the thirties as what, in a certain sense, he always had threatened to become – a full-fledged mythologist, endeavoring to propagate a consistent set of beliefs capable of shaping an ethos. Obvious tendencies in this direction were clearly apparent in *The Waste Land,* where he had cobbled together a mythic structure for his poem from pieces of Frazer, Jesse Weston, the Bible, the myth of Tiresias, and the Upanishads. And in the following year, 1923, he suggests that Joyce's turn to mythology in *Ulysses* points the way for any artist of the future who would organize the modern chaos:

> In using the myth, in manipulating a continuous parallel between contemporaneity and antiquity, Mr. Joyce is pursuing a method which others must pursue after him. They will not be imitators, any more than the scientist who uses the discoveries of an Einstein in pursuing his own, independent, further investigations. It is simply a way of controlling, of ordering, of giving a shape and a significance to the immense panorama of futility and anarchy which is contemporary history.[1]

But Eliot's interest in an overarching metaphysic that would be prior to the plurality of experience can be dated at least as early as his encounter in 1911 or shortly thereafter with the work of F. H. Bradley, subsequently the topic of his doctoral dissertation (1916). In *Appearance and Reality,* the book that had been the main focus of the dissertation, Bradley had begun by arguing along post-Kantian lines that our typical conceptual apparatus – cause, space, time, things, and self – could be shown to be self-contradictory and, taken as a whole, constituted the world of mere appearance. The real, by contrast, was posited as a consistent, harmonious whole, which Bradley designated the Absolute. We come nearest to an apprehension of the Absolute, not enmeshed in the fictive webs of abstract thought, but rather in immediate experience, an act of percipience in which subject and object remain undifferentiated.[2] These nodal points of experience or "finite centres" are logically prior to the self, which may contain a shifting multiplicity of them. Bradley's model is roughly analogous to the biblical one: a state of blessed preconsciousness, followed by a fall into selfhood with its benighted distinctions, all absorbed in a cosmic whole that eludes our understanding.

Here again, though now executed in the densely technical language of a professional philosopher, is an attack on the primacy of self that was concurrently attracting Eliot to Maurras. The connection suggests itself even more strongly when we consider that Maurras, though not properly speaking a philosopher, edged toward a kind of quasi-philosophy in his metaphysical speculations, and Bradley, an entrenched Tory, was fully aware of the political implications of his work, something even more palpable in his *Ethical Studies* and *Principles of Logic,* both conceived as vigorous attacks on the utilitarian liberalism of John Stuart Mill, which he abhorred. (The existence of other forces at work in philosophical endeavor occurs to Bradley in his witty ironization of metaphysics as "the finding of bad reasons for what we believe upon instinct, but to find these reasons is no less an instinct.")

Why Maurras ultimately subsumed the more sophisticated thinker as a formative influence on Eliot, rather than vice versa, has to do with a difficulty Eliot voices in his *Monist* article of 1916, "Leibniz' Monads and Bradley's Finite Centers." In this piece, Eliot shows his dissatisfaction with Bradley's blank notion of the Absolute (Bradley: "The Absolute is not personal, nor is it moral, nor is it beautiful or true.")[3] and its hasty, unexplained absorption of individual instances of experience:

So Bradley's universe, actual only in finite centres, is only by an act of faith unified. Upon inspection, it falls away into the isolated finite experiences out of which it is put together. Like monads they aim at being one; each expanded to completion, to the full reality latent within it, would be identical with the whole universe. But in doing so it would lose the actuality, the here and now, which is essential to the small reality which it actually achieves. The Absolute responds only to an imaginary demand of thought, and satisfies only an imaginary demand of feeling. Pretending to be something which makes finite centres cohere, it turns out to be merely the assertion that they do. And this assertion is true so far as we here and now find it to be so.[4]

Aware that he had not provided any demonstration of how particular instances of error and contradiction are overcome in the Absolute, Bradley could only offer as explanation: "For what is *possible,* and what a general principle compels us to say *must be,* that certainly *is.*"[5] But the general principle, namely, that the harmonious whole that the metaphysician seeks must exist, is, as Bradley himself admits, reliant on a leap of faith, a leap Eliot was not prepared to make at this time and even later would choose to make from more conventional platforms.

Maurras, by way of contrast, provides the dialectic missing in Bradley. In his account of classicism, regions are united in the monarchy, and nations themselves in the larger Latin tradition, compounded not only of political institutions but of religious ones as well, and buttressed by literary decorum.[6] Thus, the Absolute has an identifiable content made up of the sum of its parts. Error – romanticism – though it causes temporary disruption and should be eradicated as quickly as possible, has historically always redounded to the greater good by inducing a salutary purgative of the system. On the basis of Maurras's account, one can develop a theory of the relationship between the smallest component, the individual, and an Absolute that manifests itself as continuous cultural inheritance, and this is precisely what Eliot began to do in "Tradition and the Individual Talent":

> The existing order is complete before the new work arrives; for order to persist after the supervention of novelty, the *whole* existing order must be, if ever so slightly, altered; and so the relations, proportions, values of each work of art toward the whole are readjusted; and this is conformity between the old and the new.[7]

Alternatively, the relationship between the tradition and those with no discernible talent is the subject of the poetry from "Prufrock" through *The Waste Land* and generates the dominant tone of ironic contrast. Of course, Maurras's version of tradition ultimately fails to qualify as mythology because he lacks the religious faith necessary to make the whole cohere, but this Eliot could supply himself.

For Eliot, then, as a committed Christian, mythology will be far more than just the literary method suggested in the comments on *Ulysses*. He is intent on ordering not only the literary representation of reality but the reality itself. Paul Elmer More, a former ally of Babbitt who joined Eliot in the move toward religion, acknowledges that it was politics that led Eliot to religion in the first place: "[Eliot] underwent a kind of conversion, due largely I believe to the influence of Maurras and the Action Française."[8] Political enthusiasm is not rejected but *aufgehoben* in the new dispensation: "Religious beliefs . . . are on a different plane . . . There is a form of faith which is solely appropriate to a religion; it should not be appropriated by politics."[9] In elevating his preferences to the level of mythology, Eliot gains in two ways: First, the irrational elements in the French reactionary case that had been forced to present themselves as the product of the highest reason need no longer sustain the charade; a mythology, by its very nature, may appeal to the irrational to compel assent. Second, the all-encompassing nature of Eliot's enterprise may now more freely and openly reveal its scope (if not always its true motivations). Specifically, as a *Christian* mythologist, Eliot gains even more. Christianity, though some would argue that it was every bit as outmoded as Maurras's politics, nevertheless was at least in place and respectable. Further, there could be little question that it was not a purely French phenomenon.

Understandably enough, however, from the very beginning of his formal commitment to Christianity – and this never changes though it does become more discreetly assimilated – Eliot's religious orientation betrays signs of its Maurrasien genesis. His Anglo-Catholicism is defined chiefly over against political opponents: the sublunary left with its godless vision of mundane utopia. Given his resolution of the world into supernaturalists and naturalists, he recognizes a certain intellectual kinship with those on the other side of the divide who, unlike the trimmers, see that a choice must be made: "Where you find clear thinking you usually find that the thinker is either a Christian (if he is a European) or an atheist; where you find muddy thinking you usually find that the thinker is something between the two, and such person is in essentials a Modernist."[10] This being the case, he conceives a grudging respect for communism, the most thoroughgoing of naturalist myths, and a worldview that, like his own, is intended to resolder the human community fragmented by liberalism. Georges Sorel had already pointed out in *Réflexions sur la violence,* one of the *Criterion*'s "classics," that revolutionary socialism had accumulated the compelling force of a religion and had thereby risen to the status of a "myth," a closed system immune to refutation. Moreover, the easy transition of French Catholics from Christianity to communism must have underlined the parallelism to Eliot, who observes: "The great merit of Communism is the same as one merit of the Catholic Church, that there is something in it which minds on every level can grasp. Marx may not be intelligible, but Communism is. Communism has what is now called a 'myth.' "[11]

Indeed, Eliot, who seems almost perpetually to create in recoil, sets out quite consciously to model a Christian countercommunism: "[Toryism needs] a religious foundation for the whole of its political philosophy. Nothing less can engage enough respect to be a worthy adversary for Communism."[12] Further, Eliot was greatly impressed with communism's asceticism, its ability to inspire self-sacrifice in its adherents, something that struck him as a bracing antidote to the flabby world of liberal indulgence. And clearly, were it not for the fact that communist art was so uniformly dreary – Eliot never ceases to regard artistic quality as an index of the politics that produces it – he might have been even more admiring. Finally, however, if he is not to fall into Maurras's trap, Eliot must inquire about the *truth* of a myth, and this is where communism, despite its attractions, fails:

> I have ... much sympathy with communists of the type with which I am here concerned; I would even say that, as it is the faith of the day, there are only a small number of living people who have achieved the right *not* to be communists. My only objection is the same as my objection to the cult of the Golden Calf. It is better to worship a golden calf than to worship nothing; but that, after all, is not, in the circumstances, an adequate excuse. My objection is that it just happens to be mistaken.[13]

Only the supernaturalist myth of Christianity will count as orthodoxy.

It is, in effect, this orthodoxy coupled with its counterfeit, heresy, that comes to replace "classic" and "Romantic" as a means of organizing the world. The transition from one set of terms to another is first apparent in the unpublished Clark lectures delivered at Cambridge University in 1926, the year before Eliot's conversion. In the third of these eight lectures devoted to metaphysical poetry, Eliot endeavors to show that medieval Christianity, despite the presence of a strong mystical element, represented the ideal fusion of thought and feeling. Making his case, he distinguishes between the analytic mysticism of Richard of St. Victor, Aquinas, and Dante on the one hand and the flux-borne Bergsonian mysticism of St. Theresa and the Jesuits on the other: "The first is what I call classical, the second romantic."[14] This sort of move by Eliot is familiar enough; what is new is an additional term of opprobrium, "heresy," which creeps into the argument to denote the most pernicious deviants from the Latin tradition. Chief of these, at least in terms of the mystics, is Meister Eckhardt: "In the XIV century Meister Eckhardt and his followers – appropriately in Germany – reasserted the God of the Abyss; the God, in short, of Mr. D. H. Lawrence."[15] Heresy thus shows the same historical flexibility as romanticism, as well as the same broad applicability to a variety of fields, and offers an advance in having men who were canonized by the Vatican rather than condemned by it as primary sources of authority.

By the time Eliot delivered the Page–Barbour lectures at the University of Virginia six years later – subsequently published as *After Strange Gods: A Primer of Modern Heresy* (1934) – he is ready to slough off almost altogether the old classic–Romantic distinction, announcing as if newly discovered what at some level he always knew: "The differences represented by these two terms are not such as can be confined to a purely literary context. In using them, you are ultimately bringing in all human values, and according to your own scheme of valuation."[16] The conjunction of classicism, royalism, and Anglo-Catholicism now appears to the more rigorous and confident Eliot to have been little more than a personal association, doubly to be rejected insofar as it suggested that religion was an equal partner of the other two:

> Some years ago, in the preface to a small volume of essays, I made a sort of summary declaration of faith in matters religious, political and literary. The facility with which this statement has been quoted has helped to reveal to me that as it stands this statement is injudicious. It may suggest that the three subjects are of equal importance to me, which is not so, it may suggest

that I accept all three beliefs on the same grounds, which is not so, and it may suggest that I believe that they all hang together or fall together, which would be the most serious misunderstanding of all . . . and I now see the danger of suggesting to outsiders that the Faith is a political principle or a literary fashion, and the sum of all a dramatic posture.[17]

But if previously classicism was a cloak for political preferences, now one cannot help but notice that, in the new order, religion assumes this function. Conservatism, it turns out, is necessary to protect orthodoxy from the anarchic attacks of liberals whose adulterations historically have been "greedily received by a democratic, thoughtless public."[18] And in the preface we are told that orthodoxy today is rendered virtually speechless "in a society like ours worm-eaten with Liberalism."[19] Here, then, is the real enemy once more, this time identified with heresy rather than romanticism. That essentially nothing much has changed is further detectable when all the predictable literary renegades, England's rural moralists – Hardy, George Eliot, and worst of all, D. H. Lawrence – are brought to trial yet again and found guilty of the familiar charge of rampant individualism. If there is any difference at all, it is that the inquisitorial winnowing of the literary tradition is done with a mean-spiritedness quite distinct from even the occasional flippant arrogance of the younger Eliot.

Eliot's purging of heretics goes far beyond the literary sphere, however, and he immediately alerts his readers (originally listeners) that it would be a grave mistake to assume that his choice of subject matter indicates the full scope of his concern: "The three lectures which follow were not undertaken as exercises in literary criticism. If the reader insists upon considering them as such, I should like to guard against misunderstanding as far as possible . . . I ascended the platform of these lectures only in the role of moralist."[20] And Eliot makes it quite clear that he expects his particular moral scrutiny to encounter great sympathy from his southern audience. Of course, if the real thrust of Eliot's remarks were to chastise on behalf of his limited version of *religious* orthodoxy, then one could hardly imagine a less receptive forum for a Torquemada of Anglo-Catholicism than the overwhelmingly Protestant, largely Baptist South. But Eliot has cannily sized up the substantial *political* affinity of his own reactionary position and that of many of his auditors. Three years earlier, a group of twelve southerners including three of the New Criticism's future luminaries, Allen Tate, John Crowe Ransom, and Robert Penn Warren, had contributed to a book of essays championing Southern Agrarian life against the despotic sway of northern industrial capitalism. Unlike the frantic, scurrying North, where deracination seemed a small price to pay for material success, the Old South, according to these authors, offered the alternative life of a settled and leisurely contemplation of beauty. Slavery, when they grudgingly acknowledged it at all, appeared to them to be more an unfortunate accident of the Old South than the economic base that supported porchfulls of white-clad colonels and their ladies. "It is impossible," writes Ransom, "to believe that its [slavery's] abolition alone could have effected any great revolution in society," nor is it at all clear that slavery was nearly as bad as crusading Yankees make out, for it was "more often than not, humane in practice."[21] All things considered, southern reverence for "the amenities of life" seemed to more than compensate for the foible of slavery, and it is on this basis that Ransom admonishes: "The South is unique on this continent for having founded and defended a culture which was according to the European principles of culture; and the European principles had better look to the South if they are to be perpetuated in this country."[22] Eliot apparently picked up on this hint and brought the volume *I'll Take My Stand* to the attention of the *Criterion*'s readers in a favorable review of April 1931. Before his Virginia audience he mentions the book by name and, with approval, says that he hopes to see more of the same from these writers. He then goes on to praise the South, ominously, for its regional purity: "You are further away from New York; you have been less industrialised and less invaded by foreign races."[23] But exactly what this means shocks when it comes shortly thereafter:

> The population should be homogeneous; where two or more cultures exist in the same place they are likely either to be fiercely self-conscious or both to become adulterate. What is still more important is unity of religious background; and reasons of race and religion combine to make any large number of free-thinking Jews undesirable.[24]

Eliot, then undergoing a painful separation from his wife, later attempted to suggest that he hadn't been quite himself during these lectures. Had it not been both for the fact that his poetry of earlier years too readily showed us the odious, squatting "jew . . . spawned in some estaminet in Antwerp" and for his life-long attachment to the rabidly anti-Semitic Maurras, the excuse might have carried more weight. Had his southern audience at the time been willing to acknowledge that history did not stop at Appomattox, they might have noticed that Eliot's remarks came only a few weeks after Hitler's seizure of power and been less appreciative than presumably they were.

At his best, though, during these years Eliot moved beyond this name-calling to try to evolve a considered defense of orthodoxy. In terms of poetry this led him to join in the debate, occasioned by I. A. Richards's work in the twenties, on the nature of truth in poetry and the type of belief to be expected of the ideal reader. Richards had pushed for a severance of poetry from any correspondence theory of truth by positing a radical distinction between poetic language and scientific language:

> A statement may be used for the sake of the *reference,* true or false, which it causes. This is the *scientific* use of language. But it may also be used for the sake of the effects in emotion and attitude produced by the reference it occasions. This is the *emotive* use of language.[25]

Poetry makes, then, not statements, but "pseudo-statements." These are designed to elicit a complex interplay of affects in the reader that, when the work of art is well constructed, result in a refreshed psychological equilibrium. If the reader were to grapple with the irrelevant question of belief in the poet's utterances, this could only impede the exercise in mental health: the crudity of assent or denial would interrupt the more delicate and subtle emotive response. "We must," concludes Richards categorically, "free poetry from entanglement with belief."[26] Reflecting the enormous popularity of Freud in the postwar years, Richards's own emphasis on the psychology of the reader emitted a lunar glow that made it seem, to many, brighter than it actually was. Further, to those who felt increasingly trapped by the trumpeting contention of "isms," Richards's quiet and studied attention to the private world of emotion made of poetry a welcome oasis. It was, accordingly, in the spirit of Matthew Arnold's fond hope that the emotions aroused by poetry might do service for the lost ardors of religion that Richards assures us, "Poetry is capable of saving us."[27]

Between, on the one hand, Richards's rejection of poetry as statement making and his corresponding freeing of the reader from the
burden of evaluating the poet's philosophy and, on the other hand,
the insistence on poetry as propaganda voiced by, for example, vulgar Marxists, a wide space remained for Eliot to stake out his own
position. Here, though, as in almost all that Eliot produces in the
decade after his conversion, the steady refinement of his thought is
placed in service of a narrowing of sympathy. In a 1927 review of
Richards's *Science and Poetry*, Eliot begins, promisingly, by establishing
his basic differences from the author. He quite rightly takes Richards
to task for putting forth a purely psychological theory of value while
making no attempt to complement it with any *moral* theory of value.
Like Nietzsche, who had derided George Eliot for wanting to retain
the old Judeo-Christian morality while no longer believing in the
God who authorized it, Eliot (though with vastly different intention)
turns on Richards for, in effect, going one step further: he would
retain the psychological well-being traditionally attendant on the
moral life while abandoning all interest in what that life should look
like. Eliot thus scores heavily and fairly against Richards as spokesman for an age all too blithely committed to substituting mental
health for salvation: "Poetry 'is capable of saving us,' he [Richards]
says; it is like saying the wall-paper will save us when the walls have
crumbled."[28] Yet lest his reaction to Richards should seem to place
him in the camp of those who saw in poetry only its doctrine, in an
essay on Shakespeare in that same year, Eliot writes, "In truth, neither Shakespeare nor Dante did any real thinking – that was not
their job; and the relative value of the thought current in their time,
the material enforced upon each to use as the vehicle of his feeling,
is of no importance."[29] This rejection of the poet's worldview as in
any way decisive situates Eliot, all of a sudden, in a position very
close to Richards. The similarity appears even greater when Eliot
continues on to sketch what sounds like a completely emotive theory
of poetry. In holding up for comparison the line of Dante, "la sua
voluntade e nostra pace," and Shakespeare's, "As flies to wanton
boys, are we to the gods; / They kill us for their sport," Eliot claims
that although the philosophy behind Dante is superior, Shakespeare's poetry is equally great:

> But the essential is, that each expresses in perfect language,
> some permanent human impulse. Emotionally, the latter is just
> as strong, just as true, and just as informative – just as useful

and beneficial in the sense in which poetry is useful and beneficial, as the former.[30]

Guardedly, Eliot does not tell us, as Richards had done, just what
the use of poetry is except to say later that "it provides 'consolation':
strange consolation." This is cryptic and inadequate at best and indicates that Eliot's own thoughts on the subject, in the process of
being reworked, are as yet inchoate.

The year 1929 finds Eliot still wrestling with the problem of truth
and belief, though now more willing to acknowledge the possibility
that a poet's intellectual apparatus matters: "My point is that you
cannot afford to *ignore* Dante's philosophical beliefs, or to skip the
passages that express them most clearly; but that on the other hand
you are not called upon to believe them yourself."[31] What this
means, as it turns out, is that the reader must try to "understand"
the philosophy and to entertain the poet's worldview as "possible."
Such a stance, closer to Husserlian bracketing than Richards's pseu-
dostatements, represents an advance in sophistication, but still leaves
Eliot himself uncomfortable. He is almost certainly aware that Dante
had avowed didactic designs on his reader and therefore *intended*
more than this theory allows (Eliot will in later years snipe at those
who teach the Bible as "literature"), but knows equally well that
there would be little left of classical literature if we were to insist on
this kind of concordance between author and reader. As a result, no
sooner has he set down his thoughts than he is busy pointing out
their inadequacy in a lengthy footnote. Apparently with St. Thomas's
credo ut intelligam in mind, Eliot admits that belief and understanding
may be implicated with each other in ways that his theory ignores:

> But if you yourself are convinced of a certain view of life, then
> you irresistibly and inevitably believe that if any one else comes
> to "understand" it fully, his understanding *must* terminate in
> belief. It is possible, and sometimes necessary, to argue that full
> understanding must identify itself with full belief.[32]

And, in support, he provides personal testimony that as his belief in
the truth of Dante increased, so has his poetic appreciation:

> And the statement of Dante seems to me *literally true*. And I
> confess that it has more beauty for me now, when my own ex-
> perience has deepened its meaning, than it did when I first read

it. So I can only conclude that I cannot, in practice, wholly separate my poetic appreciation from my personal beliefs . . . Actually, one probably has more pleasure in the poetry when one
shares the beliefs of the poet.[33]

This modest assertion seems faithful to experience and shows Eliot
in an increasingly rare, winning moment as a man grappling with
reality rather than pontificating on it. The objections he raises
against his own theory, however, return him to the starting block.

The instant of weighing possibilities is brief, for when Eliot takes
up the matter in the following year, the ossification of thought that
characterizes so much of his work of the thirties is in evidence. In
"Poetry and Propaganda" (February 1930), annoyed in equal part,
first, that the philosopher Whitehead had claimed to learn from
Shelley and Wordsworth and, second, that what he learned was
termed a "doctrine" (of organic nature), Eliot is moved to make "a
fresh start" on the problem. A long way from his remarks of 1927,
where he considered the poet's ideas as nothing more than an indifferent vehicle for transporting emotions to the reader, he now is
prepared to acknowledge that a great many poets, and among these
the best, must be labeled "propagandists." The important distinction to be made, he goes on, is between "responsible" and "irresponsible" propagandists. And to understand this distinction he
believes it helpful to group poets into three categories on the basis
of how they obtain their ideas: (1) The philosophic poet like Lucretius and Dante "who accepts one philosophy of life so to speak in
advance, and who constructs his poem on one idea"; (2) the poet
like Shakespeare and Sophocles "who accepts current ideas and
makes use of them, but in whose work the question of Belief is much
more baffling and evasive"; and (3) poets like Goethe and Blake
who, playing the role of philosopher *and* poet, "have their own ideas
and definitely believe them."[34] Because the second group is so difficult to pin down in terms of a system of beliefs, Eliot feels it would
be misleading to see them as anything we might reasonably call propagandists. Of the two remaining groups, it is the first that he wants
to call "responsible," the third "irresponsible." The basis for this
radical sorting out is not derived from appeal to literary history –
Goethe, it seems safe to say, has been canonized, Blake at least be-
atified – but, as it looks, from a consideration of their power to
convince ideologically. Eliot explains: "The philosophies of Lucre-

tius and Dante, different as they are from each other, are still potent to influence mankind. I cannot imagine any reader today being affected in his theological view by Milton [representative of the class of Goethe and Blake]."[35] At first glance, the notion that Lucretius enjoys a currency absent in Milton or Goethe or the Romantics sounds preposterous, so much so, in fact, that Wellek, rightly suspicious of Eliot here, concludes that the opposite fear is what motivated his statement: "Lucretius' version of Epicurus is dated and innocuous, while Shelley's revolutionary faith and Goethe's paganism and naturalism (badly misinterpreted, I think) constitute an immediate challenge to orthodoxy."[36] Wellek is one of the few to see what is at stake in such remarks by Eliot, but nonetheless goes a bit askew in his analysis. Lucretius, as propounder of a pure materialism, would undoubtedly have been seen by Eliot as an ancestor of communism, which he regarded as the most rigorous materialistic position available in the modern world and one that obviously enjoyed massive subscription. This, then, would account for the potency Eliot senses in Lucretius as well as his respect, already noted, for the coherent "naturalist" view. But Wellek is surely correct to detect something amiss in the assessment of the Protestant–Romantic–liberal lineage as powerless, for Eliot had battled against just this tradition for fifteen years. Now his strategy is to summarily dismiss as impotent that which he and those who shared his animus could not overcome. This maneuver is repeated elsewhere when he explains why Shelley, whose ideas he finds "repellent," lacks the ability of Dante and Lucretius to persuade:

> It is not the presentation of beliefs which I do not hold, or – to put the case as extremely as possible – of beliefs that excite my abhorrence, that makes the difficulty. Still less is it that Shelley is deliberately making use of his poetic gifts to propagate a doctrine; for Dante and Lucretius did the same thing. I suggest the position is somewhat as follows. When the doctrine, theory, belief, or "view of life" presented in a poem is one which the mind of the reader can accept as coherent, mature, and founded on the facts of experience, it interposes no obstacle to the reader's enjoyment, whether it be one that he acccept or deny, approve or deprecate. When it is one which the reader rejects as childish or feeble, it may, for a reader of well-developed mind, set up an almost complete check.[37]

The inability to persuade, then, is not to be understood as referring to the common reader, but to those, like Eliot, of "well-developed mind." Since Eliot, more than most, realized that a society of such minds could not exist, he became increasingly insistent, as will be seen, that taste would have to be imposed from above.

Eliot's attempted balance between the emotive-aesthetic and doctrinal evaluations of poetry shifts, then, in the thirties toward the latter. The last effort to accommodate both in anything approaching parity occurs toward the end of "Poetry and Propaganda":

> Yet we can hardly doubt that the "truest" philosophy is the best material for the greatest poet; so that the poet must be rated in the end both by the philosophy he realizes in poetry and by the fulness and adequacy of the realization. For poetry – here and so far I am in accord with Mr. Richards – is not the assertion that something is true, but the making that truth more fully real to us; it is the creation of a sensuous embodiment. It is the making the Word Flesh, if for poetry we remember that there are various qualities of Word and various qualities of Flesh.[38]

But even here, while the evaluation of doctrine need not be temporally prior to the consideration of its poetic rendering, the doctrine itself, as the imagery of incarnation indicates, is ontologically prior. A poem allows us to experience its particular truth in its emotive density; it allows us to *feel* what it means to *believe*. While it is certainly possible that the affects aroused in readers, even in the case of responsible propaganda, lead them to the belief, nonetheless it is belief that is the poem's telos. This being the case, even within the category of responsible propaganda, which had only recently been large enough to include Lucretius as an equal partner of Dante, Eliot is compelled now by his own logic to create distinctions. As a Christian he simply cannot admit that Lucretius is as "true" as Dante, but as erstwhile champion of classicism he cannot bring himself to impugn the wellspring of the tradition. As a result, he is reduced to a solution painful to anyone who truly cares about the integrity of the classics: "It is high time that the defence of the Classics should be . . . permanently associated where they [*sic*] belong, with something permanent: the historical Christian Faith."[39] Once again the literary tradition is reformulated, though fewer were listening to Eliot this time.

Given this line of development, Eliot's ultimate stance of these years seems virtually inevitable. In the 1935 essay "Religion and Literature," he summons Christians, living in an unfortunately pluralistic age, to join him in maintaining "standards and criteria of criticism over and above those applied by the rest of the world."[40] This higher criticism, confident in its superiority, enjoins the faithful "to scrutinize their reading, especially works of the imagination, with explicit ethical and theological standards."[41] And the continuation of the passage reveals the now severely diminished role of aesthetic judgment: "The 'greatness' of literature cannot be determined solely by literary standards; though we must remember that whether it is literature or not can be determined only by literary standards." Artistic criteria, then, are to be invoked for little more than a generic sorting out, a distinctly secondary exercise.

Perhaps the best way to see what this sort of evaluation amounts to in practice is to look at Eliot's own critical work of the thirties, and especially at his estimations of Lawrence, who, of all his contemporaries, seemed to him to have squandered the greatest gifts in worship of tawdry idols. What is immediately clear, first of all, in Eliot's appraisal of Lawrence is that he does not misread him. He is acutely aware of just what is at stake for Lawrence and adept at judging the relative importance of the variety of his interests. All too well Eliot understands the lifetime effort to shrug off the mortmain of overbearing maternal solicitude and how this shapes Lawrence's corpus. Recognizing the tendency for this problem to become all-consuming, he fully appreciates the difficulty of dialogue for Lawrence when this is more than just the self talking to the self. But when all this has been said, we still find the following sort of commentary – which looks to be and ought to be marginal – at the center of Eliot's appraisal:

> I may make this [Lawrence's ignorance] clearer by instancing a peculiarity which to me is both objectionable and unintelligible. It is in using the terminology of Christian faith to set forth some philosophy or religion which is fundamentally non-Christian or anti-Christian. It is a habit towards which Mr. Lawrence has inclined his two principal disciples, Mr. Murry and Mr. Aldous Huxley. The variety of costumes into which these three talented artists have huddled the Father, the Son, and the Holy Ghost, in their various charades, is curious and to me offensive. Per-

haps if I had been brought up in the shadowy Protestant un-
derworld within which they all seem gracefully to move, I might
have more sympathy and understanding[42]

As with his earlier treatment of the Romantics, though now much
more pointedly, all of Eliot's praise for Lawrence's artistry seems in
the end as little more than a rhetorical set-up to demonstrate a potentially responsible propagandist gone irresponsible. Doctrine decides – "The false prophet kills the true artist."[43]

What of Eliot's own poetry during this period? What influence did
the preoccupation with orthodoxy have on his own creative expression? Would he be willing to admit himself into the ranks of the
responsible propagandists? In moving toward an answer to these
questions, the best starting place is the most obvious point of connection between the dictates of the prose and the practice of the
verse: the use of tradition. Whereas in Eliot's preconversion poetry
tradition shows up as a jumble of shards, crying out to be reassem-
bled (a more honest rendering of the felt difficulty of fitting together the pieces of Maurras's creation than is indicated by the
essays), the postconversion poetry gains in coherence by understanding tradition to be the specifically Christian. This is not by any means
to say that the various personae are now one with the tradition. In
After Strange Gods, Eliot had distinguished between the solutions of
prose and the problems of poetry: "In one's prose reflexions one
may be legitimately occupied with ideals, whereas in the writing of
verse one can only deal with actuality."[44] But at least now the personae see the ideal; they are no longer under the double burden of
recognition *and* fulfillment. Syllables of liturgy, which once bubbled
up in Eliot's poetic deserts to create distant oases, now join together
to make a clearly discernible promised land.[45] The partial vision of
the stuttering "Hollow Men" – "For Thine is / Life is / For Thine
is" – gives way to the calm, though deeply felt, need for forgiveness
and the clear enunciation of contrition that concludes "Animula":
"Pray for us now and at the hour of our birth." Correspondingly,
the focus of the poetry has subtly shifted from the spiritual limitations of the personae to the religious reality. In the early work,
whether, for example, Prufrock can get an answer to (or even ask)
his "overwhelming question" looms up with paramount importance;
in contrast, whether or not an answer is forthcoming to the question
of the half-comprehending Magi at the Nativity – "were we led all

that way for / Birth or Death?'' – is dwarfed by the event itself. Eliot's early manifesto of artistic impersonality – "The more perfect the artist, the more completely separate in him will be the man who suffers and the mind which creates" – extends now, in its distrust of the (merely) individual, to include the reactions of the personae as well. The truth of orthodoxy remains essentially independent of its power to convert the human heart and, for Eliot, despite his own wrestlings and those of his poetic personages, far more important and interesting. This movement away from contingency is further reflected in the diction of the later poetry. In the early work Eliot had prided himself in the sharp rendering of physical immediacy. With an unflinching eye he recorded the minutiae of urban rot in a tonic rebuttal to idyllic Georgian landscapes. The detritus of the modern state's *Massenmenschen* clogged drainpipes and, by inference, souls. But the later work, impatient with the concrete, uses earth as little more than a vantage point for spiritual meditation. The specific rounds of human degeneracy are now deemed insignificant in comparison with larger universal patterns, and to capture these Eliot uses a much more abstract diction. The difference can be seen clearly in a comparison of pre- and postconversion treatments of winter:

> The winter evening settles down
> With smell of steaks in passageways.
> Six o'clock.
> The burnt-out ends of smoky days.
> And now a gusty shower wraps
> The grimy scraps
> Of withered leaves about your feet
> And newspapers from vacant lots;
> The showers beat
> On broken blinds and chimney-pots,
> And at the corner of the street
> A lonely cab-horse steams and stamps.
> And then the lighting of the lamps.
>   ("Preludes")

Before the time of cords and scourges and lamentation
Grant us thy peace.
Before the stations of the mountain of desolation,
Before the certain hour of maternal sorrow,
Now at this birth season of decease,

Let the Infant, the still unspeaking and unspoken Word,
Grant Israel's consolation
To one who has eighty years and no to-morrow.
                                    ("A Song for Simeon")

The heavily Latinate vocabulary of the second passage appeals to
Eliot for another reason, its connection with the Christian Middle
Ages. Having once claimed, in a youthful effort to rally the English
to Maurras's cause, that England was a Latin country, he now seems
determined to make it one by introjecting a language that can act
as a conduit for medieval modes of thought. What is to be gained is
apparent in his essay on Dante, where he compares Dante's strongly
Latinized Italian to the attenuated language of other European masters: "The Italian language, and especially the Italian language in
Dante's age, gains much by being the product of universal Latin.
There is something much more local about the languages in which
Shakespeare and Racine had to express themselves."[46] The advantage of Dante's language, we are told, consists in the fact that it can
effortlessly draw on the whole repository of scholastic philosophy.
This in turn provides Dante with a religious tradition so readily at
hand that the material world portrayed in his poetry is forever pointing allegorically to greater and greater depths. Shakespeare, according to Eliot, would not have been able to produce the luminosity of
the *Inferno*'s opening:

> Nel mezzo del cammin di nostra vita
>   mi ritrovai per una selva oscura,
>   che la diritta via era smarrita.

These remarks are persuasive but, oddly, don't prevent Eliot from
apparently attempting what was impossible for Shakespeare. Ronald
Bush has perceptively noted the willed aspect of Eliot's efforts to
write in this condensed religious mode, a quality nowhere more in
evidence than in the line just quoted: "Now at this birth season of
decease."[47] It is perhaps not altogether unfair to see the forced nature of this line as emblematic of the enormous pressure Eliot had
to exert throughout his life to contrive the conditions, the tradition,
by which he might live.

But eager to absorb others into his vision, Eliot's poetic interest
during the thirties began to turn from the lyric to the more broadly
engaging drama. Having built his own reputation on a poetry the
complex allusiveness of which deterred all but a highly educated

elite, he knew full well that even his starker, more accessible religious verse was not likely to have widespread appeal. (In fact, he would undoubtedly have been uneasy to think that it might.) The drama, however, born in religious ritual and cutting across class lines, might still enjoy popular favor without sacrificing artistic seriousness. Indeed, it seemed to Eliot at this point that along with the celebration of the Mass, drama could provide a way of reestablishing a meaningful sense of community otherwise absent in the liberal state:

> The most useful poetry, socially, would be one which could cut across all the present stratifications of public taste – stratifications which are perhaps a sign of social disintegration. The ideal medium for poetry, to my mind, and the most direct means of social "usefulness" for poetry, is the theatre.[48]

A further reason for this increasing preference for drama is that the personal statement implied by the lyric – and here he would have humbly included his own, despite the straining for impersonality – was by nature suspect to Eliot. Even the most chiseled lyric verse, he feared, may be no more than a cri de coeur, the very excess he had for so long despised in the Romantics. Moreover, drama required not only a distancing of the poet from his expression, but a contention of ideas that Eliot believed would of necessity reveal "imperfectly conceived philosophies."[49] Truth would out in the crucible of drama, or at least the spuriousness of the false would stand revealed. With this in mind, it would certainly have seemed to him no accident that the English Romantics found themselves almost utterly incapable of producing anything in this genre.

Eliot's own initiation into more publicly oriented forms of poetry came with the welcome commission to write the choruses and dialogue for a church fund-raising pageant of 1934. Since the money was to go for the construction of churches in London suburbs, the contrast between the sprawling City of Man and the neglected City of God provided an obvious point of tension, one of which Eliot took full advantage. In the finished product, entitled *The Rock*, representatives of secular doctrine make shadowy appearances and one by one are brushed aside by the right thinking. The communist "agitator," a ranting descendant of Dickens' Slackbridge, and the most persistent and dangerous of worldly antagonists, would siphon off church funds for low-income housing. This plausible attempt to advance the brotherhood of man at the cost of denying the fatherhood of God Eliot exposes as spiritually bankrupt. Even in economic matters the agitator is shown to be muddled as the foreman of the building crew, armed with Major Douglas's theory of social credit, argues him into submission. Less dangerous to the faithful because more obvious are the Fascist and the capitalist, who, though both ostensibly support the church, do so for transparently instrumentalist reasons. Finally, and somewhat gratuitously, from within the ranks of Christianity, Eliot feels obliged to summon up for bashing once again the dreaded Protestant. (Despite pointed reminders by Catholics that the Church of England was itself Protestant, Eliot never ceased to regard it as continuous with the Roman tradition.)[50] Here he resurrects the image of the fire-breathing Lutheran preacher and his iconoclastic offspring, the desecrating Puritans of 1640. Champions of four bare walls and a sermon, they too, across the ages, obstruct the Anglo-Catholic edifice.

Thus, in a work as apparently innocuous as a church fundraising pageant, Eliot has managed to air nearly all his political concerns. In short, he has created a piece of propaganda in the guise of an ecclesiastical exercise. This practice, so typical of Eliot's religiously oriented writing, both prose and verse, that it might be said to constitute a method is not always easy to detect, for generally the political urgency will be camouflaged by the appearance of being completely above such mundane squabbling. In the poetry, the contrast between the spiritual and the secular gives shape to the antithetically balanced line that becomes the hallmark of Eliot's verse in the thirties and forties. The first chorus in *The Rock* is marked by this device, which gives the impression of rendering moot all the political contention that follows:

> The endless cycle of idea and action,
> Endless invention, endless experiment,
> Brings knowledge of motion, but not of stillness;
> Knowledge of speech, but not of silence;
> Knowledge of words, and ignorance of the Word.
> All our knowledge brings us nearer to our ignorance,
> All our ignorance brings us nearer to death,
> But nearness to death no nearer to GOD.
> Where is the life we have lost in living?
> Where is the wisdom we have lost in knowledge?

> Where is the knowledge we have lost in information?
> The cycles of Heaven in twenty centuries
> Bring us farther from GOD and nearer to the Dust.

The cosmic irony achieved by playing off true (religious) wisdom against ephemeral information is a common enough poetic motif, but rarely has a poet been simultaneously so apparently contemptuous of the City of Man yet so embroiled in the debate over its organization.

The nature of orthodoxy and its power to attract and hold the lower stratum of society in its orbit is examined in the much more subtle *Murder in the Cathedral* of the following year. The play had been commissioned by the Bishop of Chichester, who had been very favorably impressed with a performance of *The Rock*, and again Eliot accepted without hesitation. The fact that the production was to be mounted within fifty yards of Becket's actual assassination was stirring in itself, perhaps doubly so for Eliot, who could not fail to have noticed the parallel with Greek tragedy that traced its origin, thematically and geographically, to the festival commemorating the slain Dionysus. Moreover, the martyrdom of Becket, recapitulating that of Christ, is *the* myth of Christianity.[51] For all these reasons, the use of a chorus, congenial to Eliot in any case because of its abstraction of the personal, seemed almost compelled by the classical associations. Wedding form and function, Eliot's purpose will be to show that Thomas's struggle for orthodoxy – doing the right thing for the right reason – bears on the spiritual well-being of the chorus of uneducated women of Canterbury in the same way that the Greek tragic hero's moral disposition affects the health of the polis. Unlike the situation in Greek tragedy, however, in which the chorus often comments perceptively on the career of the protagonist and thereby is all the more intimately involved in his or her fate, Eliot's chorus has absolutely no understanding of Thomas's agon with the tempters. Comprehension of orthodoxy, according to Eliot, is available only to the very few; the many, dimly patient, wait to receive its benefits in a mystical descent:

> These things had to come to you and you to accept them.
> This is your share of the eternal burden,
> The perpetual glory.

As a result of this view, Eliot's chief problem as a dramatist – and shortly as a social theorist – is how to establish a dialectic between classes in the Christian commonwealth.

The preponderance of critical opinion of *Murder in the Cathedral*, though largely laudatory, finds the play's main weakness to be precisely in this lack of any vital interaction between Thomas and the chorus. Katherine Worth's remarks in this regard may stand for others:

> The chorus are not involved in any human relationship with Becket real enough to move belief in his having power to affect their lives. They are only a collective voice, not living people with a stake in the action. Becket addresses them, typically from a physical height above them, in the pulpit, but hardly speaks to them. Whether his awareness of them affects his own inner development is extremely debatable . . . Eliot admitted to having difficulty imagining the chorus.[52]

But Worth and those who rightly join in her objection to the lack of interchange between Thomas and the chorus uniformly regard the failure as a technical one: Eliot, new to the theater and with few modern models to follow, simply didn't know quite how to incorporate a chorus into the dramatic action. Significantly, however, no one was troubled by the chorus in *The Rock,* which spoke as "the voice of the church." Indeed, it was *The Rock*'s choruses of which Eliot was most proud, and justly so. The problem of conceptualization involved in the chorus of *Murder* is due rather to the fact that Eliot has no real sympathy with "the scrubbers and sweepers of Canterbury" and even less belief that the remote and rarefied Thomas could learn anything from them. Conversely, his effect on them is attraction at a distance, the magnetism of his martyrdom aligning the lives of these women like iron filings. In language heavy with sexuality, now sublimated, the chorus confesses the error of their ways:

I have consented, Lord Archbishop, have consented.
Am torn away, subdued, violated,
United to the spiritual flesh of nature,
Mastered by the animal powers of spirit,
Dominated by the lust of self-demolition,
By the final utter uttermost death of spirit,
By the final ecstasy of waste and shame,
O Lord Archbishop, O Thomas Archbishop, forgive us,
                                      forgive
us, pray for us that we may pray for you, out of our shame.

Even these rawly physical progenitors of the animalistic, underbred Sweeney can be made to stop short here at the prospect of saintly abnegation. Of course, Thomas knows full well that these sentiments will fade in time, for as he reminds the chorus, "Human kind cannot bear very much reality." Yet he also knows, and Eliot would have us know, that this in no way diminishes the grandeur of his sacrifice. What we are left with then is a tenuous and unconvincing relationship between the self-sufficient orthodoxy of the spiritual elite and the mores of the great mass of believers. Aware of the difficulty, Eliot will do a great deal more systematic thinking on the problem by the time he readdresses it in his major cultural criticism of the late thirties and forties.

It would be misleading, however, to leave the impression that Eliot's only social concern is the corrigibility of the lower orders. The action in the play is motivated, after all, by the political conflict between church and state. If that conflict, overshadowed by Thomas's private struggle with pride, is less than coruscating, it is only because the issue is so firmly decided for Eliot. Though Hegel might have claimed, with the very similar *Antigone* primarily in mind, that the tragic situation arose from the conflict of two partial truths each of which believed itself to be the whole truth, this is manifestly not the case with *Murder*. Truth here is plainly all on one side. Indeed, it is precisely Thomas's inflexibility on this issue that lends him the tremendous dignity he enjoys throughout. Surrounded by timeservers, he stands alone as champion of the church's primacy, Eliot's own isolating position. The second tempter, who is the most eloquent voice on behalf of political efficacy, is effortlessly answered:

> Those who put their faith in worldly order
> Not controlled by the order of God,
> In confident ignorance, but arrest disorder,
> Make it fast, breed fatal disease,
> Degrade what they exalt.

The audience's temptation, one of which Eliot is quite aware, is, while admiring Thomas's singleness of purpose, to regard his position as politically fossilized, a quaint curiosity. To prevent this reaction, Eliot, in the play's most daring move, forcefully implicates the audience in the action. We are the heirs, not of Thomas with whom we all too comfortably identified, but of the assassins. As the third knight points out – and even in his self-serving speech, this we are meant to be stung by – the modern liberal state *required* the removal of such men as Thomas:

> Unhappily, there are times when violence is the only way in which social justice can be secured. At another time, you would condemn an Archbishop by vote of Parliament and execute him formally as a traitor, and no one would be called a murderer. And at a later time still, even such temperate measures as these would become unnecessary. But, if you have now arrived at a just subordination of the pretensions of the Church to the welfare of the State, remember that it is we who took the first step. We have been instrumental in bringing about this state of affairs that you approve. We have served your interests; we merit your applause; and if there is any guilt whatever in the matter, you must share it with us.

Eliot's challenge is unmistakable here, but just as obviously it is now incumbent on him to demonstrate what an alternative society informed by Christian orthodoxy would look like. And it is precisely this task he takes up in *The Idea of a Christian Society* and *Notes Towards the Definition of Culture*.

4

ARCHITECT OF A CHRISTIAN ORDER

As long as Eliot faced his enemies as a classicist pitted against Romantics, he engaged them on the field of history. However outmoded and outmatched his values may now seem retrospectively, he – and his French sources – genuinely believed that those who held these values might prevail as architects of the twentieth century. It was they, after all, who had the weight of tradition behind them. Maurras, who never abandoned the field, continued to contend as a fascist, enjoying a brief moment of ascension under the Vichy government, followed by imprisonment and ignominy. Eliot, more flexible because younger and considerably less embittered, wisely refused this path. Instead, he ceded contemporary history to the heretics and tried to gather a saving remnant around him in anticipation of a better day. That this day would come he was confident, since for him the essence of the tradition, orthodoxy, was a continuous stream whose journey, as it now appeared, happened to be in part underground. So sure was he of ultimate vindication that whereas the earlier, classical Eliot had tried in various forums to shape his age, the later, dogmatic Eliot, employing a form of ventriloquism popular in the thirties, gives the impression that history speaks through him:

> The World is trying the experiment of attempting to form a civilized but non-Christian mentality. The experiment will fail; but we must be very patient in awaiting the collapse; meanwhile redeeming the time: so that the Faith may be preserved alive through the dark ages before us; to renew and rebuild civilization, and save the World from suicide.[1]

What it meant specifically to redeem the time was that Eliot and the like-minded would put together a social blueprint against the day when men would realize that God was not dead but merely obscured. To this end Eliot participated first in the 1937 ecclesiastical conference entitled "Church, Community, and State"; later, and more importantly, from April 1938 to June 1943 he served as an active member in a gathering of Christian intellectuals known collectively as the Moot. This group, inspired by the work of Jacques Maritain, took its task to be the creation of a "Church within the Church," a Christian elite, "something analogous to 'the Party,' but wholly different from the Nazi or Communist Party."[2] Yet it was, in truth, not wholly different, for what it shared with the other more notorious parties was the belief that history, at some point, would have to be helped along.

The exact nature of this intervention was central to almost all of the Moot's proceedings. If not in the papers delivered, then invariably in the responses, the question that occupied (and ultimately paralyzed) the group was whether they ought to advocate active revolution – understandably the position of Karl Mannheim and Adolf Löwe, both refugees from Hitler's Germany[3] – or engage in a more subtle and conspiratorial indoctrination. (My use of "conspiratorial" is based on their own sense of themselves: they refer to themselves in their newsletter as "collaborators," and one of the original names proposed for the group was "The Christian Conspiracy.") Undoubtedly influenced by the example of Maurras, whose classicism, translated into practical politics, emerged transmogrified as fascism, Eliot was steadily an advocate of the latter course. His suspicion of revolutionary political action was buttressed, it should be added, by a healthy aversion to anything that smacked of totalitarianism, and in this regard he played the useful role of watchdog throughout the group's brief history. In response to Christopher Dawson's call for a totalitarian Christian order enforced by an all-powerful Church, Eliot responded bitingly, "The best thing a totalitarian state could do would be to abdicate."[4] Eliot's alternative is not, however, the democratic circulation of ideas – he was equally adamant that ideas of any subtlety simply could not be understood by the masses – but the imposition of values abstracted from the masses' ideal selves:

These should not be values imposed by the power of a personality or the doctrines of a "party," but elicited by a kind of representative character; and should have reference not necessarily to what people think they want, but to what they really

want and what they can recognise that they ought to want – to
people not always just as they are, but as they would like to be.[5]

The uneasy balance here between coercion and respect for the individual sounds, as Kojecky perceptively notes, oddly like a prescrip-
tion for Rousseau's dirigisme: "On le forcera à être libre." Perhaps
as Nietzsche, a more seasoned polemicist than Eliot, once observed,
we must choose our enemies carefully, for we come to resemble
them.

Meanwhile Eliot continued as editor of the *Criterion*, though the
almost complete estrangement of his interest from the current literary scene in favor of "theology, politics, economics, and education" and the steadily abstract manner in which even these fields
were discussed robbed the journal of the excitement it had generated while on the cutting edge of events.[6] Like the Catholic Church,
Eliot now appeared to be thinking in terms of millennia, showing
scant interest in the ad hoc maneuverings of time's slaves. In issue
after issue, what Eliot knew or cared to teach remained the same:
we must establish principles consistent – or at least not inconsistent
– with the instauration of the Kingdom of God. The role of Christian
vates did indeed have the positive effect of allowing him to offer a
salutary reminder that responsible politics ought to have a vision,
but at the same time this loftiness often manifested itself as a dis-
turbing aloofness from specific evils. Nowhere was this more apparent than in his response to the Spanish Civil War, when he urged
his readers not to be frightened by "the bogey of fascism" into supporting the Popular Front.[7] Christians must take the long view, and
given the fact that the information may be incomplete and that human action, in any event, will invariably be tainted with error, neu-
trality is the best policy:

> And those who have at heart the interests of Christianity in the
> long run – which is not quite the same thing as a nominal re-
> spect paid to an ecclesiastical hierarchy with a freedom circum-
> scribed by the interests of a secular State – have especial reason
> for suspending judgment.[8]

Giving Eliot the benefit of the doubt that had the preponderance
of right been on the side of Franco, he would have urged the same
abstention, it seems at least fair to say that from his supernaturalist
vantage point, important political distinctions inevitably became dan-
gerously blurred.

In January 1939 Eliot ceased publication of the *Criterion*. As he himself freely acknowledged in his farewell commentary, the shift of his own interests had made literature seem secondary – fatal in what purported to be a literary review. His earlier hope that Europe might be remolded by its best literary minds now, in the penumbra of World War II, seemed to him deluded. As partial explanation he points out that these things had not been clear in 1922 when he began his editorship, for "only from about the year 1926 [the date of the Action française's condemnation] did the features of the post-war world begin clearly to emerge."[9] One is tempted, however, to say that had Eliot not demanded so much from literature in his classical phase, he would not have been so despondent of its value subsequently. But it remains the case that Eliot's confidence in poetry to inaugurate a new order by recreating sensibilities evaporates as the thirties wear on. The formerly held belief that a poet might write against the historical grain now seems remote: "At the moment when one writes, one is what one is, and the damage of a lifetime, and of having been born into an unsettled society, cannot be repaired at the moment of composition."[10] Tradition (expanded far beyond literary tradition to include the whole unfolding of a people's history) has almost completely absorbed the individual talent. True, the poet qua cultural critic may envision a future, but the poet qua poet is bound to "actuality." And in full flight from the liberal cult of personality, Eliot obliquely criticizes his own earlier attempt to integrate these disparate talents: "For a poet to be also a philosopher he would have to be virtually two men: I cannot think of any example of this thorough schizophrenia, nor can I see anything to be gained by it: the work is better performed inside two skulls than one."[11] Not only is the poet incapable of playing the role of Shelley's "unacknowledged legislator of the world," but he or she is also ill suited for the more modest Arnoldian task of offering a "criticism of life" – this must be left to the Christian social philosopher. What is crucial here is that this psychic division of labor into what may be crudely called feeling and thought registers Eliot's loss of faith that the dissociation of sensibility can ever be remedied *in the individual*, the ostensible locus of his original concern. Not only must the dissociated self await historical remedy, but even then it will only find its complementary attributes in fellow members of society.

Thus, it is incumbent on Eliot to offer some outline of what this new social order might look like, and this he does in *The Idea of a Christian Society* (1939), delivered as a series of lectures just before,

and published just after, the outbreak of World War II. This book –
as evidenced by the title – reveals Eliot standing above the immediate
hurly-burly of contemporary events as a Christian Platonist. His use
of "Idea" as a transcendent reality perhaps fated to be realized only
imperfectly on earth is obviously indebted to the Greek philosopher:

> In using the term "Idea" of a Christian Society I do not mean
> primarily a concept derived from the study of any societies
> which we may choose to call Christian, I mean something that
> can only be found in an understanding of the end to which a
> Christian Society, to deserve the name, must be directed. I do
> not limit the application of the term to a perfected Christian
> Society on earth; and I do not comprehend in it societies merely
> because some profession of Christian faith, or some vestige of
> Christian practice, is retained.[12]

Platonic, too, is the use of this "Idea" to castigate existing forms of
social organization: communism, fascism, and liberal democracy all,
in varying degrees, fall short of the Christian ideal. And Eliot, as he
looks to puncture the smugness of the Western democracies that
believe themselves different in kind from totalitarian systems, insists
that the difference is only one of degree. Echoing the traditional
communist reading of the prevailing Western philosophy of liberalism, Eliot regards it as the decaying product of unfettered capitalism,
of "an age of free exploitation," and therefore just as implicated in
the materialist heresy as the ideology of the "pagan" communists
and fascists themselves. Perceptively (and Eliot is often a telling critic
of the liberal cause) he attacks liberalism for its lack of a telos. Because liberalism is a freedom *from* and not a freedom *for*, it is in
grave danger of leading the democratic mass toward "that which is
its own negation: the artificial, mechanised, or brutalised control
which is a desperate remedy for its chaos."[13] Thus, fascism and communism appear to Eliot as merely the logical extension of a rudder-
less, democratic materialism. It is with this in mind that he presents
the reader with his concluding either/or: "If you will not have God
(and He is a jealous God) you should pay your respects to Hitler or
Stalin."[14]

The overarching question of the book is thus the one that had
been exercising Eliot ever since his days as a "classicist": can a particular religion and politics be said to entail one another and what
would the connective ligaments look like? (The relationship of all

this to art he takes up at length in the later *Notes Towards the Definition of Culture*.) But having learned from the miseries of the Action française, he exchanges Maurras's starting point in politics for an ostensibly more orthodox one:

A usual attitude is to take for granted the existing State, and ask "What Church?" But before we consider what should be the relation of Church and State, we should first ask: "What State?" Is there any sense in which we can speak of a "Christian State," any sense in which the State can be regarded as Christian? . . . What I mean by the Christian State is not any particular political form, but whatever State is suitable to a Christian Society, whatever State a particular Christian Society develops for itself.[15]

Although this gives the impression that a smorgasbord of possible states exists for Christians to choose among, such apparent pluralism is belied by Eliot's essential thinking on the matter. It is quite clear that the state may not be liberal, nor democratic in any ordinary sense of the word. From the records of the Moot we know that a tiered society directed by a Christian elite was the working premise, and this is amply borne out in Eliot's text as well.[16] The state, in turn, is envisioned by Eliot as merely the framer and enforcer of laws consistent with the wisdom and well-being of this elite: "I conceive then of the Christian State as of the Christian Society under the aspect of legislation, public administration, legal tradition, and form."[17] While he undoubtedly believes that such a society would redound to the good of the mass as well, it is equally clear that this is only because it is to be a silent partner in the creation and administration of the commonwealth.

In delineating the sort of alternative social structure entailed by the desired alignment with the Christian ideal, Eliot again makes use of a Platonic stratagem. Having posited the dissociated sensibility – some men are characterized by the capacity for thinking, others by the capacity for feeling – Eliot translates psychic distinctions into social functions that quickly crystallize as classes. This move had been adumbrated in *After Strange Gods,* where he distinguished between "tradition" and "orthodoxy":

I hold – in summing up – that a *tradition* is rather a way of feeling and acting which characterises a group throughout generations; and that it must largely be, or that many of the elements in it must be, unconscious; whereas the maintenance of *orthodoxy* is a matter which calls for the exercise of all our conscious intelligence.[18]

In *Idea*, this unconscious–conscious distinction becomes the basis for sorting out those molded by the culture from the molders. As it turns out, it is tradition – an unthinking adherence to the "myth" of the society as it elaborates itself in daily life – that binds the majority of people together and guarantees the regularity of their behavior: "For the great mass of humanity . . . as their capacity for *thinking* about the objects of faith is small, their Christianity may be wholly realized in behavior: both in their customary and periodic religious observances, and in a traditional code of behavior towards their neighbors."[19]

This, then, forms Eliot's large lower class, whom he designates "the Christian Community." Like Plato's class of artisans, they are being most fully human when exercising a steady temperance. They should remain dimly aware of their own ultimate unworthiness but not be agitated by this knowledge: "While they should have some perception of how far their lives fall short of Christian ideals, their religious and social life should form for them a natural whole, so that the difficulty of behaving as Christians should not impose an intolerable strain."[20] The poor women of Canterbury in *Murder* had testified that when actually forced to think through the religious significance of events, "the strain on the brain of the small folk" was nearly unbearable, and it is this overloading of circuitry that Eliot's scheme is, among other things, designed to prevent. Conversely, these women – who may be taken as a fuller embodiment of what is merely sketched in *Idea* – do react with almost preternaturally keen instincts to the prevailing religious atmosphere. They may not be able to parse orthodoxy but they can smell it, or its absence. When it is absent, the habitual, mindless pattern of their lives, which Eliot regards as the deepest impress orthodoxy can make on them, begins to disintegrate.

The problem, of course, is even more urgent in the twentieth century than it was in the twelfth, for the power of the mass, unleashed by the laissez-faire logic of the liberal, bourgeois state, is volcanic. Eric Hobsbawm has recently argued that the lineaments of the modern state in the late nineteenth and early twentieth centuries have evolved in an effort to neutralize democratization: "What indeed, would happen in politics," the privileged wondered, "when the masses of the people, ignorant and brutalized, unable to understand the elegant and salutary logic of Adam Smith's free market, controlled the political fate of states."[21] Eliot shares this fear of the masses, but for quite other reasons. No friend of the free market himself, he is perplexed instead by the incipient reign of vulgarity and tastelessness. His preference for sociological distinctions to political ones suggests as much:

> To substitute for "democratic" a term which for me has greater concreteness, I should say that the society which is coming into existence, and which is advancing in every country whether "democratic" or "totalitarian," is a lower middle class society: I should expect the culture of the twentieth century to belong to the lower middle class as that of the Victorian age belonged to the upper middle class or commercial aristocracy.[22]

Had Eliot identified this lower-middle-class culture as being largely imposed from above, he would have evolved the more sinister reading of the contemporaneous Frankfurt School, which detected in all this the machinations of a "culture industry." Instead, although he is aware of exploitation of the masses' desires, he sees the desires themselves as self-generated and in dire need of proper tutelage:

> I mean by a "lower middle class society" one in which the standard man legislated for and catered for, the man whose passions must be manipulated, whose prejudices must be humoured, whose tastes must be gratified, will be the lower middle class man. He is the most numerous, the one most necessary to flatter. I am not necessarily implying that this is either a good or a bad thing. that depends upon what lower middle class Man does to himself, *and what is done to him.* (italics added)[23]

The burden of thinking – and hence of the maintenance of order – falls to the guardians of the myth, who vigilantly scrutinize it in all its variousness for consistency with the orthodox kernel of truth that lies obscurely at the center. As long as the myth remains in vibrant contact with this truth, Eliot seems to feel that the refractory desires of the masses will respond in conformity. This highly conscious minority of guardians, referred to as the "Community of Christians," constitutes Eliot's elite:

> The Community of Christians – a body of very nebulous outline
> – would contain both clergy and laity of superior intellectual
> and/or spiritual gifts. And it would include some of those who
> are ordinarily spoken of, not always with flattering intention, as
> "intellectuals."[24]

Eliot is borrowing here from Coleridge's idea of a "clerisy," a body
of scholars drawn from all denominations who "were to be distrib-
uted throughout the country, so as not to leave even the smallest
integral part or division without a resident guide, guardian, and in-
structor."[25] This body of the learned would act as repositories and
nurturers of culture in the midst of a civilization that had come to
seem to Coleridge ever more "but a mixed good, if not far more a
corrupting influence."[26] But Eliot, again having learned from the
debacle of the Action française, is careful to exclude from his Community of Christians those intellectuals who, while insisting on orthodoxy, privately deny its truth. His elite will consist of only
"consciously and thoughtfully practicing Christians."[27] This insistence on sincere devotion is, moreover, obviously functional within
the system, for the elite not only cultivate the myth but also supervise
its inculcation. Here Eliot is aware, from the example of communism, that a cultural revolution presupposes thorough indoctrination, and he does not shy away from imitation. The difference is that
his regime will not dispense propaganda, but truth: "There is likely
to be, everywhere, more and more pressure of circumstance towards
adapting educational ideals to political ideals, and in the one as in
the other sphere, we have only to choose between a higher and a
lower rationalisation."[28] The ultimate goal of education in Eliot's
utopia will be to ensure that "there is a unified religious–social code
of behavior."[29] At this point, however, it is difficult not to sense that
we have returned to something very like the religiously restrained
masses of Maurras and Machiavelli, minus the cynicism. The Order
of hierarchy has been reaffirmed and is to be maintained by the
noble lie of Christianity, sanitized through Eliot's faith, to reemerge
as the noble truth.

Having at long last done what his French mentors could not –
sketch a consistent case for the metaphysically based natural right of
hierarchy – Eliot is understandably not eager to bring in politics,
which relies for its energy on the conflicting claims of antagonistic
interest groups. Instead, "politics" is so thoroughly absorbed by the

culture, for Eliot, that the word itself seems too crude to indicate
the subtle internal self-adjustments of the organic life of a people.
For those who might insist that an imperceptible politics is nonetheless a politics, Eliot has little patience. In *Notes Towards the Definition of Culture* (1948), his last and most fully developed statement
on social organization, he waspishly disqualifies from further discussion of culture those who hold such a view:

> I dare say that some readers will draw political inferences from
> this discussion: what is more likely is that particular minds will
> read into my text a confirmation or repudiation of their own
> political convictions and prejudices. The writer himself is not
> without political convictions and prejudices; but the imposition
> of them is not part of his present intention. What I try to say is
> this: here are what I believe to be essential conditions for the
> growth and for the survival of culture. If they conflict with any
> passionate faith of the reader – if, for instance, he finds it shock-
> ing that culture and equalitarianism should conflict, if it seems
> monstrous to him that anyone should have "advantages of
> birth" – I do not ask him to change his faith, I merely ask him
> to stop paying lip-service to culture.[30]

To try to see through culture to its political skeleton is tantamount
on Eliot's view to a materialistic indictment of religion itself, for
culture and religion are practically coterminous, distinguishable only
for the sake of analysis, much like form and content: "We may go
further and ask whether what we call the culture, and what we call
the religion, of a people are not different aspects of the same thing:
the culture being, essentially, the incarnation (so to speak) of the
religion of a people."[31] Eliot here has arrived at what, from a radically different perspective, Marx would have called pure ideology:
the derivation of all human activity from above.

That Eliot is taking great pains to exclude any overt mention of
politics is further evident when he provides an extensive sample of
the variety of things to be comprehended in the term "culture":

> It includes all the characteristic activities and interests of a peo-
> ple: Derby Day, Henley Regatta, Cowes, the twelfth of August, a
> cup final, the dog races, the pin table, the dart board, Wensley-
> dale cheese, boiled cabbage cut into slices, beetroot in vinegar,
> nineteenth-century Gothic churches and the music of Elgar.[32]

If this list were truly a representative one, it would be difficult to see why Eliot should even have bothered to take on the subject of culture, for there is little here he has much stake in defending. Moreover, given his claim that culture is incarnated religion, he leaves himself open to the potential embarrassment of having to demonstrate how Christianity is embodied in "boiled cabbage." In light of this, it is nearer the truth to see this catalog of culture as constituting a list of the things he is willing to *tolerate* in return for a conception of culture that can qualify as common yet have at its center things closer to his heart. Behind this descriptive view of culture as "the whole way of life of a people" is a normative view struggling to get out:

> A class division of society planned by an absolute authority would be artificial and intolerable; a decentralisation under central direction would be a contradiction; an ecclesiastical unity cannot be imposed in the hope that it will bring about unity of faith, and a religious diversity cultivated for its own sake would be absurd. The point at which we can arrive, is the recognition that *these conditions of culture are "natural" to human beings;* that although we can do little to encourage them, we can combat the intellectual errors and the emotional prejudices which stand in their way. (italics added)[33]

In keeping with the long tradition of conservative organicism from Burke and Maistre onward, Eliot observes strikingly that "only God can plan culture"; yet it is equally clear that the Christian elite has access to the blueprint and may insist on certain specifications.

Much as he had posited a Community of Christians within the larger Christian Community, Eliot is here attempting to create a restrictive notion of culture within the all-embracing original definition. This more rarefied culture will be distinguishably "higher" than that of the masses – yet continuous with it. To see what Eliot has in mind here, we need only look at how he envisions the role of art in his alternative schema. Since Eliot's rejection of the modern world originally assumed the shape of aesthetic revulsion and, even with his growing political sophistication, societies often seem to be judged more by their potential for creating and nourishing a vigorous and sophisticated art than for the distribution of justice, this is obviously no small matter for him. The difficulty he faces, however, is that once having adopted an anthropological use of the concept culture to designate the whole way of life of a people, he must somehow retrieve "art" from mass entertainment if he is not to abandon one of his dearest concerns. Or to place the problem in the old familiar terms of romanticism and classicism, he must import the distinctions of classicism into what is essentially a Romantic-*völkisch* vision of *Gemeinschaft*.

But, not without a certain irony, Eliot has to rely on a Romantic remedy to salvage classical culture. The source of the solution is traceable to the German idealists Fichte (Maurras's town crier of Teutonism) and Schelling, who posited a world spirit or mind that spun the material world from itself in order to apprehend itself. The journey, through history, of the world spirit was toward just this apprehension, and the instrument of self-knowledge was the human mind or, more accurately, the most highly refined human minds. To these minds, spirit shone luminously through substance: the cycle of knowledge was completed. That these rare minds, at the pinnacle of consciousness, were likely to be possessed by the artistic genius was conceded by Schelling and eagerly believed by the German Romantic poets. Subsequently imported wholesale to England by Coleridge, this belief sustains Eliot's cultural pyramid: "We should not consider the upper levels as possessing more culture than the lower, but as representing a more conscious culture."[34] This culture within the culture must necessarily be exclusionary: "For it is the essential condition of the preservation of the quality of the culture of the minority, that it should continue to be a minority culture."[35] Thus unencumbered by having to appeal to a mass audience, this higher culture aspires toward the point where spirit would come to know itself fully so that art and religion coalesce; there the religious consciousness recognizes its pure artistic (cultural) incarnation:

> Esthetic sensibility must be extended into spiritual perception, and spiritual perception must be extended into esthetic sensibility and disciplined taste before we are qualified to pass judgment upon decadence or diabolism or nihilism in art. To judge a work of art by artistic or by religious standards, to judge a religion by religious or artistic standards should come in the end to the same thing: though it is an end at which no individual can arrive.[36]

Indeed, it seems that it is only Eliot's inherent distrust of the individual that keeps him from arriving at something very like a concept of the Romantic genius here.

Instead, this dual use of "culture," which also creates a dual tradition, is used by Eliot to justify a hereditary class structure:

> If we agree that the primary vehicle for the transmission of culture is the family, and if we agree that in a highly civilised society there must be different levels of culture, then it follows that to ensure the transmission of the culture of these different levels there must be groups of families persisting, from generation to generation, each in the same way of life.[37]

While the two cultures are to be mutually nourishing, it is difficult, given Eliot's obvious sympathies, to see much percolating from below.[38] The masses seem instead to serve largely as a stable scaffolding for the activities of the elite, whose accomplishments may trickle down, imperfectly understood. Nor is education – liberal democracies' tool of equalization – desirable for the lower orders, for it merely deranges community by creating kaleidoscopically changing meritocracies with each generation: "It would disorganize society, by substituting for class, elites of brains, or perhaps only of sharp wits."[39] Although the lower classes are to be consoled with the knowledge that they too have a culture, it is clear that this culture is less enriching. The very disparity of cultures is, in fact, used by Eliot to justify political power, which he disingenuously views as something of a burden: "In a healthily *stratified* society, public affairs would be a responsibility not equally borne: a greater responsibility would be inherited by those who inherited special advantages."[40] The ability to generate and appreciate high culture thus delineates a political entity.

In this interplay between the artistic and the political, we can see Maurras's classicism, a third of a century after its discovery by Eliot, brought to fruition. A static society of fixed classes has been posited virtually outside of time; the only movement is the flash of epiphanic insight enjoyed by the few. The appeal of Eliot's construct, and there is much about it that is appealing, is the same as that found in Maurras's writings: the capitalistic calculus of self-interest is replaced by a strong sense of commonwealth, and the *felt* life of the whole is taken seriously as something essential to its well-being. All of this needed to be said, even if once again, and Eliot says it eloquently and persuasively. Further, his rebuttal to Karl Mannheim's alternative scheme of professional elites is convincing: doesn't the creation of specialized cadres each ignorant of the work of the others merely defer, not resolve, the problem of modern atomism? But despite the keenness of his criticism of liberal bourgeois society and its surgeons, his own remedy presupposes much of what he would do away with. As Raymond Williams has correctly pointed out, Eliot insists on the traditional class structure while overlooking the fact that these classes were formed by the economic system he purportedly disdains.[41] And even if Eliot were to reply that the classes he would champion are the more stable ones characteristic of feudalism, who would want to follow him in this direction, assuming it were possible? Of course, by claiming a God-directed priority for culture, Eliot hopes to make economics as well as politics seem incidental, but this too would set the intellectual clock back in a way acceptable only to those who believe we had *nothing* to learn from Marxian analysis.

In his most subtle exposition of these ideas, *Four Quartets*, this is precisely what Eliot does ask of us, though he asks so quietly and, at times, humbly that almost no one has noticed. Moreover, since the *Quartets* are written in the mode of religious vision, it might easily seem a violation of the devout man's most intimate relationship, that with his God, to ask about political motivation. This is especially the case where such a man seems to renounce the concerns of his politically engagé earlier life and, in a gesture of mutual forbearance, indicates that the reader should do so too:

> We cannot revive old factions
> We cannot restore old policies
> Or follow an antique drum.
> These men [royalists], and those who opposed them
> And those whom they opposed
> Accept the constitution of silence
> And are folded in a single party.
>
> ("Little Gidding," III)

But with all due deference to Eliot's religious sensibility, this sort of move – the calling of a truce while he attacks from above – has been typical of his work in the thirties and forties. We are steadily being admonished to place our faith in God rather than parliaments, but the God always turns out to be that of Charles I. This is not to assert, by any means, that Eliot's faith may not in some sincere way transcend politics, but rather to remind that it always *includes* politics.

This incorporation of the political within the religious is accomplished primarily through the intricate interweaving of symbolic patterns throughout the *Quartets*. The most comprehensive of these

symbols and the one that comes closest to serving as an organizing
principle is that of the rose. We encounter it first in "Burnt Norton,"
I, where the rose garden figures forth the realm of the alternative
past of choices not made, now distant and apparently existing only
in the speculative imagination, for "If all time is eternally present /
All time is unredeemable." Tentatively, however, the protagonist lets
himself be led into the garden and encounters a rarefied atmosphere of heightened intensity. In an image that recalls Donne's
visually transfixed lovers in "The Ecstasy," the roses stare back at
their observer "and the unseen eyebeam crossed." The suggestion
of exquisite love here is supported by the parallel of Eliot's rose
garden with that of *The Romance of the Rose,* a place difficult of access
but almost boundless in promised delight.[42] Up to this point the
roses have been associated with secular love even if of a very special
kind; the visitor has been moving through the garden in a ritualized
"formal pattern" with the roses, the stylized minuet of courtly love.
But just as Dante whose presence is felt everywhere in the *Quartets,*
had moved – personally and poetically, from courtly to divine love,
with the mystic rose as his culminating image – Eliot, making use of
this tradition, associates his roses too with divine illumination as his
protagonist enjoys a brief, stunning moment of revelation in the
garden. On the basis of this experience we are given a different
assessment of time:

> Time past and time future
> What might have been and what has been
> Point to one end, which is always present.

While cryptic enough on the face of it, the import of this gnomic
wisdom becomes clearer in "Burnt Norton," II, where some elabo-
ration is provided:

> At the still point of the turning world. Neither flesh nor
>   fleshless;
> Neither from nor towards; at the still point, there the dance
>   is,
> But neither arrest nor movement. And do not call it fixity,
> Where past and future are gathered. Neither movement from
>   nor towards,
> Neither ascent nor decline. Except for the point, the still
>   point,

There would be no dance, and there is only the dance.
I can only say, *there* we have been: but I cannot say where.
And I cannot say, how long, for that is to place it in time.

Almost like a Poundian vortex where movement is concentrated in a stationary nodal point, Eliot posits an ingathering of energy, dynamic in its ability to transfigure what comes before and after, static in its suspension of ordinary chronology. It is in such moments, then, that the past, seemingly unalterable at the beginning of "Burnt Norton," can be redeemed and linked – beyond cause and effect – with a newly envisioned future.

This is a highly personal statement, and even when Eliot expands his frame of reference to the spiritual malaise of twilit London in "Burnt Norton," III, nothing that might be considered political advocacy is evident. It is not until the two last quartets that the rose begins to accrete new meaning. In "The Dry Salvages" Eliot, borrowing from Hinduism, refers to the future as "a Royal Rose," but it is a future that is described in terms that are in part appropriate to the past, for the rose is "pressed between yellow leaves of a book that has never been opened." This notion of "a Royal Rose" belonging to both past and future is picked up in "Little Gidding," now however with more definite historical associations. Bearing in mind that Little Gidding was visited by Charles I during his defeat by Parliament, we are led to connect the royal rose with the white rose of the Stuarts.[43] Moreover, since Little Gidding was a community of Anglican contemplatives (destroyed by the Puritans as was Charles I), there is the neat dovetailing of Eliot's religion and politics. And we find that the past of Charles I bears relevance to the future as Eliot addresses the reader who might wish to follow Charles's footsteps:

        If you came this way,
Taking the route you would be likely to take
From the place you would be likely to come from,
If you came this way in may time, you would find the hedges
White again, in May, with voluptuary sweetness.
It would be the same at the end of the journey,
If you came at night like a broken king,
If you came by day not knowing what you came for,

> It would be the same, when you leave the rough road
> And turn behind the pig-sty to the dull façade
> And the tombstone.

The locale is both a particular and a spiritual landscape, and much like Virgil and Dante, who both place entrances to the otherworld on the map of Italy, Eliot here identifies Little Gidding as the English equivalent:

> There are other places
> Which also are the world's end, some at the sea jaws,
> Or over a dark lake, in a desert or a city –
> But this is the nearest, in place and time,
> Now and in England.

The "still point of the turning world" may be spatially indeterminate, but in England at least, one can only get there from the place consecrated by throne and altar.

With this in mind, we begin to see that the *Quartets'* view of time as following cyclical patterns organized around moments of rose-inspired transfiguration is a rebuttal to the liberal position of linear progress. This is certainly easy enough to overlook since throughout most of the four poems the implicit criticism of the liberal belief in secular redemption seems an almost inadvertent by-product of the call to higher things. However, Eliot himself is not content to leave the criticism completely implicit. In "Dry Salvages," II, the liberal view of time, so often in the past vilified by the French reactionaries, is directly addressed as a wearisome, earth-bound heresy:

> It seems, as one becomes older,
> That the past has another pattern, and ceases to be a mere
>   sequence –
> Or even development: the latter a partial fallacy,
> Encouraged by superficial notions of evolution,
> Which becomes, in the popular mind, a means of disowning
>   the past.

That Eliot is going out of his way to take issue with the liberal conception of time is further apparent if we dare to question one of the basic presuppositions of the *Quartets*, namely, that Christianity entails a cyclical view of history. A moment's reflection should reveal that this is at the very least difficult to square with the central tradition of Christianity, which, like liberalism, posits movement along a continuum. The Fall, the Incarnation, the Crucifixion, and the Second Coming are all unique milestones in earthly affairs, and while, as the medieval church fathers taught us, we might analogously recapitulate certain of these events, in no stronger sense could Christian history be seen as cyclical.[44]

The cyclical view of history is, however, completely in harmony with Eliot's class-bound view of the ideal society as advanced in *The Idea of a Christian Society,* that is, the same sort of people doing the same thing in the same place from generation to generation. And this kind of regularity, especially valued when it occurs in the lower orders, is held up approvingly in the *Quartets* as an alternative to the meandering pointlessness of the modern London masses. In "East Coker," I, Eliot stands on the site of his ancestral home and sees with the imagined eyes of his sixteenth-century ancestor, Thomas Elyot, who four centuries before had recorded his pleasure in watching as heavy-footed peasants danced in circles. The shared satisfaction of the two onlookers is due to the fact that the orderly rounds of the lowly are taken by both Eliots to be a reflection of macrocosmic order. To highlight the continuity of this family tradition, the easy fusion of Eliot and his namesake is registered in the diction as modern usage is elided with that of the Renaissance:

> On a Summer midnight, you can hear the music
> Of the weak pipe and the little drum
> And see them dancing around the bonfire
> The association of man and woman
> In daunsinge, signifying matrimonie –
> A dignified and commodious sacrament.
> Two and two, necessarye coniunction,
> Holding eche other by the hand or the arm
> Which betokeneth concorde. Round and round the fire
> Leaping through the flames, or joined in circles,
> Rustically solemn or in rustic laughter
> Lifting heavy feet in clumsy shoes,
> Earth feet, loam feet, lifted in country mirth
> Mirth of those long since under earth
> Nourishing the corn. Keeping time,
> Keeping the rhythm in their dancing

As in the living in the living seasons
The time of the seasons and the constellations
The time of milking and the time of harvest
The time of the coupling of man and woman
And that of the beasts. Feet rising and falling.
Eating and drinking. Dung and death.

Had Lawrence written these same lines, we might have sensed the throbbing, almost arterial, connection of these folk and the earth from which they make their living. Eliot is instead impressed with the *pattern* of their movements or, more precisely, seems relieved that these rude creatures can be marshaled into a pattern at all: "rustic," "clumsy," and "country" are not words of even arm's-length fondness in Eliot's mouth. The sacred, epiphanal rose, which guarantees their obedience through time, has, one suspects, rarely if ever shown itself to these souls.

That this whole section, typically taken as the gentle meditation on the passing of time by the man of faith, has a palpable political design on us can be substantiated by going to *The Governour* of Thomas Elyot, the source of the lines just quoted. The central thesis of his book is laid out vigorously and unmistakably in the opening chapters, where Elyot immediately launches into a diatribe against democratic notions of the public good and follows with a lengthy encomium to political hierarchy as consistent with God-given order. We may choose, he warns, between the chaos of egalitarianism on the one hand, or a king on the other. The supporting arguments from biblical patriarchy and insect organization were commonplace enough even in the Renaissance and likely to be persuasive only to the already persuaded. But perhaps this very lack of originality, allowing the book to serve as a ready warehouse of virtuous-sounding commonplaces for the governing class, is what ensured its considerable popularity in the sixteenth century. Of its many readers, not the least was the future James I, who would have found ample encouragement for his adamant insistence on divine right in Elyot.[45] It is fair to say, then, that in appealing to this work, Eliot is not just making use of an obscure family document in praise of dancing but of something that was a well-recognized part of the literature in defense of monarchy and hierarchy. And as we know from *The Waste Land* and elsewhere, Eliot does not simply import lines out of context, but rather takes his allusions as a sort of shorthand for invoking a world against which the modern world may be compared.

Further confirmation that Elyot's ordered universe provides a touchstone in Eliot's poem lies in their common appeal to the notion of the four elements, which with Christian modification, survived from its origin in Empedocles down through the Renaissance. These elements are the stuff of which the *scala naturae* is formed, as Elyot points out a few pages into his book:

> Behold the four elements whereof the body of man is compact, how they be set in their places called spheres, higher or lower according to the sovereignty of their natures, that is to say, the fire as the most pure element, having in it nothing that is corruptible, in his place is highest and above other elements. The air, which next to the fire is most pure in substance, is in the second sphere or place. The water, which is somewhat consolidate, and approacheth to corruption, is next unto the earth. The earth, which is of substance gross and ponderous, is set of all elements the lowest.
>
> Behold also the order that God hath put generally in all His creatures, beginning at the most inferior or base, and ascending upward . . . so that in everything is order, and without order may be nothing stable or permanent; and it may not be called order, except it do contain in it degrees, high and base, according to the merit or estimation of the thing that is ordered.[46]

That Eliot is quite consciously structuring his poem vertically by means of the gradations described by Elyot is perhaps nowhere clearer than in the account of the dancing peasants. These country folk seem almost purely compounded of Elyot's "gross and ponderous" earth, "of all elements the lowest" and perpetually on the verge of losing human form altogether, reabsorbed into nature: "Feet rising and falling. / Eating and drinking. Dung and death." At the same time it is the fire, that "most pure element" around which they are dancing, but seem to partake of very little, that organizes their life at its best.[47] (How fire and the rose are symbolically related will be discussed shortly.) Nor is this interplay of the elements an isolated example. As Helen Gardner pointed out in her classic explication of the *Quartets*, the four elements occur systematically in each of the separate poems, with each quartet being dominated by a different element.[48] She does not, however, find it at all odd or even worthy of some discussion that a twentieth-century poet should employ this antiquated "physics" to account for what she calls "the material of mortal life."[49] Perhaps her unwillingness to press Eliot here offers one of the clearest examples of the weakness in applying largely New Critical methods to a poet who was so deeply grounded in historical controversy.

Whereas the element of fire figures fleetingly in "East Coker," it dominates "Little Gidding," which borrows its name from a spiritual home of deeper significance than the ancestral one of "East Coker." Moreover, since Eliot's purpose is to move from the purely personal to the communal, the Anglican retreat of Little Gidding serves as "beginning" for the society as a whole (despite the ecumenical gestures in section III). The poem itself is set in "midwinter spring," the nadir of the year but a time in which the appearance of a brief, bright sun offers hope of renewal. As the sun seems to blaze into hibernating souls, Eliot, systematically translating the natural cycles into Christian idiom, is put in mind of the "pentecostal fire" that burned over the heads of the apostles, revivifying them spiritually. From there, the reader need only make a short associative leap to conjure up the episcopalian miter, symbol of the pentecostal fire of which bishops are the direct heirs. And once we recall that Charles I was a noted champion of the episcopacy, almost all of Eliot's values come to seem as natural as the sun itself.[50] Among other things – but prominent among them – this fusion of Eliot's religious and political convictions is what is being ratified in the transcendent claim of the poem's last lines:

> All manner of thing shall be well
> When the tongues of flame are in-folded
> Into the crowned knot of fire
> And the fire and the rose are one.

If one should protest that this particular set of values has long been laid to rest and therefore can hardly be seen as natural, Eliot neatly relies on the double nature of fire as both destructive and transmutative to suggest otherwise. In the most daring set of images in the *Quartets*, Eliot first likens the fire-bombing planes of the Luftwaffe to the flame-bearing dove of the Holy Spirit and then reverses the comparison:

> After the dark dove with the flickering tongue
> Had passed below the horizon of his homing
>   ("Little Gidding," II)

The dove descending breaks the air
With flame of incandescent terror
Of which the tongues declare
The one discharge of sin and error.
                    ("Little Gidding," IV)

Clearly it is only by succumbing to the second of these doves that
we can wrest something from the ashes of the first ("Sin is Behovely,
but / All shall be well"). This notion of the power of fire to redeem
man's destructive impulses – Northrop Frye has described the *Quartets* convincingly as purgatorial[51] – is put to service to intimate that
the Puritans' destruction of both the chapel at Little Gidding and
the person of the king has not eradicated the inhabiting spirits but
sent them abroad in more refined form as symbols: "What they had
to leave us – a symbol: / A symbol perfected in death." Though
Eliot might counter by saying that this passage refers as well to the
Puritans, themselves defeated, it is difficult to see what of symbolic
significance they have left us in terms of the poem. The effort to
include them seems to be made in an attempt to absorb and neutralize them rather than grant them status on an equal footing. Any
doubts that Eliot's amnesty is insincere should be dispelled by a look
at the 1947 essay on Milton, where he insists, "The fact is simply
that the Civil War of the seventeenth century . . . has never been concluded."[52]

To redraw all of the old battle lines, it remains only for Eliot in
the *Quartets* to incorporate his aesthetics into the mystery of the fire
and the rose, and this he does brilliantly. The danger, which occasions the brilliance, is that if the old classicism is conjoined in too
bald a fashion to what is now presented as virtually mystical truth,
the whole compound will come to seem partisan in a way that Eliot
certainly does not wish. To avoid just this appearance, he inserts in
section V of each of the first three poems a steady lament on the
inherent failure of art, including his own poetry, to give adequate
utterance to the complexity of revelation. This, of course, is in keeping with the overall tone of humility, but more importantly looks
like a dismissal of classicism from the sacerdotal status it had always
enjoyed in Eliot's estimation. No sooner, however, has the possibility
presented itself that Eliot is at last dissolving, in part, his old trinity
of preferences than he begins slowly to reconstitute it. In "Little
Gidding," I, we are exhorted to kneel before the site of the chapel,

for "the communication / of the dead is tongued with fire beyond the language of the living." And in the next section we discover exactly what this means for the poet as he encounters a "familiar compound ghost" (the religious parallel is fully intended) made up of his masters, especially Dante. The ghost speaks presumably with fire-consecrated tongue, thereby allowing the literary tradition to take on the glory of the religious; moreover, since the poet has in-corporated the tradition into his own work – as far back as "Tradi-tion and the Individual Talent," we were told that the best part of a poet's work may be that in which "the dead poets, his ancestors, assert their immortality most vigorously" – this tongue also becomes his in a secular parallel to pentecostal immanence:

> So I assumed a double part, and cried
>   And heard another's voice cry: 'What! are *you* here?'
> Although we were not. I was still the same,
>   Knowing myself yet being someone other –
>   And he a face still forming; yet the words sufficed
> To compel the recognition they preceded.

Having sanctified *his* version of the literary tradition as well as his own part in it, Eliot promptly calls for an end to the thirty-year de-bate in which he has been engaged. This self-serving charity, which would have the effect of defusing any further dissent, is urged by the ghost as he gently rebukes the poet for clinging to the old aesthetic battle standards:

> And he: 'I am not eager to rehearse
>   My thought and theory which you have forgotten.
>   These things have served their purpose: let them be.
> So with your own, and pray they be forgiven
>   By others, as I pray you to forgive
>   Both bad and good.

Eliot tacitly acknowledges that much more was at stake in the debate than aesthetic preferences by invoking the full force of Christian forgiveness, bizarrely incommensurable with the settling of a mere literary squabble.[53] Thus, he seems willing to abandon his formerly held classicism and all it stood for. But again, and perhaps this can-not be stressed too much, Eliot's method is to indicate that he is giving up his old aesthetic and political allegiances in favor of a transcendent religious point of view, while camouflaging the fact that his religion entails these allegiances. Indeed, one often wonders what, beyond perhaps a certain world weariness, would be left of Eliot's religion after the subtraction of these elements.

The most subtle implication of the aesthetics and politics with the religious vision occurs in the climax of the *Quartets,* the last section of "Little Gidding":

> What we call the beginning is often the end
> And to make an end is to make a beginning.
> The end is where we start from. And every phrase
> And sentence that is right (where every word is at home,
> Taking its place to support the others,
> The word neither diffident nor ostentatious,
> An easy commerce of the old and new,
> The common word exact without vulgarity,
> The formal word precise but not pedantic,
> The complete consort dancing together)
> Every phrase and every sentence is an end and a
> > beginning,
> Every poem an epitaph.

The first two and a half lines of the passage establish the religious motif of circularity that has been employed throughout, appealing to notions of personal birth and rebirth, as well as to the public cycle of ecclesiastical ritual as it acknowledges the revolving seasons of the divine calendar, the cosmic pattern. To move from here to the consideration of language that follows does not constitute a radical ellipsis but, in the mind of the man who defended Maurras's religious bona fides on the basis of his prose style, an obvious extension of the discussion of spiritual discipline. Only when God is properly understood as the Word (and this involves Loyola-like ascesis for Eliot) can our own words be said to observe decorum in its profoundest sense of right measure. To employ Derridean terms, if one must, Eliot's universe is unrepentantly "logocentric." The Word that orders our words also organizes the users of words, as Eliot hints in the anthropomorphism of the last part of the passage. The patterned dance of the "common" word "without vulgarity" should recall the similar dance of the well-behaved peasants in "East Coker"; now, however, the elite has joined in, careful of their dignity yet not condescending: "The formal word, precise but not pedantic." The resultant culture, maintained in common yet with obvious distinctions, parallels the social schema he was to lay out in *Notes Towards the Definition of Culture* a few years later.[54] To locate Eliot's source for establishing this odd intimacy between the hierarchy of the sentence and the sociopolitical hierarchy, we need only turn to Maurras:

> Just as decadence in literature had disposed man to permit the decadence of the country, so the renaissance of the classical techniques produced hopes and desires for reconstruction in fields quite removed from art and language. The degradation of our tongue, the tortured rhythms, that kingdom of words where subversion engenders total dislocation, all this reminds us of the subversion born of other crises. Sibling in blood to what philologists call a "personal style," the literature of personal individualism tended to consign to oblivion all readers but the author himself. How could such a literature not be slanted in favour of a social system which puts the citizen in opposition to the state and, in the name of a state which would preside over its own destruction, incites its citizens now to the frenzy of insurrection, now to the torpor of civic indifference.[55]

Eliot, by the time of the *Quartets,* would never have worded the argument so provocatively – or obviously. Maurras's raw polemics had always hurried Eliot away from the nuanced discriminations with which he felt most comfortable. Indeed, the most persuasive case for his position is found in the *Quartets,* where it occurs by indirection and allusion, where the connection is whispered to the reader. But this should not blind us to the fact that Maurras's original insight in this as in so much else was the axis along which Eliot organized his thought throughout his career. Maybe that too was part of the meaning of "in my beginning is my end."

5

VISIONS AND REVISIONS

In part because of his belief that drama was the art best suited to
the cultural integration of all strata of society, in part because the
"demon" that once drove him to "meditative verse" seemed to have
been, if not exorcised, at least tranquilized by church ritual, Eliot
abandoned nondramatic poetry entirely following the war. The
graceful harmonies of the *Four Quartets* had superseded the synco-
pated rhythms of *The Waste Land* to the satisfaction of Eliot if not
always to that of such earlier champions as Pound, for whom disgust
with the modern world had gone beyond being a stimulus to a career
and become the career itself. Moreover, for Eliot, speaking with the
authority of the church and the reputation of his own poetic achievement, the more personal voice of meditative verse now seemed out
of place. He had become the tradition that future individual talents
would have to reckon with. While this may seem a premature ossification of great gifts, it is in keeping with a view Eliot had maintained about himself. Having always regarded his body as a stained
and ill-fitting suit of clothes, he tended to present himself, from early
in his career, both in his choice of poetic personae and in private
life, as much older and more enfeebled than he actually was. Now,
although he had two decades of life still left, he seemed to begin
considering himself with a posthumous eye. This is evident not only
in his turning away from the young man's art of the lyric, but in
his prose work as well. His essays of this period generally add little
to what had been said earlier, but show rather a concern to mol-
lify the harshness of certain judgments, in keeping with the ostensibly conciliatory spirit of the *Quartets,* and to smooth out the rough
edges in his own slowly forged positions. Unheard before, a tone
he occasionally strikes in these essays (especially when the essay
was originally delivered as a lecture) is that of mildly amused de-
tachment, much like that of someone not wanting to admire a well-
done bust of himself too obviously. On hearing that he was to be

awarded the Nobel Prize for Literature in 1948, Eliot, though pleased with his much deserved honor, observed wryly, "The Nobel is a ticket to one's funeral. No one has ever done anything after he got it."[1] Whether a function of character or destiny, the prophecy was largely borne out.

The one significant contribution to his overall vision for a new social order that Eliot did make after becoming Nobel laureate was the 1949 comedy *The Cocktail Party*. This play represented his most sustained effort to reach a widely diverse audience while still being deeply serious, or as he put it in the conclusion to *The Use of Poetry and the Use of Criticism*, "He [the poet] would like to be something of a popular entertainer, and be able to think his own thoughts behind a tragic or a comic mask."[2] By the time of *Notes Towards the Definition of Culture*, this wish to combine the exoteric and the esoteric in drama came to be seen as the most effective artistic means of achieving a common culture. There would be something to hold both groundling and sophisticate as they sat together in communal experience. Nor were the pleasures to be totally disjunct, for in keeping with Eliot's notion of gradations of apprehension, the less astute mass of playgoers would unconsciously imbibe what their cleverer neighbors savored consciously. Here we might think – for it is almost certain Eliot did – of the Catholic Mass, where an ability to comprehend the Latin may add to one's experience, but the inability does not prevent a genuine spiritual response.

If one were to judge solely by the vast interest inspired by *The Cocktail Party*, then Eliot would seem to have achieved his desired purpose. The play attained popular success first on Broadway, then in London, and finally on American television, where it was seen by three and a half million viewers. Yet, whereas it is difficult to measure the unconscious effect of the play on the large viewing public, it is a safe bet that its mass appeal registered more a wish on the part of the audience to be brushed by the master's work then any real engagement, conscious or unconscious, with the elaborate social vision that informed it. (A few years later, it might be recalled, 14,000 Minnesotans would surround a baseball field to observe the spectacle of Eliot delivering the listener-unfriendly talk "The Frontiers of Criticism."[3]) The Edinburgh *Daily Express*'s dutifully admiring but bewildered review "Beautiful – But What's the Meaning,"[4] that appeared the morning after the premier of *The Cocktail Party* would undoubtedly have set most of its readers' heads nodding in agreement.

This is not to say that Eliot's intention to embrace in a meaningful way a varied audience *had* to be frustrated. Samuel Beckett's *Waiting for Godot*, a play that resembles Eliot's insofar as it offers up a daring blend of comedy and alienation, is reported to have made an enormous impression on the inmates of San Quentin Prison.[5] Nor is the difficulty due to the fact that one simply *must* read the social theorizing of a dramatist in order to grasp what he or she renders on stage. One can think of countless examples to the contrary, the most relevant perhaps being Sartre, whose *No Exit* stands as a Marxist counterpart to Eliot's play but does not require for its effectiveness a knowledge of Sartre's reflections on communism. The reason Eliot's play fails to make the desired impress on the wide audience it solicits is due rather to the fact that it all too accurately reflects his social theorizing and mirrors its essential weakness. Just as his social writings, and here I'm referring to *The Idea of a Christian Society* and *Notes Towards the Definition of Culture*, failed to show how the lower orders interacted with the higher except as objects of manipulation (all in the name of Christian community), so too *The Cocktail Party* fails because the organic society based on Christian love that the play implies is belied by the condescension of "the Guardians" as they coolly orchestrate the lives of the uninitiated. If the popular audience was baffled by the import of the play, the fault lay in the conception.

But to say this without glancing at particulars is to pass an unfairly summary judgment on the play, and this is especially so since it is not among Eliot's most widely known works. In fact, because *The Cocktail Party* has waned so severely in popularity after its initial attraction, a brief account of the plot might be helpful before proceeding further.

The play opens in the drawing room of Edward and Lavinia Chamberlayne, where, amidst the endless small talk Eliot has always satirized so brilliantly, we come to discover that Lavinia is not present at her own party. Edward feebly tries to convince the various guests – Celia his mistress, Alex the adventurer, Julia the irritating old busybody, Peter the aspiring artist, and a mysterious unidentified man – that everything is fine, only to confess to the unidentified man, after the others' departure, that Lavinia has left him. Surprisingly, the unidentified man knows where Lavinia is, claims to have the ability to produce her, and agrees to do so after he induces Edward to admit that he wants her back and will promise not to ask her where she has been. At this point Celia returns and, although she is at first hurt to learn that Edward actually wants Lavinia back, is soon moved to confess (the play is full of confession) that her relationship with him has been a desperate and unfulfilling attempt to concoct ecstasy. They part amicably with mutual relief. On the following day, the unidentified man returns to tell Edward that although he knows Edward will change his mind about wanting Lavinia back, events are now fated. Soon thereafter all the original guests arrive, having been informed by Julia and Alex that Lavinia requested their presence by telegram. Lavinia finally puts in an appearance and seems surprised to see the crowded room for she has invited no one. Left alone with Edward, she shows herself expert at pointing out his faults, and he reciprocates as Act 1 comes to an end.

Act 2 takes place in the consulting room of the psychiatrist Sir Henry Harcourt-Reilly, whom Edward has been persuaded to visit by Alex. Although Edward feels trapped when he recognizes Sir Henry as the unidentified man at his party, he again falls under his sway and is persuaded to describe his own anguished state. As he concludes, Lavinia arrives for an arranged consultation, annoyed to find her husband there. They soon resume their mutual recrimination only to be interrupted by the doctor who pronounces them both thoroughgoing self-deceivers. He diagnoses Lavinia as isolated because of her incapability of inspiring love, Edward because of his incapability of loving, and sends them off, presumably improved with this knowledge, to make the best of things. Far different is the case of Celia, who has been shepherded to Sir Henry by Julia. She feels the need to atone for a pressing though vague sense of sin and is disillusioned with life because (in the Platonic sense of dissatisfied, upwardly striving Eros) she cannot find an object worthy of her love. Much impressed, Sir Henry offers her the choice of either reconciliation to life as a well-meaning liberal, tolerant of all because nothing truly matters, or the terrifying, uncharted path of a demanding faith that leads one away from the world's pleasures. She chooses the latter and is taken to a preparatory "sanatorium." After her departure, Alex and Julia, whom we find have been Sir Henry's accomplices in the manipulation of events throughout, join him to consider the fate of their "patients." Act 2 ends with these three, who are fashioned "Guardians," offering a libation on behalf of the newly redirected lives.

Act 3, which Eliot admitted "only just escapes, if indeed it does escape, the accusation of being not a last act but an epilogue,"[6] gives us the results of the Guardians' efforts two years later. All the guests from Act 1 with the exception of Celia gather again at Edward and Lavinia's for yet another party. However, the change in the host and hostess is immediately evident: they now show a courteous solicitude for one another, and Lavinia, it is hinted, is pregnant. But Celia, whom we learn about by report from Alex, has undergone much more dramatic transformations. After leaving the sanatorium she has joined an "austere" order and been sent abroad as a nurse-missionary among growingly hostile natives. Refusing to abandon her patients during an uprising, she is crucified, her body left to be devoured by ants. This news of her martyrdom seems to provide the final stage for the partygoers' reeducation as each in turn measures his life against hers. Edward and Lavinia now vie in terms of guilt and responsibility, where they had once thought only of the short-comings of one another. As the curtain comes down, the Guardians are off to a neighbor's cocktail party apparently to begin again their tutelary services. Edward and Lavinia, together this time, prepare to greet their guests.

The difficulty of what Eliot is attempting here should not be un-derestimated: he is, in essence, rewriting *Murder in the Cathedral* with modern players and claiming that the life of the saint has the power to organize society in the twentieth century much as it did in the twelfth. What this implies is that society is still *latently* Chris-tian, or as Eliot put it in *The Idea of a Christian Society*: "It is my contention that we have today a culture which is mainly negative, but which, so far as it is positive, is still Christian."[7] Unsympathet-ically, one might insist that this statement is virtually a tautology, since the only positive values Eliot is willing to admit are the Chris-tian, but this would be to miss his less dogmatic, but more inter-esting point that is, our channels of thought and feeling are still essentially Christian, though we may not think or feel this to be so. (For this reason he viewed Babbitt's humanism as parasitic on the Christianity it pretended to ignore.) The transforming power of the saint – Celia in the case of the play – is due to her whole-hearted return to these nearly obliterated origins. By her example she forces the rest of us to focus on what Eliot believes are the in-evitable alternatives for the future:

I believe that the choice before us is between the formation of a new Christian culture, and the acceptance of a pagan one. Both involve radical changes; but I believe that the majority of us, if we could be faced immediately with all the changes which will only be accomplished in several generations would prefer Christianity.[8]

Regardless of whether the monkey-worshipping cannibals of Kinkanja, who appear to be a mid-nineteenth-century churchman's notion of Darwinism, are convincing representatives of the spiritual and moral status of "pagan" society, or whether one can imagine modern society with a saint anywhere near the center, the Kierkegaardian daring of Eliot's insistence that the bourgeoisie make a radical decision should be freely granted. And almost equally daring is the way in which he, unlike Prufrock, is willing to drop the question among the easy, comic commerce of the drawing room. Eliot firmly believes the choice will alter the background; he does not recast the background to press the choice as, for example, we find in the twilit reality of Beckett's no-man's-lands or Sartre's rooms with no exits.

To proceed in this way is to place tremendous confidence in the ability of the City of God to influence the modern blasé City of Man. The superstructure may have changed; the infrastructure, he insists, has remained constant. This notwithstanding, the one concession Eliot does feel obliged to make to the times is his creation of the Guardians, a conspiratorial elite who are now needed to point the connection between the smart facade of twentieth-century society and the reality of Christian transcendence, to remind us that the wineglass can also be a chalice. Without the Guardians' help, even Celia, though more spiritually gifted than they, might not have found her vocation, unaware that such a life was possible. The Guardians, then, are not creaky dei ex machina employed as a necessary evil for a larger dramatic purpose but reside near the center of Eliot's conception. They are the fullest embodiment any place in his work of what he had termed in *The Idea of a Christian Society* the Community of Christians, the highly conscious elite responsible for molding the new Christian social order:

> In any Christian society which can be imagined for the future
> – in what M. Maritain calls a *pluralist* society – my "Community
> of Christians" cannot be a body of the definite vocational out-
> line of the "clerisy" of Coleridge: which viewed in a hundred
> years' perspective, appears to approximate to the rigidity of a
> caste. The Community of Christians is not an organisation, but
> a body of indefinite outline; composed of both clergy and laity,
> of the more conscious, more spiritually and intellectually devel-
> oped of both. It will be their identity of belief and aspiration,

their background of a common system of education and a common culture which will enable them to influence and be influenced by each other, and collectively to form the conscious mind and the conscience of the nation.[9]

As a result of the importance Eliot accords to his elite, then, the success of the play and, by extension, of his social theory will depend on his detailed conception of them.

In their broadest outline, the Guardians, as their name suggests, are borrowed from Plato and show the continued influence of the philosopher on Eliot, though he rarely acknowledges him in his prose. What Eliot finds congenial in Plato is both the belief that true freedom comes only through the repression of one's lesser self and the corollary contempt for a (Millian) notion of freedom as wide-bordered self-expression. Consequently, for Eliot as for Plato the Guardians are conceived of as internal as well as external censors, a regulatory element of the psyche as well as a group whose members are characterized especially by that element. A crucial difference does exist, however, because of Eliot's distaste, developed in discussion with Mannheim, for the idea of a *professional* elite. Whereas Plato's guardians are sorted out for their future duty from early childhood and constitute a sharply defined, barracked class determined solely by their performance of that duty, Eliot's Guardians, as the passage on the Community of Christians just quoted makes clear, are drawn from a variety of walks of life. Theoretically, this would allow Eliot to superimpose the contours of his spiritual aristocracy across existing class lines, but in the event, nowhere in his work does he give the slightest indication that he expects to find Chaucer's Plowman or, finding him, would be moved to duplicate Chaucer's unmitigated admiration. (That Lawrence's spiritual aristocracy is skewed toward the lower class accounts for more than a little of Eliot's distrust of him.) Practically, the double life of Eliot's elite allows them to remain invisible when they choose, gathering information and altering events like a sort of Christian CIA.

Beyond this difference, Eliot must make one further update in what he takes from Greek thought, and that is the addition of the will, a faculty not, properly speaking, included in Plato's view of the psyche. If, as Plato has Socrates say, it would be impossible to know the good and not to do it, then the positing of an independent will would seem to be largely redundant. Psychic conflict for Plato consists of a tension between reason and the constantly impeding demands of the emotions, with the intermediate third element of spirit functioning as ally of reason to the extent that it has been properly disciplined (by an education based on the dictates of reason). It was only later when the Judeo–Christian tradition became philosophically self-reflective enough to anatomize the psyche that the need for a will was felt. As creatures made in the image of a God who chose to create and thereby to set a chain of events in motion – far different from the self-thinking thought of Aristotle's divinity – we were seen as possessing a similar capacity of effective volition.

It was left to the great medieval theologians to sort out exactly how this newly elaborated faculty operated, especially how it interacted with the chief faculty identified by the Greeks, our reason. In response, the two main traditions that developed were the voluntarist – based chiefly on Augustine, which posits the will as our primary faculty, the reason as its agent – and the rationalist – based chiefly on Aquinas, which posits the reason as primary, the will as its agent. Viewed in terms of the most basic distinction, the difference in the two outlooks hinges on their respective confidence in the irrational. As Hannah Arendt points out in her masterful intellectual history of the dynamics of willing, Augustine ultimately came to see the will as moved by love, understood as "the specific gravity of bodies," the desire that directs our attention, and finally our movements, toward the desired object.[10] The will, on this view, is that which propels us toward our telos, our highest happiness, steadfast union with the beloved. To rest in love of God would be, of course, the absolute achievement of our designed end. Aquinas, demurring, retains a Greek suspicion of desire, according to which it was inextricably implicated with the lower wants of the emotions and, even when sublimated, was still suggestive of a lack (of the desired object), hence a deficiency. Instead, following the Greeks, he argues that "man's ultimate happiness is essentially to know God by the intellect; it is not an act of the Will."[11]

Of these two positions, it is the second, or more properly the second as filtered through the lens of Maurras, that was more appealing to Eliot, and its appeal is deeply indicative of what he took the essence of Christianity to be: an exercise in discipline of the will, that faculty whose association with the vulgar vagaries of desire taint it as potentially Protestant and Romantic. In *The Cocktail Party*, it is Edward, the ineffectual adulterer, who explains how his own drifting will, moored only by a dull sense of convention, lacks the supervision of a well-developed internal "guardian":

The self that can say 'I want this – or want that' –
The self that wills – he is a feeble creature;
He has to come to terms in the end
With the obstinate, the tougher self; who does not speak,
Who never talks, who cannot argue;
And who in some men may be the *guardian* –
But in men like me, the dull, the implacable,
The indomitable spirit of mediocrity.
The willing self can contrive the disaster
Of this unwilling partnership – but can only flourish
In submission to the rule of the stronger partner.

In contrast to the aimless Edward is the emerging saint, Celia. Relatively indifferent, as she says, to the claims of conventional morality, but endowed with a powerful guardian, she demonstrates her genius by turning from adultery and embarking on a life of askesis whose logical culmination is the brutal annihilation of her body: the desire-driven will is stilled, with a vengeance.

But beyond the fact that it can so totally master the will, what exactly *is* this internal guardian? If it "never talks" and "cannot argue," to read it as something akin to "reason" makes a strained case. Here, a return to Aquinas will help. He distinguishes between "intellect" and "reason," the first our capacity to apprehend self-evident universal truths, the second our capacity to deduce discursively from these principles. But Aquinas includes among the truths that manifest themselves to the intellect – and here we can see again his effort to contain the irrational – those of revelation.[12] Our intuition of the divine, while not rational, is intellectual. (Jacques Maritain, whose work Eliot admired, has many fine pages on the nature of this knowledge that precedes and enables philosophy.) What this amounts to, then, is a spiritual unconscious, or if that sounds misleadingly somatic after Freud, a spiritual preconscious. And it is almost certainly this Thomistic agency on which Eliot patterns his internal guardian, which, consistently enough, compels though it "never talks" and "cannot argue."

Such a reading of the internal guardian goes a long way toward explaining the vague intimations that cryptically motivate characters throughout the play. When Edward first realizes he wants Lavinia back but cannot say exactly why, Sir Henry, recognizing the prompting of Edward's dwarfed guardian, replies: "The fact that you can't give a reason for wanting her / Is the best reason for believing that you want her."[13] When Celia, in turn, similarly tries to account for her conversion – "I don't in the least know what I am doing / Or why I am doing it. There is nothing else to do: / That is the only reason" – Sir Henry once again responds, "That is the only reason." In both instances once a choice has been made to heed the promptings of the internal guardian, what follows is fated. The external Guardians suddenly become endowed, or endow themselves, with the power to manage these lives absolutely, much like vampires who puppeteer their hosts, but must first be invited over the threshold:

> *Edward:* I have half a mind to change my mind now
>   To show you that I am free to change it.
> *Unidentified Guest:* You will change your mind, but you are
>   not free.
>   Your moment of freedom was yesterday.
>   You made a decision. You set in motion
>   Forces in your life and in the lives of others
>   Which cannot be reversed.

Likewise, once Celia agreed to accept a life of renunciation, Sir Henry knew by means of a vision that he was preparing her for a violent end: "That was her destiny."

There is in all this the impulse, which must be admired, to envision a society where commitments other than just the financial are binding. Eliot, like Marx, deplored the spidery cash nexus. And in the past two centuries much of the appeal of social criticism from both left and right has been due to the undeniable force of this complaint. But Eliot, again like Marx, was not careful enough to guard against the alternative evil of *compelled* community. In each case there is no space allotted in society outside the organizing myth. Consequently, the world of *The Cocktail Party* is nearly as coldly repellent as totalitarian regimes erected in Marx's name. There is scarcely a moment in the play in which the "patients" are not under observation by the Guardians, who appear in perpetual relay at the door and wheedle information on the telephone. The Guardians' light banter, the vehicle for most of the comedy, is chilling when their ulterior purpose is considered: Julia's playful "I am going to make you dine alone with me / On Friday, and talk to me about everything"; Alex's witty "You know, I have connections – even in California" are comments, seen in their total context, that suggest

something of the smiling sadism of total control. By Act 3 the network of surveillance becomes Orwellian when even one of the non-
descript caterers of Lavinia's party turns out to be Julia's snitch.

Nearly as oppressive as the unrelieved vigilance is the tone of the
Guardians when they get down to business. The following interview
between Sir Henry and Edward is representative of the steady *de haut
en bas* used in addressing the Chamberlaynes:

> *Reilly:* I could make you dream any kind of dream I suggested,
>   And it would only go to flatter your vanity
>   With the temporary stimulus of feeling interesting.
> *Edward:* But I am obsessed by the thought of my own insignif-
>   icance.
> *Reilly:* Precisely. And I could make you feel important,
>   And you would imagine it a marvelous cure;
>   And you would go on, doing such amount of mischief
>   As lay within your power – until you came to grief. . . .
> *Edward:* If I am like that I must have done a great deal of harm.
> *Reilly:* Oh, not so much as you would like to think.
>   Only, shall we say, within your modest capacity.
>   Try to explain what has happened since I left you.

Eliot may have meant this to sound refreshingly forthright like the
blunt truths spoken by crusty old Captain Shotover in Shaw's dark
comedy *Heartbreak House,* but if so, he has failed.

The failure is more than just a failure of tone, however; it is a
failure in the feelings that generate the tone. At the most basic level,
the character of Sir Henry, like Eliot's play and like his project for
the recreation of a Christian society, radiates no love. There is never
a moment in the play when Sir Henry demonstrates any warmth for
the Chamberlaynes. Granted, he is concerned enough to place them
back on the path of married forbearance, but even this seems more
an act of social sanitation than Christian fellowship. Addicted to the
mundane, the Chamberlaynes simply do not inspire Eliot or the
Guardians. If the nonelect behave themselves, this is all one can
reasonably ask of them. Though Sir Henry tells Celia, as she weighs
the satisfactions of the commonplace life against the life of severe
spiritual exercise, that "Neither way is better / Both ways are necessary," this is an unconvincing attempt to *assert* a common culture
in which the spiritually obtuse need not occupy inferior status. In

light of Sir Henry's description of quotidian life, the notion of equivalence rings particularly hollow:

> [The non-elect] Maintain themselves by the common routine,
> Learn to avoid excessive expectation,
> Become tolerant of themselves and others,
> Giving and taking, in the usual actions
> What there is to give and take. They do not repine;
> Are contented with the morning that separates
> And with the evening that brings together
> For casual talk before the fire
> Two people who know they do not understand each other,
> Breeding children whom they do not understand
> And who will never understand them.

Precisely the sort of people, in other words, from whom Eliot made a career of distancing himself, both in his poetry and in his personal life.

But what of Celia? Is there a demonstration of love for her, perhaps all the stronger for its having been denied the Chamberlaynes? Certainly we notice that she is treated by Sir Henry with a great deal more respect, the respect due to one that, as Julia points out to him, will transcend the understanding of her teachers: "But what do we know of the terrors of the journey? / You and I don't know the process by which the human is / transhumanised." Moreover, she enjoys a sense that her decision, when finally reached, is her own, unlike Edward, who is never quite sure whether his decision to have Lavinia back was not implanted. Finally, when Sir Henry hears the report of Celia's death, he registers "satisfaction," naturally, we assume, deeper than that produced by a survey of the Chamberlaynes' life. But it is hard to see how there is anything here one would want to call "love." And though this might not be a charge fatal to a vision based on Lockean social contract, it is to one purportedly based on Christianity.

It might, of course, be objected that it is Celia the saint who manifests a love that the others can only aspire toward. After all, she sacrifices herself as a nurse-missionary, a life that, at the play's end, is universally recognized as exemplary. Even the Guardians, as has been mentioned, recognize her as their ultimate spiritual superior. However, the difficulty with taking Celia's brief career as a nourishing fountain of *caritas* is that we never *see* her in this role. Dramatically, it is difficult to outweigh the lengthy presentation of misguided lives – including Celia's earlier life – with a brief mention that she has, in some far off locale, acted nobly. Indeed, even in the description of her time in Kinkanja, the report of her death overshadows the sketch of her service, which suggests that it is her suffering rather than the nurse's touch guided by love that occupies Eliot.

This supposition is supported by the observation that martyred sensuality, though not always as gruesome as here, was a theme that fascinated Eliot from the days of his earliest unpublished poems.[14] The young man who felt the need to write the lewd "King Bolo and His Great Black Queen" could atone by entering into the mutilated bodies of male saints in such poems as "The Death of St. Narcissus" and "The Love Song of St. Sebastian."[15] Even in the mature poetry we find St. Augustine, having succumbed to the demands of the flesh (and surrounded in *The Waste Land* by numerous examples of rancid sexuality ahistorically juxtaposed), crying out for the surgery of asceticism: "Burning burning burning burning / O Lord Thou pluckest me out / O Lord Thou pluckest / burning." Yet beyond the laceration of the male, there remained, too, a residual hatred of woman as temptress. In "The Love Song of St. Sebastian," St. Sebastian, after groveling at the feet of the desired woman, arises to strangle her. Thus, we may find less than appealing the "satisfaction" Sir Henry experiences at the news of the former adulteress Celia's murder, especially given the hints throughout the play of his lascivious impulses.[16] There is a certain dark logic in the fact that the most attractive female character Eliot created is visited with the most ghastly of deaths.

In "What the Thunder Said," the final movement of *The Waste Land,* the admonition from beyond was "give, sympathize, control"; of these, for Eliot, it is the last that remained greatest. The restraint implicit in Aquinas's rationalism, exaggerated by Eliot, results in the diminished spirituality of a crabbed asceticism. The critic Lesley Chamberlain correctly observes:

It is a good lesson Celia teaches us, that heady, probably superficial emotions lead us into the situations in which we learn a deeper sobriety, but how can we accept it taught through a drama about love which is well nigh drained of flesh and blood? ... Eliot's crucifixion of Celia drew together the worst of the Christian beliefs which shaped his idiom and raised to them what should have been a celebratory pyre, but the flame did not ignite, and the end of Celia is like the death of Alissa in Gide's *La Porte étroite,* a novel which sets out to illustrate the murderous coldness of Christian fanaticism.[17]

Behind this unlovely Christianity we ought to hear the voice of Hulme insisting that because of man's corruption through Original Sin, "it is only by tradition and organization that anything decent can be got out of him." Behind Hulme we ought to hear the deeper voice of Maurras calling endlessly for a society in conformity with the transcendent principle of Order. It is these voices that Celia hears before her conversion:

> It sounds ridiculous – but the only word for it
> > [her nagging unease]
> That I can find, is a sense of sin
>
> . . .
>
> It must be some kind of hallucination;
> Yet, at the same time, I'm frightened by the fear
> That it is more real than anything I believed in.

The remedy: to join a "very austere" order. The outcome: mutilation and "transhuman[isation]."

The cold *caritas* of the play is evident in the postwar essays as well, in which Eliot vainly endeavors to embrace former enemies in a new spirit of catholicity. Taking earnestly the ghostly admonition in "Little Gidding" to "pray they [your thoughts and theories] be forgiven / By others, as I pray you to forgive / Both bad and good," Eliot sets out in these pieces to reestimate and elevate the major writers of the Protestant tradition – but he simply cannot bring himself to do so. While it is true that much of the negatively charged terminology that characterized the prewar polemics is dropped, this is the extent of Eliot's effort at reconciliation. Nothing essential ever is actually newly conceded; no vice reveals itself as a hidden virtue. Indeed, how could the situation be otherwise since Eliot believed to the end of his life that "we can hardly doubt that the 'truest' philosophy is the best material for the greatest poet; so that the poet must be rated in the end both by the philosophy he realizes in poetry and by the fulness and adequacy of the realization"? While Eliot now shows himself more willing to enter alien churches for the music, he never changes his mind about the inferiority of their philosophy.

Perhaps nowhere is this plainer to see than in comparing the 1947 essay on Milton with the 1936 attack it was intended to soften. In the earlier piece, conceived at the time of his greatest intolerance, Eliot wonders whether anything can be salvaged of Milton given the general reprehensibility of his character and everything he believed in: "As a man, he is antipathetic. Either from the moralist's point of view, or from the theologian's point of view, or from that of the political philosopher, or judging by the ordinary standards of likableness in human beings, Milton is unsatisfactory."[18] Only by severing the sense of Milton's poetry from the sonorous roll of his long periods, Eliot finally decides, can one find anything of merit. Considered as pure sound, the poetry of *Paradise Lost* displays to advantage the blind Milton's hypertrophied musical sense. Considered in terms of its meaning, it is an audacious heresy: "So far as I perceive anything, it is a glimpse of a theology that I find in large part repellent, expressed through a mythology which would have better been left in the book of *Genesis,* upon which Milton has not improved."[19] In the final analysis, however, Eliot finds that even the beautiful music of Milton's poetry has had a persistent harmful effect on subsequent poets, for his verse, in its abstraction and complex syntax, stands at the farthest possible remove from anything resembling colloquial English. Both philosophically and poetically, then, in 1936 Milton presented a clear and present danger.

By 1947 Eliot was prepared to offer a recantation of the earlier piece.[20] And had this recantation involved an explicit (or even implicit) acknowledgment of the virtues of Milton from the aforementioned point of view of moralist, theologian, and political philosopher, this would have signaled *the* major turning point in Eliot's thinking. But because Eliot refuses to value Milton in this way after creating a platform from which he might have done so, the essay is crucial instead in demonstrating the continuity of his thought. Indeed, he indicates early in the essay that he retains his old "antipathy" to Milton, something he shares with Samuel Johnson, who had likewise been a political opponent of the republican poet. Whereas, however, Johnson's politics soured his reading of the poetry, Eliot endeavors to lay his own animus aside and "attend to the poetry for the poetry's sake." What causes the reader to blink on reading this assertion is not that Eliot is willing to make this distinction, but that he seems to be offering it as an advance, after having made precisely the same distinction in "Milton I." Despite the gesture of magnanimity, then, Eliot still cannot bring himself to reconsider any more of Milton than he did in the first essay. In "Milton II" as in "Milton I," it will be only after turning his nose from the noxious odor of Milton's meaning – and thereby disqualifying him from the ranks of great poets – that Eliot may draw breath enough to praise what is left.

Moreover, Eliot goes out of his way to let the reader know that what he *won't* discuss in Milton is that aspect which would have been of crucial importance. Milton's political and religious stance, and the opposition to it, remain the two primary poles of tension in English society:

> The fact is simply that the Civil War of the seventeenth century, in which Milton is a symbolic figure, has never been concluded. The Civil War is not ended: I question whether any serious civil war does end. Throughout that period English society was so convulsed and divided that the effects are still felt . . . It is now considered grotesque, on political grounds, to be of the party of King Charles; it is now, I believe, considered equally grotesque, on moral grounds, to be of the party of the Puritans; and to most persons to-day the religious views of both parties may seem equally remote. Nevertheless, the passions are unquenched.[21]

Despite his promise in *Four Quartets* not to pound the antique drum any more since from the larger Christian perspective both factions of the Civil War "are folded in a single party," the implicit advice in the passage is that we make sure of what actually is inscribed on our banners, not that we cast them into the dust. Accustomed from long usage to thinking of his religion in as partisan a way as his politics, and to seeing both as mutually nourishing, only fitfully did he impose on the Anglican God to indulge in the promiscuity of forgiveness.

Thus, by the time Eliot gets around to a consideration of the technical aspects of Milton's poetry, it is obvious that we are playing for small stakes. Within these limits, Eliot does have some perceptive remarks to make about Milton's style. He helpfully advises us to think of the sentence and especially the paragraph rather than the line as the typical unit of Milton's verse. He also points out Milton's gift for imagistically rendering large intangibles: "vast size, limitless space, abysmal depth, and light and darkness." Finally, in a backhanded compliment Eliot notes that Milton's lack of interest in or understanding of human psychology serves him well in the creation of Adam and Eve, where more particularized portraits could only

have risked trivialization. Yet when he attempts a summarizing statement about Milton's style, Eliot, despite himself, speaks in the language of political opprobrium: "There is no cliché, no poetic diction
in the derogatory sense, but a perpetual sequence of original acts of
lawlessness." (Eliot's prototype for this kind of charge may be found
in Maurras's attack on the decadent style of romanticism: "The deg-
radation of our tongue, the tortured rhythms, that kingdom of words
where subversion engenders total dislocation, all this reminds us of
the subversion born of other crises.")[22] Later, he identifies Milton
the poet as "probably the greatest of all eccentrics," employing a
term he had first used in the Blake essay in warning of Milton's
dangerous influence as a Puritan mythologist outside the great
Latin–Catholic tradition. In the end, try as he might, Eliot is never
able to fully divorce Milton the artist from Milton the dissenter. Even
the game for small stakes looks rigged.

In 1955 Eliot endeavored to extend the amnesty to another eccentric, Goethe, though he had never considered him as large a
figure or as dangerous a one as Milton. That he was even moved to
a reappraisal at this late date was more a function of occasion, it
seems, than conviction, for his revisionary lecture "Goethe as the
Sage" was delivered in Hamburg on receipt of the Hanseatic Goethe
Prize. At work, too, was undoubtedly the larger diplomacy of rein-
tegrating Germany back into the European community about which
Eliot cared so deeply, and an appeal to Goethe as a good European
was an obvious means to this end.

Prior to the lecture Eliot's judgments of Goethe had always occurred in passing, the very casualness of which matched his dismis-
sive opinion of him as a European Olympian. In a 1933 essay on
Shelley and Keats, he showed a unique disregard for Goethe's own
lyric genius as he placed him inappropriately with the seventeenth-
and eighteenth-century French moralists: "Of Goethe perhaps it is
truer to say that he dabbled in both philosophy and poetry and made
no great success of either; his true role was that of the man of the
world and sage – a La Rochefoucauld, a La Bruyére, a Vauvenargues."[23] In the 1944 essay "What Is a Classic?" Goethe is excluded for being too local a talent, especially given that the locale
was Germany:

Yet, because of its [Goethe's poetry's] partiality, of the imper-
manence of some of its content, and the germanism of the sensibility; because Goethe appears to a foreign eye, limited by his

age, by his language, and by his culture, so that he is unrepresentative of the whole European tradition, and like our own nineteenth-century authors, a little provincial, we cannot call him a *universal* classic.[24]

The Hamburg revision of these opinions is, like the Milton essay, unpersuasive, but for different reasons. We are being asked to believe, if we take the lecture at face value, that at the age of sixty-six Eliot suddenly has promoted Goethe from the company of Vauvenargues to that of Shakespeare and Dante. While such a vertiginous reassessment might be plausible on the basis of arguing that meager acquaintance was remedied by intensive, though belated, study, Eliot never makes such a claim. In fact, sprinkled throughout the essay is the admission that others know Goethe much better than he. And this may itself be something of an understatement given the fact that Eliot, who possessed a virtually unrivaled genius for illustrative quotation especially when it came to demonstrating strength and weakness by brilliant juxtaposition of parallel passages from the works of poets, *never* quotes Goethe in a 9,000-word essay devoted exclusively to him. We are vaporously reminded again and again that Goethe was a wise man, but given no shred of evidence. It comes as little surprise to discover that Eliot confessed privately to Ronald Duncan as he was preparing the Goethe lecture, "I can't stand his stuff."[25]

Eliot reserves another of these arm's-length embraces of his old age for Shelley, the author whose ideas he once labeled "repellent" and his poetry for that reason "unreadable."[26] In the 1950 essay "What Dante Means to Me," Eliot, as he enumerates his own debts, notes approvingly that Dante had a great influence on Shelley as well. Having himself tried to find an English equivalent for Dante's terza rima in "Little Gidding," II, and admitting that it "cost me far more time and trouble and vexation than any passage of the same length that I have ever written," Eliot is prepared to admire Shelley's admittedly superior attempt in the unfinished *Triumph of Life*. Again, however, as in the treatment of Milton, this is to abstract the style of Shelley's poem from what Eliot chooses not to discuss: any relationship the poetry might bear to "the thought of Dante, to his view of life, or to the philosophy and theology which give shape and content to the Divine Comedy."[27] The only difference in this case is that because Shelley adopted Dantean technique, his style, momentarily, seems to have escaped the contamination of his own philosophy. There is even a hint, remotely dropped, that his thought might have been positively affected by disciplining himself to the Dantean rhyme scheme. In the only comment Eliot makes on the meaning of Shelley's verse, he draws attention to several negative lines on Rousseau as "interesting." (Almost every other reference to Rousseau in Shelley's works, it should be mentioned, showed him to be an admirer.) In sum, then, Shelley merits passing praise for allowing himself, in however limited a way, to imitate orthodoxy.

In one of the last essays he wrote, "To Criticize the Critic" (1961), Eliot surveyed his own prose and offered a reading of it quite different from the one I have presented in the preceding paragraphs and the book as a whole. Contrary to the view I have put forward, the force of Eliot's final comment on his critical career is to depoliticize it, both early and late. Most striking in this regard is his own account of two long-lived phrases he first used as a champion of classicism, "objective correlative" and "dissociation of sensibility." Since Eliot felt that these phrases, removed from their original context, had developed a sort of ghostly, ill-defined afterlife, his own explanation of what he had intended ought to be quoted in full:

> What I wish to suggest, however, is that these phrases may be accounted for as being conceptual symbols for emotional preferences. Thus, the emphasis on tradition came about, I believe, as a result of my reaction against the poetry, in the English language, of the nineteenth and early twentieth centuries, and my passion for the poetry, both dramatic and lyric, of the late sixteenth and early seventeenth centuries. The "objective correlative" in the essay on Hamlet may stand for my bias towards the more mature plays of Shakespeare – *Timon, Antony and Cleopatra, Coriolanus* notably – and towards those late plays of Shakespeare about which Mr. Wilson Knight has written illuminatingly. And the "dissociation of sensibility" may represent my devotion to Donne and the metaphysical poets, and my reaction against Milton.[28]

What is remarkable here are the lengths to which Eliot is prepared to go to efface all traces of the Maurrasien-classical political commitment encoded in the two phrases. (Several pages later he claims that it was "only the more literary essays of Charles Maurras" that influenced him and gives the impression that this influence was operative only until 1918. He seems to have forgotten, or wants to have forgotten, that as editor of the *Criterion* in 1926 he recommended as an essential text of the new classicism Maurras's *L'Avenir de l'intel-*

ligence, a work conceived in opposition to the Dreyfusards and one whose thesis is that there exists a war between blood and money; and forgotten, too, that he vigorously defended Maurras's politico-religious position in 1928 against the Vatican and its sympathizers.)[29] He is now willing to portray himself from the beginning as having been a crypto-Romantic responding solely to "emotional preferences," in effect an ally under the skin of the enemies he spent three decades excoriating.

Of course, if we were to return to the historical origins of the tradition of which Eliot is the heir, the conservative reaction to the French Revolution, then, as I have indicated earlier, Eliot might indeed qualify as a late Romantic. His statement then would constitute the insight that the politically colored classicism that he adopted was itself basically a romanticism that obscured and finally turned against its own provenance. But clearly Eliot does not intend anything like this by his "confession," which serves the purpose of precluding investigation along these very lines. The "emotional preferences" that motivate him propel him exclusively, in his example, to and from various poets. There is no hint of these same desires inspiring political or religious choices. His attraction to or repulsion from a particular poet is almost exclusively a response to literary qualities. This is confirmed later in the essay when he points out that he has been discussing "that part of my own critical prose which is most nearly definable as 'literary criticism.' "[30]

Building on the assertion that his judgments originated in emotional reactions, Eliot claims (apparently as explanation) that his criticism was in essence merely a lengthy rumination on the way other poets related to his own poetic practices: "But I am sure that my own theorizing has been epiphenomenal of my tastes, and that in so far as it is valid, it springs from direct experience of those authors who have profoundly influenced my own writing."[31] Such a statement, by giving the impression that taste exists on a plane beneath normative judgment and that validity can only be ascertained in personal terms, further wraps Eliot's critical production in a cocoon of subjectivism. Of course, questions of truth and interpretation were a major concern of Eliot's throughout his intellectual life, and to construct an overarching theory accounting for all his comments is far from simple or perhaps even desirable (these issues will be taken up at greater length in Chapter 6), yet this statement is, at the very least, misleading in its emphasis. Even as a young man in the first invigorating shock of realization that he was a far more subtle reader than the well-published nineteenth-century "appreciators" who still held sway in London, he rejected the role of the sensitive soul whose nuanced responses would be of interest for their own sake. To set himself apart from his predecessors, he took as epigram for the opening essay in his first collection of critical writings, *The Sacred Wood*, Rémy de Gourmont's "Ériger en lois ses impressions personnelles, cest le grand effort d'un homme s'il est sincère." As the essay over which the epigram stood – "The Perfect Critic" – made clear, criticism must begin with the critic's impressions, but these impressions ought to be instantaneously taking shape as a structure through the process of comparison and analysis. The critical utterance that is the culmination of this process is a distillation of impersonal truth from the matrix of personal impression: "The end of the enjoyment of poetry is a pure contemplation from which all the accidents of personal emotion are removed."[32] This is, of course, a regulative ideal (the accomplishment of a hypothetical "perfect critic"), and Eliot was elsewhere willing to concede that, in reality, individual impressions may provide different paths toward this goal,[33] but the goal tended to be constant: "the elucidation of works of art and *the correction of taste*" (emphasis added).[34]

Eliot's contention that his view of individual poets and literary history in general was really nothing more than workshop criticism – a poet talking too loudly to himself – is even less convincing if we look specifically at one of his own examples, the phrase "dissociation of sensibility." His claim that the phrase registered nothing more than his emotional preference for the poetry of Donne rather than of Milton is belied by the fact that, over the years, he progressively *loosened* the connection with Milton's poetry:

> In the seventeenth century a dissociation of sensibility set in, from which we have never recovered; and this dissociation, as is natural, was due to the influence of the two most powerful poets of the century, Milton and Dryden. (1921)

> In the seventeenth century a dissociation of sensibility set in, from which we have never recovered; and this dissociation, as is natural, was aggravated by the influence of the two most powerful poets of the century, Milton and Dryden. (1932)

> I believe that the general affirmation represented by the phrase "dissociation of sensibility" . . . retains some validity; but I now

agree with Dr. Tillyard that to lay the burden on the shoulders of Milton and Dryden was a mistake. If such a dissociation did take place, I suspect that the causes are too complex and too profound to justify our accounting for the change in terms of literary criticism. All we can say is, that something like this did happen; that it had something to do with the Civil War; that it would be even unwise to say it was caused by the Civil War, but that it is a consequence of the same causes that brought about the Civil War; that we must seek the causes in Europe, not in England alone; and for what these causes were, we may dig and dig until we get to a depth at which words and concepts fail us. (1947)[35]

If we are to accept Eliot's account of the phrase in *To Criticize the Critic*, then we would have to imagine that he reversed the direction his analysis pursued over a quarter of a century and ended by taking a position completely personal and grounded purely in affective response to poetry, a position more extreme than even the early attribution of causality to Milton and Dryden. That original remark assumed at least that a cultural change had occurred and, since Eliot placed the rupture specifically at the time of the Revolution, that it had involved politics as well as poetry. Further, we would have to replace his scrupulously tentative claim of 1947 that the ultimate causes of the dissociation resided at "a depth at which words and concepts fail us" with the glib assertion that the dissociation was no more than a handy way of talking about his impressions of two poets.

Alongside these remarks, which unpersuasively distance Eliot from almost all connection with politically charged classicism, let us place two postwar references to Maurras, the first of which, appearing in French in a small right-wing French journal, rarely finds its way into Eliot scholarship. In the April 25, 1948, issue of *Aspects de la France et du Monde,* Eliot joined other European admirers of the imprisoned Maurras in a section entitled "L'Hommage de l'étranger." There he acknowledges the tremendous influence of Maurras on him and other like-minded young people: "Maurras, for certain of us, represented a sort of Virgil who led us to the gates of the temple." The allusion here is to Dante's Virgil, who, excluded from entering Paradise himself because of his pagan beliefs, nevertheless led Dante the pilgrim to the threshold. This mild rebuke of Maurras's religious eccentricity – Eliot calls it "an idealization of the pre-Christian mediterranean world" – should not, he tells us, blind us to his valuable political ideas, especially "his conceptions of the monarchy and of hierarchy . . . [which are] kin to my own, as they are to English conservatives, for whom these ideas remain intact despite the modern world."[36] And we must not overlook, as Eliot reminds himself in perusing "the magisterial pages" of the man who was convicted of betraying the Resistance in his newspaper, that the prose is in every way worthy of the content and not the least of Maurras's virtues. As he did in 1928 when he tried to exonerate Maurras in the face of Vatican condemnation in part on the basis of his verbal decorum, Eliot clearly still believes that the classical style establishes one's essential bona fides.

Despite the disconcerting avoidance of any mention of Maurras's political career in his "Hommage," a later, second reference demonstrates amply that Eliot was not blind to the lesson of a man condemned by the church he supported and, after World War II, imprisoned as a traitor by the country of which he had always regarded himself the one true champion. The acerbic French activist never seemed to realize, or realizing to care, that unpopular politics might require protective coloration. It is this failure of strategy to which Eliot draws attention in a lecture before the London Conservative Union in 1955:

I think of a man whom I held in respect and admiration, although some of his views were exasperating and some deplorable – but a great writer, a genuine lover of his country, and a man who deserved a better fate than that which he had in the end to meet. I know it is easy to criticize a man for not being another man than the man he was; and we should be particularly reserved in criticism of a man whose political setting was that of another country from our own. But with the reservations compelled by this awareness, I have sometimes thought that if Charles Maurras had confined himself to literature, and to the literature of political theory, and had never attempted to found a political party, a *movement* – engaging in, and increasing the acrimony of the political struggle – if he had not given his support to the restoration of the Monarchy in such a way as to strengthen instead of reducing animosities – then those of his ideas which were sound and strong might have spread more widely, and penetrated more deeply, and affected more sensibly the contemporary mind.[37]

Pointing to Plato and Aristotle, whose influence is so all-pervasive in the West that it is almost impossible to visualize our culture without them, Eliot ventures the opinion that "the profounder and *wiser* the man, the less likely is his influence to be discernible." Hence, Eliot outlines the *idea* of a Christian society, but organizes no Camelots du Roi, and at the end of his career smudges the tracks he left in following the man who did. It is in this light that one must consider the late, revisionist essays.

6

ELIOT AND THE NEW CRITICISM

The all-pervasive influence that Eliot sought came not as he had hoped through his social theorizing, which even at its best constituted primarily an eloquent protest against what *is* rather than a plausible (or for most, desirable) sketch for what *might be*. Rather, his more durable legacy came in the literary criticism, especially of the early years. This is by no means to say that Eliot failed in his larger aspirations, for as I have tried to show, the early criticism grew out of and embodied extraliterary concerns. Indeed, if one accepts the thesis that Eliot's late Christianity is one with a great deal of political baggage, then there is not a significant difference in ideological assumptions between the early Eliot and the late Eliot, of Eliot the literary critic and Eliot the Christian propagandist. That Eliot should have made his deepest impress when his agenda was most implicit substantiates his retrospective opinion that unpopular revolutionaries need to veil their full intents if they hope to succeed.

The difficulty of isolating the transmission of certain of Eliot's ideas is complicated, though, by the fact that Eliot himself rejects the notion that he has fathered the American New Criticism, the school most commonly seen as, at least in part, his offspring. In 1956, long after New Criticism's theory and practice were well established, Eliot spoke disparagingly of it as "the lemon-squeezer school of criticism" and claimed that beyond giving some of its practitioners voice in the *Criterion,* he failed "to see any school of criticism which can be said to derive from myself."[1] The New Critics, for their part, even if they were generally convinced of Eliot's paternity, were not always grateful children. John Crowe Ransom, one of the oldest New Critics and the one who gave popular currency to the name in *The New Criticism* (1941), found Eliot to be too "historical" and lamented his "theoretical innocence."[2] The dyspeptic Yvor Winters, for whom reason all too often seemed to be circumscribed by the boundaries of his own skull, did not spare Eliot in his general indictment of almost all rival thinkers:

> Eliot is a theorist who has contradicted himself on every important issue that he has touched . . . one might account for them [the contradictions] by a change of view if he showed any consciousness of contradiction; but many of them occur within the same book or even within the same essay.[3]

Similarly, though more gently, William Wimsatt, the most scrupulous of New Critical theorists, finds that the seminal essay "Tradition and the Individual Talent" derived currency from its "highly ambiguous" central proposition of the impersonal poet, and he goes on to remark that this ambiguity registered a lifelong inconsistency on this point in Eliot's thinking.[4]

Beyond the fact that Eliot and the New Critics were not completely enthralled with one another, Eliot harbored grave reservations about I. A. Richards, the critic usually paired with him as a formative influence on New Criticism.[5] Eliot could not accept Richards's emotive theory of poetry whereby the value of a poem was determined by the complexity of responses aroused in the reader and the poem's success in bringing about a state of psychic equilibrium in the reader by harmonizing these responses. After having radically severed the emotions of the poet from the act of writing a poem ("The more perfect the artist, the more completely separate in him will be the man who suffers and the mind which creates"), Eliot was certainly not about to look favorably on a theory that made the delicate disposition of the reader's emotions the criterion of value. Moreover, Richards's claim that poetry, by inducing these states, "is capable of saving us" did not, as was mentioned earlier, impress Eliot, who looked for salvation in more orthodox places: "It is like saying the wall-paper will save us when the walls have crumbled."[6]

In a 1957 interview, Robert Penn Warren, looking back on what seemed to him the lack of a common theory in the New Critics, wondered how they came to be lumped together in the first place: "Let's name some of them – Richards, Eliot, Tate, Blackmur, Brooks, Leavis (I guess). How in God's name can you get that gang into the same bed? There is no bed big enough and no blanket would stay tucked."[7] And we need only to add the name of Winters to make these bedfellows seem all the odder. Even subtracting for the fact that Warren, regarded as a New Critic himself, chooses to deny that there ever was anything called New Criticism at the very moment when it was passing out of favor (an ungainly means of retreat currently in vogue with deconstructionists), one can see what he took to be evidence. In light of all these difficulties, then, how can lines of connection be established between Eliot and the New Criticism with any confidence?

Instead of beginning with the respective theories and methodologies per se, perhaps a more fruitful point of departure would be to try to establish what Eliot and the New Critics were reacting against. Since enemies tend to be simplified as monoliths of wrongdoing, there is much more likely to be a higher degree of agreement on problems than on solutions. Viewed as attempts to combat a situation perceived in common as undesirable, the various approaches might take on a coherence not otherwise readily apparent. This is especially the case with Eliot and the New Critics, for as I hope to show, their literary theories and versions of literary history are shaped in common by a profoundly reactionary stance. Because it should be unnecessary at this point in the book to rehearse in any detail the argument for Eliot's reactionary concerns, let me turn instead to those of the New Critics and employ Eliot's position as the understood point of reference.

In reconsidering the New Critics (and despite Robert Penn Warren, I will assume for the moment that the designation has validity), one must first get beyond two fashionable misconceptions about them. The first is that voiced most pointedly by historically oriented scholars who attack the New Critics for having wrapped themselves in the cocoon of formalism. This view was put forward originally by Edmund Wilson in regard to the undesirable influence of Eliot's criticism and subsequently attached itself with leechlike persistence to the New Criticism.[8] In what follows I will try to demonstrate that this charge, without a good deal of serious qualification, is misleading and tends to make the New Critics politically conservative by default, whereas they were actually conservative in a much more active way. The second charge, commonly leveled by the deconstructionists, has much less merit. The New Critics, they contend, were champions of linguistic "reference" who believed that the words of a work of art constrained meaning to such an extent that there could be only one correct reading. By means of this charge, the deconstructionists set up the New Critics as strawmen profoundly corrupted by the ignorant certainty of "logocentrism." Perhaps needless to say, this ill-conceived attack serves only a polemical purpose, for it is hard to imagine how the New Critics, who made a cult of ambiguity, paradox, and irony, could possibly at the same time have insisted that there could be only one correct reading of a work.[9] Over and over again they maintained that the language of literature bore only a metaphoric relationship to the world and that even the best critic was engaged in no more than "skilled guesswork" as he or she sorted through "interpretive possibilities."[10]

The deconstructivist attack constitutes a parody of a complaint, itself not well founded, that was common in the late sixties and early seventies, namely, that the New Criticism was the literary analogue of natural science. Common to both the New Criticism and science, it was argued, was the radical separation of subject and object, with the object being accessible only to cold, empirical methodology. Typically, the New Critics were portrayed in their practices as soulless technologists who mirrored the larger problems of a society out of touch with its vital energies.[11] They treated works of literature the way oil companies treated the earth. In his book arguing for a more loving hermeneutical approach, Richard Palmer finds the New Criticism to be a kind of "rape" of the text representing "the modern technological way of thinking and the will-to-power that lies at its root."[12]

The justification offered for this linkage was based on the New Criticism's insistence on the integrity of the work of art, an artifact existing apart from biography and – for all except Richards – the emotive states of the readers. In "The Intentional Fallacy" (1946), Wimsatt severed the work from any consideration of the author's intent by maintaining that evidence from origins was an example of what philosophers routinely regarded as the genetic fallacy. A few years later, in "The Affective Fallacy" (1949), he severed the work of art from evaluation based solely on the reader's private emotional response. Such an approach would leave us in a morass of impressionism and relativism, he argued. Instead of relying on the "sincerity" of the reader, we should demand that he or she give a precise account of the reasons for emotions; this should lead us back to the work, where our attention belongs, and thus universalize the response.

While this direction of our attention to the words on the page might be called more "scientific" than the rhapsodic appreciations it was intended in part to guard against, we should not overlook the fact that it was also intended as a corrective to the philological studies that dominated academic criticism in the early part of the century. Because the New Critics were dominant for so long, we tend to forget that originally they had to fight a strongly entrenched system and found the way slow and painful.[13] As Allen Tate makes clear in a 1940 lecture, the very complaint they had against these older critics who surrounded the work with great masses of philological and historical data was that they were slavishly aping scientific methodology:

> We no longer believe in the specific quality of the work of literature, the quality that distinguishes it from a work of history or even science. As men of letters we no longer, in fact, believe in literature; we believe rather that the knowledge offered us in even the most highly developed literary forms has something factitious and illusory about it, so that before we can begin to test its validity we must translate it into an analogy derived from the sciences. The historical method is an imitation of scientific method: we entertain as interesting and valuable that portion of the literary work to which we can apply the scientific vocabularies.[14]

The New Critics were clearly, then, every bit as suspicious of criticism that pretended to scientific objectivity as they were of the subjectivity implied by impressionistic readings.

But this rejection of a scholarship that aspired to scientific exactitude was only one aspect of a much wider animus against modern science harbored by the New Critics, and an understanding of this resentment will bring us close to the essential antagonism they shared with Eliot. We should first bear in mind that although the brand of literary criticism espoused by the New Critics came to dominate the American academy, they were fighting a lost cause on all wider fronts. This is easy to overlook because of the customary tendency of humanities professors to exaggerate the link between intramural and extramural power, as witness those who did not hesitate to imagine the New Critics agents of global technological oppression. In actuality, the New Criticism was essentially an elegy to a lost world; its practitioners were cultural pessimists appalled by most of the developments of the twentieth century. Specifically, they lamented the industrialization of America, the bazaar of dispensable commodities spawned by capitalism, and the reign of liberal democracy with its triumphant vulgarity of taste. Hovering between cause and symbol, "science" was their catchword for this general malaise.

The most pointed of the New Critics in elaborating this case was Ransom, who spoke out aggressively as a champion of southern regionalism, praising the Old South as a place of ritual and rich tradition felt in the bone.[15] In opposition to the leisurely minuet of southern life, he set that of the encroaching North, propelled by raw acquisitiveness and armed with the tools of science. This ruthless progressivism did violence not only to venerable folkways but also to the integrity of the land, which the agrarian South had always respected. Of course, all of this is familiar enough in the English tradition and might have been found virtually verbatim, say, in Lawrence's agony over the coal industry's desecration of the land and rural life of Nottinghamshire. But what Ransom imports to the argument, enlarging it beyond a strictly social criticism of industrial rapaciousness that could have been made as easily by communitarians on the left, is Eliot's credo of 1927, which underscores its reactionary bent:

> A natural affiliation binds together the gentleman, the religious man, and the artist – punctilious characters, all of them, in their formalism. We have seen one distinguished figure in our times pronouncing on behalf of all three in one breath. In politics, royalism; in religion, Anglo-Catholic; in literature, classical. I am astonished upon discovering how comprehensively this formula covers the kingdom of the aesthetic life as it is organized by the social tradition. I am so grateful that it is with hesitation I pick a little quarrel with the terms. I would covet a program going something like this: In manners, aristocratic; in religion, ritualistic; in art, traditional. But I imagine the intent of Mr. Eliot's formula is about what I am representing . . . The word for our generation in these matters is "formal," and it might even bear the pointed qualification, "and reactionary."[16]

While Ransom's restatement of Eliot shows an increase in decadence – Eliot would never, for example, admit to valuing the church *primarily* because of its ritual, an effete version of Maurras's mistake – what the two credos share is a profound distrust of the ascent of the common man, with his unrestrained emotions. For Ransom, form is to be valued because it delays the gratification of instinct: poets must trim their inspiration to fit the inherited patterns of poetry, the bereaved submit to church ritual rather than throw themselves upon the corpse, and gentlemen gallantly delay possessing women until an elaborate courtship has been performed. This cod-

ification increases the worth of things, as Ransom explains in the
case of courtship:

> The form actually denies him [the gentleman] the privilege of
> going the straight line between two points, even though this line
> has an axiomatic logic in its favor and is the shortest possible
> line. But the woman, contemplated in this manner under re-
> straint, becomes a person and an aesthetic object; therefore a
> richer object.[17]

These traditions, or rather tradition, since both Eliot and Ransom
see the various aspects as mutually reinforcing, provide the only safe-
guard against the vulgar urgency of the tasteless masses of "carbun-
cular clerks" coupling with jaded typists and the corresponding
throwaway culture that caters to other "needs." Ransom and the
New Critics generally blame science for positing a world of exploit-
able matter, whereas Eliot blames romanticism for its glorification
of rampant individualism, but the real object of opprobrium is the
same.

Eliot clearly recognized the kindred political and social criticism
of Ransom and regarded it approvingly.[18] As has been mentioned,
both in the *Criterion* and in his notorious 1933 lectures at the University of Virginia, which were later published as *After Strange Gods*,
Eliot praised the appearance of *I'll Take My Stand* (1930), a collection
of essays of backward-yearning southerners, including Ransom, Tate,
and Warren. Tate sets the tone of the volume in a querulous piece
arguing that the South succumbed to northern values because it had
not evolved a feudalistic religion to go with its feudalistic economy
and social organization. Its mistake was not the practice of slavery –
of this we hear no mention – but in having adopted Protestantism,
the religion properly belonging to the capitalistic North. As a result
it was not medieval enough to withstand "the post-bellum tempta-
tions of the devil," the tawdry goods spawned by "the scientific
mind."[19] (Twenty years later Tate converted to Roman Catholicism.)
Ransom, in his contribution, does bring up the problem of the Old
South's slavery, but dismisses it as "more often than not, humane in
practice."[20] Far worse, he indicates, is the problem of modern
uprootedness from the land and shifting populations, the "deracination" brought about "by the blandishments of such fine words as
Progressive, Liberal, and Forward-looking."[21]

The feudalistic agrarianism presented in this collection almost certainly connected in Eliot's mind with Maurras's praise of medieval French social organization: semiindependant, indigenous, rural communities held together by the throne and altar. Unfortunately, Eliot chose to fill out the comparison between medieval France and antebellum South by the introduction of Maurras's anti-Semitism, an element that had never surfaced in the southerners' defense of their disappearing culture. His comment to the Virginia audience, later regretted, that the South's advantage lies in its distance from New York with its industrialization and "foreign races" (i.e., undesirable "free-thinking Jews"), was apparently an attempt to play to the fear of deracination expressed by Ransom. A decade later – this time minus the anti-Semitism – Eliot took the model of decentralized indigenous communities bound together by an all-pervasive religious culture as the basis for social renewal in *Notes Towards the Definition of Culture*. Arguing on behalf of "regionalism," he considers that

> on the whole, it would appear to be for the best that the great majority of human beings should go on living in the place in which they were born. Family, class, and local loyalty all support each other; and if one of these decays, the others suffer also.[22]

Eliot also takes over Tate's flaccid argument that the feudalism of the Old South was essentially spiritual and therefore is at a great disadvantage in trying to justify itself in the flat accents of political discourse. Tate complained, "The Southerner is faced with the paradox: He must use an instrument, which is political, and so unrealistic and pretentious that he cannot believe in it, to re-establish a private, self-contained, and essentially spiritual life."[23] Eliot echoes:

> The champions of local tradition . . . are inclined to formulate the remedy wholly in political terms; and as they may be politically inexperienced, and at the same time are agitated by deeper than political motives, their programmes may be patently impracticable. And when they put forward an economic programme, there, too, they are handicapped by having motives which go deeper than economics, in contrast with men who have the reputation of being practical.[24]

That one may freely grant that there are reservoirs of being outside the compass of politics and economics without being willing to concede that feudalistic relations evolved from such sources is an option neither Tate nor Eliot seems to allow. Their own political prefer-

ences are constantly presented as merely crude and misleading trans-
lations of spiritual positions.

The political and cultural affinities of Eliot and the New Critics
yield similar views of history, which in turn color their view of both
literary history and the evaluation of particular authors. Eliot's anti-
republican stance, which gets recorded in his notion of a "dissociation of sensibility," I have already discussed at some length.
According to Eliot, the collapse of the old monarchy, spelling a final
end to medieval modes of social organization, had a disastrous effect
on psychic wholeness, recorded nowhere more plainly than in the
degeneration of poetry. If Eliot stresses the virtues of the Metaphysical poets, it is because they are our last example, and hence most
accessible model, of the integration of thought and feeling that typ-
ified classical and medieval authors. This belief in a radical change
of consciousness occurring in the seventeenth century is accepted
almost universally by the New Critics, who differ among themselves
only as they emphasize one or another aspect of the subsequent loss.
(Winters places the break slightly earlier, at the end of the sixteenth
century.) Similarly, they hold up Metaphysical poets as embodiments
of the lost world and find the lack of their poetic virtues in poets of
subsequent ages to be indices of a general decline. For both Eliot
and the New Critics, then, literary history is an epiphenomenon of
cultural history, a cultural history interpreted from a politically reactionary perspective.

The wholesale absorption of Eliot's view of historical rupture can
be seen most clearly in Brooks. In 1927, the year of his conversion,
Eliot wrote an essay, now not much read, on John Bramhall, Bishop
of Derry under Charles I and Primate of Ireland under Charles II.
A good part of the reason for the essay's relative obscurity is that
Bramhall himself was hardly a riveting figure, being of interest to
church historians, but not many others. Occasionally he receives
brief mention in accounts of Thomas Hobbes, with whom he entered
into debate on the issues of freedom of the will and the relationship
between church and state.[25] Yet even here Bramhall's objections to
Hobbes are preserved only for the responses Hobbes made to them.
For Eliot, however, things look quite different. Bramhall emerges as
champion of the old order and, if the original debate is read correctly, vanquishes Hobbes, "one of those extraordinary little upstarts
whom the chaotic motions of the Renaissance tossed into an emi-
nence which they hardly deserved and have never lost."[26] Unfortunately, Eliot admits, the contest was adjudicated differently by

history, and the unjustly magnified Hobbes helped usher in the modern age of atheism and materialism (understood in both a philosophical and an economic sense). The resultant worldview was that of a soulless, mechanistic science:

> For a philosopher like Hobbes has already a mixed attitude, partly philosophic, and partly scientific; the philosophy being in decay and the science immature. Hobbes' philosophy is not so much a philosophy as it is an adumbration of the universe of material atoms regulated by laws of motion which formed the scientific view of the world from Newton to Einstein. Hence there is quite naturally no place in Hobbes' universe for the human will; what he failed to see was that there was no place in it for consciousness either, or for human beings.[27]

This assertion that the scientific mentality corroded what was essentially human appealed naturally to Brooks as southerner. He accepts Eliot's diagnosis completely and, having made Hobbes almost single-handedly responsible for the dissociation of sensibility, goes on to show his baleful influence on the poetic imagination.[28] Hobbes's elevation of scientific discourse reduced irony to imprecision, metaphor to fancy, and thereby spelled an end to Metaphysical poetry:

> The weakening of metaphor, the development of a specifically "poetic" subject matter and diction, the emphasis on simplicity and clarity, the simplification of the poet's attitude, the segregation of the witty and the ironical from the serious, the stricter separation of the genres – all these items testify to the monopoly of the scientific spirit . . . The imagination was weakened from a "magic and synthetic" power to Hobbes' conception of it as the file-clerk of memory. It was obviously the antirationalistic magic that Hobbes was anxious to eliminate.[29]

The nonsouthern New Critics, too, though they did not necessarily share the obsession with the evils of science, were convinced of the validity of Eliot's general theory that the seventeenth century marked the beginning of the West's decline. Wimsatt, like the postconversion Eliot, traces the falling off in terms of the disappearance of God, with the twentieth century as the absolute nadir. The slope can be seen, he maintains, in a comparison of Samuel Johnson's treatment of metaphysical absurdity in the catacomb episode of *Rasselas* with Beckett's treatment in *Godot* or *Watt:*

One main difference, which may disguise the parallel for us, is that the modern versions of the descent take place at a level which is, to start with, subterranean, the very sub-cellar or zero level of modern man's three century decline from the pinnacles of theology and metaphysics. Johnson's descendental exercise, with its saving theological clause in the Catacombs, takes place at a level still near the top of the metaphysical ladder.[30]

Again following Eliot, Wimsatt displays a certain fascination with Johnson as the first to peer into the abyss of modernity. He was tainted enough to undervalue the Metaphysicals of the previous century, yet still whole enough, as Eliot stressed, to have "abominated Hobbes," the cynical atheist.[31]

Even Yvor Winters, in general no great admirer of Eliot as a poet or a critic, buys into the theory of historical rupture. He accepts the judgment that thought and feeling began to unravel at a time just slightly earlier, as has been mentioned, than Eliot's date, and differs substantially only in what he saw to be the consequences for those who came after. For Eliot the shattered sensibility tries futilely to reassert itself by veering periodically from one extreme to the other. Thus, the Age of Reason gives way to the Romantic rebellion that in turn yields Victorian "rumination," thought ruffled at a distance by emotions that it refused to accommodate.[32] Instead of such alteration, Winters, the bellicose rationalist, sees one long attack on reason:

> The poets with whom I shall deal in this essay are the products of a rebellion against the authority of the rational mind, as that authority had been understood in the middle ages and the Renaissance. The rebellion was formulated in two closely related doctrines: the sentimentalism of the third Earl of Shaftesbury (later summarized by Pope, along with other ideas in the *Essay on Man*), and the doctrine of the association of ideas, a psychological doctrine having its beginnings in Hobbes and formulated by Locke . . . By the time we are well into the nineteenth century, both these doctrines have become folk wisdom, and their efficacy is questioned only here and there today.[33]

Winters takes Shaftesbury's "sentimentalism" to entail the belief that "our impulses are good and can lead us to virtue; that human reason is the principal source of error and evil," and takes "the association of ideas" to be its "psychological implementation" insofar as it deduced ideas from sensory impressions.[34] Leaving aside the clumsiness of this characterization of Shaftesbury and the fact that the association of ideas, as it occurs in his successors Hartley and Hume, *negates* Shaftesbury's identification of an innate moral sense, what should strike us here is the resilience of Eliot's theory, which can sustain elaborations as divergent as Brooks's and Winters's. Hobbes becomes a villain capable of spawning whatever one dislikes: excessive irrationalism or excessive rationalism. The unifying element, however, among the New Critics is that they all regret in common the passing of medieval hierarchy sustained by either: (1) orthodox religion for Tate and Wimsatt, (2) a less clearly defined "spirituality" for Brooks and Ransom, or (3) the authority of reason for Winters.

The New Critics accept not only Eliot's view of history, but also his conviction that the poet is strongly bound to his age, a conviction that relies on the Romantic elevation of poetry to the highest expression of a people's consciousness (at any given historical moment). Aside from any disparity in poetic abilities, Goethe, for example, could never have risen to the heights of Dante simply because of the historically degenerate situation in which he found himself. In outlining the requirements for a "classic," Eliot looks first to the possibilites of the age, only later to the gifts of the poet: "A classic can only occur when a civilization is mature; when a language and a literature are mature; and it must be the work of a mature mind."[35] Though poets may struggle against their age, none, it seems (the New Critics would qualify this to very, very few) are able to overcome it: "In the eighteenth century, we are oppressed by the limited range of sensibility, and especially in the scale of religious feeling."[36] The ability to *see* the limitations of the twentieth century while lacking the ability to forge independently a new sensibility occasions much of the abjectness that runs through Eliot's own poetry.

This tight fit between the poet and history would appear to violate the New Critics' warnings against the intentional fallacy, in this case by asserting that the historically determined furniture of the poet's mind sets limits to the range of his creation. Such a worry shows up in Ransom's dismay in 1941 that Eliot increasingly "uses his historical studies for the sake of literary understanding, and therefore might be called a historical critic."[37] Of course, Ransom is not alone in perceiving a falling off in Eliot's criticism in the years after his conversion, but what is misleading about the charge in this instance is that it avoids the fact that Eliot's judgments of periods and authors remained remarkably steady over his lifetime and that Ransom overwhelmingly accepted those judgments. What Ransom is reacting to in his complaint is the *overt* historicism of Eliot's later work. Would Ransom be willing to claim that his own nostalgia for an agrarian, feudalistic South had nothing to do with his own view of poetry? If so, one can only wonder how discussions of both came to find their way into the same essays or how he himself, three years earlier, might have joined in the anti-Hobbesian chorus:

> Incidentally, we know how much Mr. Hobbes affected Dryden too, and the whole Restoration literature. What Bacon with his disparagement of poetry had begun, in the cause of science and protestantism, Hobbes completed. The name of Hobbes is critical in any history that would account for the chill which settled upon the poets at the very moment that English poetry was attaining magnificently to the fullness of its powers. The name stood for common sense and naturalism, and the monopoly of the scientific spirit over the mind. Hobbes was the adversary, the Satan, when the latter first intimidated the English poets. After Hobbes his name is legion.[38]

Ransom's criticism of Eliot's reliance on history is, of course, part of his larger insistence that culture transcends politics. But it is a position belied by much of his own work. Unfortunately, it is this rather disingenuous stance that has fostered the mistaken opinion that the New Critics were themselves adamantly ahistorical.

Ransom's lead in adopting Eliot's politically inspired reestimation of literary history while suggesting that the judgments were timeless and universal was followed by all the New Critics. The virtues of the Metaphysicals – irony, paradox, and wit – are abstracted as benchmarks of all good poetry. (Winters only, demanding an identifiable ethical statement in poetry, favors the plain stylists of the previous century.)[39] Judged against these standards, romanticism's stock plummets. The individual New Critic might try to salvage a particular Romantic, but only after previously undiscovered Metaphysical features have been identified, and even then the poet is presented as an aberration. Brooks, for example, after demonstrating the wit in "London," tries to reclaim Blake in this way: "Blake is a metaphysical poet. But the elements which make him such a poet appeared rarely in the poetry of his period and never elsewhere in a form so extreme. He remains an isolated and exceptional figure."[40] Shelley, the revolutionary atheist, whose philosophy Eliot found "repellent" and whose poetry he deemed almost unreadable as a consequence, is still a disparaged figure, but now because of his ut-

ter lack of the saving grace of irony.[41] Wordsworth's simple, de-
motic poetry, "a man speaking to men," appears hopelessly
pedestrian – except where he was unintentionally paradoxical[42] –
and even Winters, who might have been attracted to a latter-day version of morally informed plain style, finds Wordsworth "heavily didactic," no more than "a very bad poet who wrote a few good
lines."[43] (Though after Winters's death a disciple of his informed
me that toward the end of his life he had mellowed somewhat and
was willing to countenance "Ode to Duty" as the one acceptable
Romantic poem.)

Thus, at two removes, Maurras's politically inspired antiromanticism shows up in the work of the New Critics, though now the battle
is fought, even more so than in Eliot, largely in terms of poetic
qualities. Ironists pummel straightforward sentimentalists on page
after page of revised literary histories. Only in unguarded moments
does the connection between poetry and extraliterary concerns become explicit, as when Winters chastises Whitman for "trying to express a loose America by writing loose poetry" and quickly extends
the criticism: "This fallacy, the fallacy of expressive or imitative form,
recurs constantly in modern literature."[44] (Although Winters's comments suggest that the poet can stand against his or her age and
should do so when the age is as degenerate as that of the modern
liberal era, the fact that Winters ultimately can produce only a handful of fairly obscure poets and friends who manage to resist is evidence of the virtual impossibility of successful revolt.) More often,
even though the New Critics subscribe fully to the ideologically motivated notion of the dissociation of sensibility, they speak as Ransom
does when he insists that questions of "ideology" ought to have
nothing to do with criticism.[45]

In the practical criticism of this school, the situation is even more
extreme. There the exclusion of politics is absolute, as is indeed
almost any mention of history beyond the most neutral explanatory
footnote. The tension is all internal, with ambiguous connotations
and paradoxical statements artfully counterweighted. The high value
placed on the reconciliation of competing pressures within a single
entity is an adaptation from Richards. In effect, the New Critics took
his psychological theory of the beneficent harmonizing of impulses
and transferred it from the reader to the more objective realm of
the work.[46] Whereas irony for Richards was the arousal in the subject
of countervailing forces, for the New Critics it became an identifiable
and eminently discussable characteristic of the work itself. The op-

portunity for ingenious burrowing this gave rise to is suggested by Tate's allusion to the vast energies latent in a poem as he defines what he means by poetic "tension":

> I am using the term [tension] not as a general metaphor, but as a special one, derived from lopping the prefixes off the logical terms *ex*tension and *in*tension. What I am saying, of course, is that the meaning of poetry is its "tension," the full organized body of all the extension and intension that we can find in it.[47]

The temptation here is, of course, to delight in complexity for its own sake, a temptation Ransom, for one, was perfectly willing to indulge in:

> The poem [Wallace Stevens's "Sea Surface Full of Clouds"] has a calculated complexity, and its technical competence is so high that to study it, if you do that sort of thing, is to be happy . . . The poem has no moral, political, religious, or sociological values. It is not about "res publica," the public thing. The subject matter is trifling.[48]

We are led back, on less engaging grounds, to Richards's notion of poetry as therapy.

Despite the seemingly arid and hermetic pleasure described by Ransom, the New Critics insisted that their theory of poetry did allow for a serious and deep connection with the extraliterary world. Their claim was much more than the almost mandatory concession that the words of poems had a denotational value that relied on the everyday realm of reference. They maintained that the figurative language of poetry – its essence – was revelatory of the deep structure of the world itself. Although they never drew the parallel precisely, this assertion stands as a direct counterstatement to Galileo's confidence that the book of nature was written in the language of mathematics. The contrast would have appealed to them, however, for the New Critics' belief in a world of metaphor was intended to dethrone science and replace it with poetry. Ultimately it was on this belief that their valorization of culture and everything that entailed depended. The difficulty, of course, was that while Galileo could point to the movement of the heavens as evidence of his claim, what could the New Critics adduce in support of theirs?

The weakest sense in which the New Critics tried to defend their position was that sketched by Brooks in *The Well Wrought Urn*. The world, in its complexity, demands a complex response, he argued.

Consequently, univocal Romantic lyrics, for example, betray the trust of poetry insofar as they suggest the adequacy of a simple response. In this regard, their emotional abstraction suffers from a deficiency akin to the scientist's rational abstraction: both belie the world's richness. Borrowing Richards's distinction between "poetry of inclusion" and "poetry of exclusion," Brooks establishes a system of evaluation based on the amount of discordant material a poem contains:

> Low in the scale one would find a rather simple poetry in which the associations of the various elements that go to make up the poem are similar in tone and therefore can be unified under one rather simple attitude – poems of simple affection, positive "external" satires, etc. Higher in the scale, one would find poems in which the variety and clash among the elements to be comprehended under a total attitude are sharper.[49]

Only a heavily ironic poetry, by constantly suggesting alternative readings, can serve as adequate simulacrum of the variousness of the real world. Not only, then, must the poet's sensibility be unified as Eliot had urged, but the connecting tissue must be byzantinely intertwined.

Criticism of this position was swift and telling, however. Brooks was jumped on, justly, by both David Daiches and Murray Krieger for the unavoidable implication that the more complexity a poem contained the better.[50] Krieger points out that the logical extension of such a position would be a poetry that duplicated the chaos of the world, nightmarishly providing the limiting case of Winters's "fallacy of imitative form." Poetry of such absolute mimesis would obviously cease to be art. To these voices was added that of R. S. Crane, who couched his complaint in Aristotelian terms. Brooks, he contends, errs by starting with a material explanation of poetry as something that is built out of ironic language rather than looking for a definition that would begin with poetry's proper function in the world.[51] As a result, when Brooks finally does speak of poetry as providing "an insight which preserves the unity of experience," this unity strikes Crane as much more that of poetic coherence than of fidelity to an external reality:

> It is not, therefore, any special principle of unity derived from the nature of the "experience" or object represented in a given

kind of poem that determines poetical structure; rather it is the presence in poems of poetical structure – i.e., ironical opposition and resolution – that determines, and is the sign of, the unification of experience.[52]

Brooks's talk of poetry's relationship to the world thus seems to Crane more of an apologetic afterthought than a premise from which he actually deduces anything.

Brooks arrived at this extreme – and extremely vulnerable – position by, in effect, taking over Eliot's preference for the Metaphysicals without wanting to link it directly to the "classical" worldview that underlay it. Eliot admired the Metaphysicals because they were the last who could scale confidently up and down the medieval Great Chain of Being. Yet sensitive to Johnson's complaint that "the most heterogeneous ideas are yoked by violence together" in Metaphysical poetry, Eliot is aware that the bold wit of their connections has a hint of bravado about it: an extravagant display of what has nearly ceased to be. Commenting on Donne's "The Ecstasy" in the third of the Clark lectures, Eliot observes "that strain to impress more than to state, which is the curse of seventeenth century verse not in England alone, but throughout Europe."[53] There is the suggestion of a willed quality to their wit, a pressure seen in much more extreme form in Eliot's own verse with its condensed phrasing and radical ellipses. By contrast, when Dante, writing at the confident pinnacle of medieval Christianity, most resembles the Metaphysicals – as, for example, in his striking rendering of the souls of suicides as tree stumps – there is an analogical naturalness to his choice which makes the comparison brilliant without seeming in the least contrived. Eliot explains this difference between the poetry of Dante and that of Donne – to the advantage of the former – by arguing that in Dante the feeling occasioned by experience leads to thought, and thought leads in turn to belief, whereas in Donne the feeling leads to thought, but thought results only in another feeling.[54] The wit of Donne is possible because there is *tension* between thought and feeling, the beginnings of a dissociation of sensibility. Indeed, it wouldn't be false to Eliot's overall point to say that it is precisely the ingenuity of Donne that holds the old medieval order together; his conceits, often admittedly brilliant, are telltale signs of the beginnings of decay. Wonderfully adapted to his own age, Donne's conceits suffer from a self-referentiality that would have been unnecessary (worse, "unorthodox," in the language of the later Eliot) in the thirteenth century. In contrast to Eliot's position here, Brooks's overestimation of wit as *the* poetic virtue occurs because he wants to fight Eliot's battles completely on literary turf. The medievalism is jettisoned. Thus, when it comes time to explain what extraliterary state of affairs endows wit with this lofty status, Brooks uncomfortably suggests that the world somehow embodies it. We are left in the end with almost a parody of the Maurrasien-Eliotic belief that classicism was the literature of cosmos.

A more sophisticated, but still overtly ahistorical and apolitical, account of poetry's relationship to the world beyond the text is put forward by Ransom. He avoids the material explanation with which Crane taxed Brooks by beginning his inquiry with the subject matter of poetry. In his most extended treatment of the topic, "Poetry: A Note in Ontology," a chapter in *The World's Body,* he distinguishes between a poetry of ideas and a poetry of things. This distinction, Ransom contends, based on the ontological status of the subject matter of poetry, is not intended as merely a heuristic device, but lies at the heart of things, "and criticism cannot go much deeper than this."[55] Much as Coleridge had declared every man to be either a Platonist or an Aristotelian, Ransom seems to believe every poem can be similarly sorted out. A poetry of ideas, he associates, as did Tate, with the abstract thought of Plato:

> Platonic Poetry is allegory, a discourse in things, but on the understanding that they are translatable at every point into ideas. (The usual ideas are those which constitute the popular causes, patriotic, religious, moral, or social.) Or Platonic Poetry is the elaboration of ideas as such, but in proceeding introduces for ornament some physical properties . . . which is rhetoric.[56]

In contrast, a poetry of things renders the textured *Dinglichkeit* of the world, "the world's body" of the book's title. Such a poetry deals in images rather than ideas, thus enabling us "to contemplate things as they are in their rich and contingent materiality."[57] Clearly, Ransom finds such poetry vastly superior to the Platonic variety which he dismisses as "bogus."[58]

Ransom's emphasis on *Dinglichkeit* serves a dual purpose, of which both aspects are deeply conservative. First, it is clearly an attempt to rescue affectively laden objects from the dispensable commodities of capitalism.[59] In this regard it bears some resemblance to Lukács's concurrent critique of reification: a seemingly fixed world of mate-

rial relations comes to alter human intercourse, as we lose the ability
to imagine other possibilites. The difference between these two appeals for a change in our relationship to the material world, however, is that Ransom, unlike Lukács, almost immediately re-reifies
the objects he would preserve. Responding to the basic difficulty of
all conservative thought, that is, how to accommodate history to sta-
sis, Ransom positions his objects both in and out of time. The objects, to be valuable, must accrete human experience (the thing as
"gathering" according to the similarly concerned Heidegger), but
at the same time they somehow remain unchangeable:

> The things are constant in the sense that the ideas are never
> emancipated from the necessity of referring back to them as
> their original; and the sense that they are not altered nor di-
> minished no matter which ideas may take off from them as a
> point of departure.[60]

He accomplishes this sleight-of-hand by taking things in this passage
in precisely the sense he disparages, that is, objects set over against
the human world (Heidegger's *Vorhandenheit*). In this way they may
be said to be the unchanging ground of human perception, the raw
data from which mutable ideas are constructed. But more important
than the apparent contradiction in Ransom's thinking – perhaps he
would find it a fecund paradox – is the fact that the external world
is ultimately frozen into a display of discrete entities, a china cabinet
of precious objects. These products of a bygone culture after which
Ransom hankers constitute the real and abiding world.[61]

The second related effect of Ransom's emphasis on *Dinglichkeit* is
that in his ardor to ban ideas from poetry, he excludes not only
crude social realism and sentimental Victorian moralizing, but theoretically all poetry that might in the broadest sense be said to be
ethical, that is, primarily concerned with human interaction. Were
this exclusion pressed absolutely, Ransom would be left with precious little in his canon, and he is fully aware of this. He acknowledges that an analysis of physical poetry "will probably disclose that
it is more than usually impure."[62] Yet it is never these impurities that
receive his critical attention. So cautious is he to keep critical discusssion riveted on objects that he redefines "metaphysical" to justify his interest in a poetry that would seem by designation to lead
beyond the physical. He first asserts that from the Middle Ages to
Dryden, the term "metaphysical" meant "miraculous," and then
claims that since Johnson took the term from Pope who took it from

Dryden, this must have been the sense Johnson intended when he applied the term to early-seventeenth-century poetry. While all of this may be true, it is Ransom's definition of the miraculous that takes us up short:

> We may consult the dictionary, and discover that there is a miraculism or supernaturalism in a metaphorical assertion if we are ready to mean what we say, or believe what we hear ... Specifically, the miraculism arises when the poet discovers by analogy an identity between objects which is partial, though it should be considerable, and proceeds to an identification which is complete.[63]

The miraculous resides in poetic technique: the bold equation of two things only partially similar. It is no wonder, then, that Ransom finds the essence of metaphysical poetry to be its conceits – extended metaphors – and one strongly suspects that Donne's parted lovers are of interest insofar as they resemble the legs of a compass rather than vice versa.[64] A static world of things seems to have assimilated human experience to itself. To find the metaphor that captures this process is to engage in the highest priestcraft.

Because Ransom, like Brooks, endeavors to keep Eliot's literary history minus the history, he is forced, like Brooks, to make grandiose claims for the poetry of the favored age and its characteristic features. Confident in his ontological speculations, Ransom goes further than Brooks, however. Whereas Brooks had vaguely and, as it were in passing, gestured toward the complexity of the world to justify the complexity of the best poetry, Ransom identifies the metaphor-forging mind of the poet as the very source of religion, with religion gaining from the association:

> From the strict point of view of literary criticism it must be insisted that the miraculism which produces the humblest conceit is the same miraculism which supplies to religions their substantive content. (This is said to assert the dignity not of the conceits but of the religions.) It is the poet and nobody else who gives to the God a nature, a form, faculties, and a history ... The myths are conceits, born of metaphors. Religions are periodically produced by poets and destroyed by naturalists. Religion depends for its ontological validity upon a literary understanding, and that is why it is frequently misunderstood.[65]

Thus, he continues on to maintain that the connection between the Metaphysical poets and the religious thinkers of the Middle Ages was a literary one:

> The metaphysical poets, perhaps like their spiritual fathers the mediaeval Schoolmen, were under no illusions about this. They recognized myth, as they recognized the conceits, as a device of expression; its sanctity as the consequence of its public or social importance.[66]

Even preconversion Eliot never made literary classicism bear this much weight, and as has been mentioned before, he grew increasingly scornful of those like Richards (and earlier Arnold) who suggested that poetry might supply the function of religion.

Ransom's *Dinglichkeit*, the veneration of illuminated objects, combines with his appropriation of religion to yield the influential idea of the poem as icon. His use of the term "icon" is derived, with significant change, from the work of University of Chicago aesthetician Charles Morris. In his *Encyclopedia of Unified Science*, Morris had distinguished between the mere sign or "symbol" used by science and the iconic sign employed in artistic media. The first of these, Morris argued, is purely referential, serving to denote the object to which it points. In contrast, the iconic sign "embodies [value properties] in some medium where they may be directly inspected (in short, the aesthetic sign is an iconic sign whose designatum is a value)."[67] But Ransom, though pleased with the obvious valorization of aesthetic representation, does not believe Morris has gone far enough in his definition of the iconic sign. If the iconic sign points to the world – though it be the values of the world – then it resembles the scientific symbol in providing a kind of knowledge. The icon, for Ransom, must do more. It does not just point to the values of the world but actually *embodies* these values. It does not just represent the value, it possesses the value: "The icon is a body imitating some actual embodiment of the value."[68] Like the well-wrought and Grecian urns it describes, the poem, too, becomes the repository of value, a precious object in its own right. Moreover, because the poem condenses metaphorically, offers as it were a distillation and heightening of values, it constitutes – and I believe this is Ransom's ultimate claim – *the* most precious object, the world's body made luminous. The icon has assumed its religious function.

Understood in this way, the idea of poetry as icon becomes the organizing theme of Wimsatt's most sophisticated work. In 1954 he collects his theoretical essays of more than a decade under the title *The Verbal Icon,* along with the following definition:

> The term *icon* is used today by semiotic writers to refer to a verbal sign which *somehow* shares the properties of, or resembles, the objects which it denotes. The same term in its more usual meaning refers to a visual image and especially to one which is a religious symbol. The verbal image which most fully realizes its verbal capacities is that which is not merely a bright picture (in the usual modern meaning of the term *image*) but also an interpretation of reality in its metaphoric dimensions. Thus: *The Verbal Icon.*[69]

Among the essays collected are the already mentioned "The Intentional Fallacy" and "The Affective Fallacy," which leave the work in splendid isolation, uncontaminated by author or reader. But it is the vagueness recorded in the italicized *somehow* of this past quotation that Wimsatt, a more philosophically conscientious theoretician than Ransom, feels obliged to dispel. How *exactly* does the icon "share the properties of, or resemble, the objects which it denotes"?

The obvious difficulty of this position is that metaphor – the essence of poetry according to Wimsatt – is a literary figure having no ordinarily identifiable status in being outside the poem. The terms of the metaphor may be found ready-to-hand in the world, but what sense does it make to speak of their *comparison* as enjoying extraliterary existence? If Wimsatt had been content to claim that poetry provided a special kind of knowledge about the world, he might have argued that metaphor was the vehicle of this (nondiscursive) knowledge. But like Ransom he is not content with this lesser claim, though for most theorists it would seem quite large enough and certainly hard enough to prove.[70] Alternatively, if Wimsatt were to fall back on the view that the metaphor is solely the poet's invention, then he would be trapped, philosophically in an idealism, artistically in a formalism, where the only criterion of value would be coherence. And clearly this is a route he does not want to take.[71]

The near mysticism that Wimsatt is left with leads him back to the Middle Ages in search of a solution. On a more serious pilgrimage than the skeptical Ransom, though, he is not content to trace literary filiations only. While he does note that the seriousness with which he takes metaphor bears comparison to the analogical language of the patristic tradition, this will not be – cannot be – the crux of his argument, for it does not explain how the language embodies what it imitates.[72] Much more to his purpose is the Thomistic conception of epiphany, the manifestation of the divine in the mundane:

> I allude to Maritain's stress on the radiance of a concrete, if ontologically secret or mysterious, kind of form, and to Father Gilby's on the substantive completeness of the poetic experience – though the latter may be rather heavily shaded toward subjectivism. It appears to me, by the way that James Joyce . . . has placed the correct accent on radiance or *claritas* – the radiant epiphany of the whole and structurally intelligible *individual* thing. It was in this direction of course that Hopkins had been working with his interest in certain Scotist technicalities which favor the individually formal inscapes of things.[73]

Although Joyce extended the use of epiphany in his work, the whole tradition has as its fountainhead the idea of the Incarnation, and Wellek is absolutely correct in seeing this as the ultimate likeness Wimsatt would establish for poetry's universalizing of the concrete.[74] Toward the end of the history of literary criticism that Wimsatt wrote in conjunction with Brooks, he freely admits as much:

> The writers of the present history have not been concerned to implicate literary theory with any kind of religious doctrine. It appears to us, however, relevant, as we near our conclusion, at least to confess an opinion that the kind of literary theory which seems to us to emerge the most plausibly from the long history of the debates is far more difficult to orient within any of the Platonic or Gnostic ideal world views, or within the Manichaean full dualism and strife of principles, than precisely within the vision of suffering, the optimism, the mystery which are embraced in the religious dogma of the Incarnation.[75]

The divinity of the world, revealed through metaphor, transubstantiates the poetic artifact, rendering it iconic. If Wimsatt could be no clearer, he could draw consolation from the precedent of religious mystery he invoked.

Wimsatt arrives at the terminus of New Critical thinking on this matter, drawing out the religious implications of Ransom's icon and the more rudimentary theorizing in the same direction of his own collaborator, Brooks. After his conversion, Tate follows suit, though he chooses to cast the whole issue rather unhelpfully in terms of the problem of Cartesian dualism. (Descartes not coincidentally was a scientist.) This allows him to romp through the Western tradition in order to demonstrate that poetry resolves the mind–body dichotomy, a vast extension of Eliot's comparatively tame idea of the dissociation of sensibility.[76] Those unsympathetic to Tate might dismiss his effortless solution as a reduction of poetry to the status of the pineal gland; he himself preferred to see it as the equivalent of religious atonement. Only Winters, as so often, stood apart from the others in shying away from grand religious claims for poetry. But again, as so often, he joins them through the back door, for his obsessive emphasis on the morality of poetry is prosecuted with a Calvinistic fervor: a sermon minus even the four bare walls.

This leaves us at some distance from Eliot's mature thinking on such matters – where he lamented the glib conflation of poetry and religion in his own earlier work of the "classical" period. If nevertheless he remained guilty of this conflation, it is religion that finally subsumes poetry and not vice versa as it had once appeared. While he might speak in quasi-religious terms of the poet "haunted by a demon . . . and the words, the poem he makes, are a kind of form of the exorcism of this demon,"[77] the ensuing relief is that of catharsis not salvation. Moreover, which of the New Critics, even in moments of extreme self-doubt, could possibly have referred to the poetic process as a "secretion" or "a mug's game"?

It is my contention that the New Critics made their vastly grander claims for the nature and function of poetry due to the fact that they never were able to sort out Eliot's early classical compound. Eliot gradually learned that it was possible to claim too much for poetry, but almost impossible to do so for religion, and his political, historical, and cultural concerns became provinces of his Anglo-Catholicism. This move required repatriation, conversion, and a somewhat eccentric view of the Anglican Church, a path not easily imitated. For the New Critics of America, especially those of the South – where, as Tate lamented, they had been worshipping at the altar of a northern faith – it was all but impossible. As a result, poetry was made to bear the New Critics' whole ideological burden: the yearning for medieval order as a stay against the science-driven modern world with its hordes of commodity-consuming democrats and easy morality. Intending their thought as remedy for a particular historical situation, yet unwilling openly to debate the sublunar implications of their position, the New Critics preferred to poeticize the world rather than politicize poetry. Metaphor was the very stuff of existence.

The methodological consequences of their impacted view of poetry led to a falling away from much of what was best in Eliot. Despite Eliot's talk of the impersonality of good poetry, few critics were more adept at getting at the essence of an author's oeuvre with free-ranging example. His essay on Tennyson is a brilliant instance. In contrast, the New Critics were theoretically excluded from any such helpful overview by their adherence to the intentional fallacy: their harvest was limited to the individual poem. Lost, too, was Eliot's comparative method in which he illuminatingly laid English poetry side by side with French or Italian counterparts (though he confessed his knowledge of Italian was not what it should have been). It took a great deal of trepidation for any New Critic to do the same, for the tremendous emphasis their hermeticism forced them to place on the connotations of words would have required virtually perfect bilingualism in order to speak with confidence of a foreign poem. This had the unfortunate academic consequence of making English departments in America unduly provincial during the reign of New Criticism, hardly something of which the editor of the *Criterion* would have approved. Finally, though there is a shared neglect of the genre of the novel, heavily implicated as it is in history, one misses in the major New Critics anything like Eliot's superb commentary on Elizabethan and Jacobean drama. The Eliot who toward the end of his life came to prefer drama to the lyric or meditative poem, as he called it, could only have found Winters's puritanical distrust of the theater benighted, though it might have confirmed his belief that the English Civil War continued. The other New Critics discussed here, while not morally offended as was Winters, nevertheless felt obviously uncomfortable equating dramatic tension with paradox, and made only passing reference to the stage. Possibly, too, in drama there was simply too much space between metaphors to account for. In all of these ways, then, the highly rarefied view of poetry embraced by the New Critics issued in a methodological narrowness at odds with the fullness of the European tradition as Eliot understood it.

Yet despite this difference, the New Criticism is essentially indebted to the French conservative legacy of Eliot for its central insights. The antiromanticism of Maurras that inspired Eliot's notion of the impersonality of the poet who searches for an objective correlative for his emotions becomes, in turn, the New Critical admonition against the intentional fallacy. This same suspicion of Romantic subjectivity generated the twin warning against the affective fallacy. Both the creation and the criticism of poetry were thereby purged of autobiography. And, of course, behind the antiromanticism is Maurras's insistence on Original Sin, the thinly veiled fear of the reign of the tasteless, restless democratic masses, perpetually revolting in both senses of the word. This fear, shared by both Eliot and the New Critics, manifested itself, for Eliot in an exclusive classicism, for the New Critics in exquisite textual strategies, which presupposed the correspondingly refined mind of the poet whose intentionality they could never openly acknowledge.[78]

Further, the antidemocratic animus of Maurras, Eliot, and the southern New Critics at least, placed them all in sympathy with the losing side in their countries' civil wars, giving rise to theories of historical and literary decline. But whereas Maurras could point with credibility to the French Revolution as a watershed of European history, whereas Eliot with less plausibility could mark the break at the time of the English Civil War, the southern New Critics could make only an extremely attenuated case for the American South's demise being of major consequence for the Western tradition. Instead – and this made possible the inclusion of those such as Winters and later Wimsatt who had no particular stake in southern agrarianism – the southern New Critics rested content with Eliot's version of a seventeenth-century breakdown. This, then, became the standard New Critical position.

But how could Americans possibly regret the demise of royalism, as had Maurras and Eliot? Faced with what looked like an insurmountable obstacle, the New Critics gestured vaguely toward Hobbes as the propagator of a modern scientific mentality, thereby bypassing historical explanation altogether in favor of a loose and unconvincing intellectual history. Of necessity, with nothing historical at stake for them in the seventeenth-century picture they inherited from Eliot, they fell back on the purely literary: metaphor was lost. This was the cause of the modern world's steady degeneration. Thus, what for Eliot had, at most, been an index of collapse, became for the New Critics the very essence of the collapse. Eliot had barely managed, even with the growing authority he carried between the wars, as well as a great deal of special pleading, to hold Maurras's classical compound together. The New Critics, at two removes from their intellectual source, could not. Literature was made to swallow history and religion, and the poem swelled to an icon. As such, it demanded a depth of veneration neither Maurras nor Eliot, even in their most purely aesthetic moments, could have granted.

CONCLUSION

The difficulty that has beset Eliot scholarship from the very beginning is how one fits together the Eliot who led an apparently apolitical aesthetic revolution and the Eliot who abruptly (or so it seemed) announced himself to be classicist, royalist, and Anglo-Catholic in 1928, a year after his secret conversion to the Church of England. How did one fit together the lyric poet of chaos and the *plus orthodoxe que les orthodoxes* champion of cultural institutions? Even those closest to Eliot were hard pressed to make sense of the split. Puzzled, Pound read the transformation in light of his own ambitious nature and chalked it up to careerism, though this did not prevent him from considering it an act of betrayal. Paul Elmer More, friend and correspondent with Eliot from the time of the conversion up until More's death in 1937 and, unlike Pound, in obvious sympathy with what Eliot had become, was unsure enough to wonder in print if the "new" Eliot's position did not entail renunciation of the past.[1]

Faced with coming to terms with the two Eliots, most critics have followed some variety of the explanation that the early Eliot had after all, despite the skepticism and cultural despair, manifested a hankering after the Absolute ever since the dissertation on Bradley. *The Waste Land* thus becomes a comprehensible landmark on the road from doubt to belief – the last dark night of the soul before the grace of conversion. The simultaneous turn to politics is regarded on the one hand by sympathetic critics as something that virtually thrust itself on Eliot amid the welter of competing ideologies between the wars, on the other hand by adversarial critics as a manifestation of the disease of late capitalism or, more loosely, as high modernism finally dropping its mask and revealing itself for what it always was: a celebration of the totalizing impositions of Western culture.

My purpose in this study has not been to categorically dismiss such readings as wrong – indeed in some instances the cases are made at such a level of generality as to make them virtually immune to falsification – but to argue that they overlook the *specific* framework of ideas that organized Eliot's intellectual and artistic career. This framework, as I have endeavored to show, is one inherited from a French reactionary tradition stretching from Joseph de Maistre to Charles Maurras. Conceived in recoil from the French Revolution and its democratic impulse, this tradition championed the old hierarchies of throne, altar, and pre-Romantic literary decorum. Only the economy of discriminations involved in these hierarchies, it was maintained, could restrict the free play of desires spawned by Original Sin. What was at stake, then, was nothing less than Order, a social organization in consonance with natural law. The threats to this dispensation were democracy, capitalism, Protestantism, and especially the Romantic spirit of untrammeled individualism that enabled the others. By the time the tradition had culminated in Maurras, this involved suspicion of the Teuton and aversion to the Jew, the first marginalized by the Latin tradition, the second parasitic upon it.

Eliot was introduced to this current of thought by Irving Babbitt at Harvard, experienced it at close range during his year in Paris (1910–11), and had it fine tuned for him by T. E. Hulme a few years later. By 1916 he follows Hulme in referring to the reactionary position as "classicism" and begins marching under this banner in full awareness that a political vision lies at its center. Of the three fronts on which the French wage their battle – the political, artistic, and religious – the early Eliot, however, advances the cause almost exclusively in terms of the artistic, a move easy to execute given the almost purely literary connotations of classicism and its negative opposite, romanticism, in England. This affords him a kind of protective coloration as he struggles to forge a workable Anglo-Saxon classicism. Indeed, it seems to me that most of the problems with which Eliot wrestled over his long career were corollaries of the difficulty in delineating exactly how his particular politics, poetry, and religion could be shown to entail one another, especially in liberal, Protestant England. In this regard, perhaps the most biting irony in Eliot's life comes in 1926, when just as he has gained enough confidence in the coherence of classicism to advance it to the readers of the *Criterion* as England's salvation, the Vatican condemns Maurras's essentially political advocacy of the church as unorthodox and dangerous. One month thereafter Eliot begins taking instruction in the Church of England, whose communion he joins the following summer. From this point on his classicism is recast, with religion given prominence. Indeed, he soon abandons the classical–Romantic terminology in favor of that of orthodoxy–heresy. It has been my contention in this study, though, that this represents merely a readjustment of the old allegiances and not a substantive change. The Christian community Eliot seeks to establish in the thirties and forties is based on the Maurrasien vision, though now of course minus the religious ambivalence that plagued Maurras. Seen in this way, there is no rupture whatsoever in Eliot's development. And it is this continuity that I have stressed throughout.

If one accepts this view of an ideologically motivated Eliot, the range of his work, both prose and poetry, takes on a new coherence. Literary history, for example, is read against a background of political history, and the judgments of particular schools of poetry and individual poets must be understood in this context. The bias that is evident in this regard organizes Eliot's poetic and dramatic work as well; thus, I locate a political vision at or near the center of works such as *Four Quartets* and *The Cocktail Party*. This has, of course, been harder to do not only because of the more metaphoric and oblique relationship of poetry to the world, but also because Eliot saw poetry as less utopian than prose: "In one's prose reflexions one may be legitimately occupied with ideals, whereas in the writing of verse one can only deal with actuality."[2] Typically, this has resulted in a sharp distinction of tone: a sublimely self-assured essayist simultaneously writing poetry of tortured, groping self-doubt. (A radical miniature of this occurs in the magisterial notes appended to *The Waste Land*.) This should not obscure the fact, however, that the questions and answers fit together and that their course runs parallel throughout Eliot's career.

The ramifications of this study are not confined to Eliot alone, for as I have tried to show in Chapter 6, the New Criticism takes over much of his politically laden critical apparatus. The French reactionary position as it is Anglicized by Eliot finds correspondence in southern agrarianism and from there infuses New Critical theory, though alembicated to almost purely aesthetic considerations. This suppression of origins leads the New Critics toward a formalistic cul-de-sac from which they are perpetually trying to free themselves. Almost inevitably, the phenomenon of a politically shaped aestheticism that painstakingly excludes reference to its own inspiration raises the issue of "false consciousness," the blindness of advocates to their own motivation. I have addressed this question in the general introductory sorting out of definitions of ideology, and more specifically in the body of my text.

As a contribution to the study of the politics of modernism, this book should serve to distinguish Eliot's antidemocratic animus from the very different strain found in Lawrence, one that derives, it seems to me, largely from Nietzsche and the German tradition of *Lebensphilosophie*. Such a contrast, however, immediately raises the broader question: can the two traditions both be said to emanate from romanticism? In the case of Eliot, one must recall that the French reactionary position he adopts began as a complaint against Rousseau for his excessive faith in reason. The Revolution laid to his charge was regarded as Enlightenment theorizing at its brutal, arrogant worst. Conversely, Maistre's defense of the ancien régime relies heavily on Romantic notions of organicism. And as he preached on page after page, we are ineradicably irrational creatures. Eliot's classicism is thus deeply implicated in the romanticism it so categorically rejects. This is evident not only in the poetry, as has often been mentioned, but also in the prose. "Tradition and the Individual Talent," the essay in which he sets forth the famous theory of poetic impersonality justifies poetry on almost purely affective grounds, and the essay itself, read with sensitivity to the volcanic pressure behind it, strikes one as a highly emotionally charged piece on behalf of coolness and distance.[3] Owing an obvious debt to romanticism, too, is the Christian communitarianism of the thirties and forties outlined in *The Idea of a Christian Society* and *Notes Towards the Definition of Culture*, which advance the ideal of a commonwealth held together by largely unconscious bonds (in the vast lower orders nearly completely unconscious). In juxtaposition we can place both Lawrence and the Nietzsche he read with youthful enthusiasm, who both offer elaborate world views, including political blueprints, based on a thoroughgoing irrationalism, metaphysical as well as psychological. Might one reasonably speak of a Romantic provenance in their cases? If so, and when taken together with the example of Eliot, would we not gain more than we lose by considering modernism a late romanticism – despite the often vehement protests of some of its practitioners? Would we then be further prepared to claim that the reactionary excesses of the twentieth century with which a number of modernists were to varying degrees implicated were at least *a* logical culmination of the premises of romanticism? Such questions have, of course, been raised before, but I hope that the rereading of Eliot I have here presented might, among whatever other benefits it may have, contribute to their reconsideration.

Finally, since so many recent works that deal with the ideological dimension of literature have struck an aggressively – at times rabidly – adversarial tone in regard to their subjects, perhaps a few words clarifying my own stance toward Eliot are still necessary. As I tried to make clear in the introduction, I am not labeling Eliot an ideologue because I happen to dislike the particular triumvirate of institutions he embraces, nor because I consider him deluded and somehow primitively pre-Nietzschean for entertaining the possibility that his values may be true ones. Where a critical note occurs in these pages, it is provoked instead by his tendency to displace and even camouflage the true locus of his concerns in the name of the higher goods he espouses. In this regard, his essay in praise of Machiavelli is instructive. To be fair, perhaps we, with a longer experience of the abuses of social and cultural engineering, are more understandably suspicious of such strategies. Yet surely Eliot, who devoted so much thought to social cohesion, might have seen – Orwell did – that the Platonic lie, even in the relatively rare instances when it is noble, erodes the very fabric it would preserve.

Where, then, do these revaluations leave Eliot studies? How will his reputation endure the change in century? First of all, it seems to me that whatever we may think of Eliot's solutions, he merits continued attention for the fullness of his response to a central problem of modernity: what sort of commonwealth is possible in a society held together only by procedure? In this regard, his continual, pointed insistence that social laissez-faire may be every bit as disastrous as economic laissez-faire was a salutary corrective to glib liberal pieties. No less than Lawrence, he was painfully aware of the thinness of modern life. The difficulty with Eliot, though, is that to create community he excludes too much. Those outside the Latin tradition, the lower social orders, and women whenever they dare display their sexual nature are all denied full participation. Though neither before nor after did he make the case as intemperately as he did in *After Strange Gods,* the call for homogeneity voiced there never ceased to be a given for his conception of the social whole. While Denis Donoghue is right to insist, as he recently did, that Eliot's reputation ought not to hang on the social criticism, he is wrong to claim that the criticism has nothing to do with the poetry.[4] As I have tried to demonstrate, there is a systematic lack of generosity, finally, of humanity, in Eliot's work – both prose and poetry – and, in the last analysis, it is this that will exclude him from the classical company to which he devoted so much of his life.

NOTES

Introduction

1 See Ronald Bush's review essay "But Is It Modern?: T. S. Eliot in 1988," *Yale Review* 77 (Winter 1988): 193–206. The revaluations of Pound and Lewis are put forward, respectively, by Kathryne Lindberg, *Reading Pound Reading: Modernism after Nietzsche* (New York: Oxford University Press, 1987), and Fredric Jameson, *Fables of Aggression: Wyndam Lewis, the Modernist as Fascist* (Berkeley: University of California Press, 1979).

2 See esp. Jean-Françoise Lyotard, *The Postmodern Condition: A Report on Knowledge,* trans. Geoff Bennington and Brian Massumi (Minneapolis: University of Minnesota Press, 1989).

3 The most valuable of these is William Chace, *The Political Identities of Ezra Pound and T. S. Eliot* (Stanford, Calif.: Stanford University Press, 1973). Also very helpful is Roger Kojecky, *T. S. Eliot's Social Criticism* (New York: Farrar, Straus, & Giroux, 1972). Though it confines itself to the time of Eliot's editorship of the *Criterion,* Joseph Margolis, *T. S. Eliot's Intellectual Development, 1922–1939* (Chicago: University of Chicago Press, 1972), captures well the European crosscurrents that influenced Eliot between the wars. More recently, Michael North has shown how right and left converge in their antagonism to modern bourgeois society by linking Eliot with Georg Lukács in his essay "Eliot, Lukács, and Politics of Modernism," in *T. S. Eliot: The Modernist in History,* ed. Ronald Bush (Cambridge University Press, 1991). He develops and expands this idea in his carefully argued consideration of the modernist aesthetic as a response to the problems of liberalism, *The Political Aesthetic of Yeats, Eliot, and Pound* (Cambridge University Press, 1991). Jeffrey Perl devotes a chapter of *Skepticism and Modern Enmity: Before and After Eliot* (Baltimore, Md.: Johns

Hopkins University Press, 1989) to Eliot's political stance. He reaches a conclusion, however, quite different from mine: "Eliot has been called apolitical and 'suprapolitical'; he himself termed his forays into social criticism 'pre-political.' The most precise adjective, however, is antipolitical. For Eliot, political controversies were at best diversions 'from things of more importance' " (93). Of course, when one expands the circle to include the politics of modernism in general, the bibliography increases substantially. Of the more recent studies of this sort, one might single out Andrew Ross, *The Failure of Modernism* (New York: Columbia University Press, 1986), and Michael Long, "The Politics of English Modernism: Eliot, Pound, and Joyce," in Edward Timms and Peter Collier, eds., *Visions and Blueprints: Avant-Garde Culture and Radical Politics in Early Twentieth Century Europe* (Manchester: Manchester University Press, 1988). Of related interest is Robert Casillo, *The Genealogy of Demons: Anti-Semitism, Fascism, and the Myths of Ezra Pound* (Evanston, Ill: Northwestern University Press, 1988). Fredric Jameson, *Fables of Aggression: Wyndam Lewis–The Modernist as Fascist* (Berkeley: University of California Press, 1979), remains an enduring provocation.

4 Raymond Boudon, *The Analysis of Ideology*, trans. Malcolm Slater (Chicago: University of Chicago Press, 1989), 17. Only slightly more sanguine about making sense of the welter of definitions are John Plamenatz, *Ideology* (New York: Praeger, 1970), and Walter Carlsnaes, *The Concept of Ideology and Political Analysis* (Westport, Conn: Greenwood, 1981), where he finds "the semantic prowess of this term . . . quite astounding" (11).

5 Karl Marx and Friedrich Engels, *The German Ideology*, in Robert C. Tucker, ed., *The Marx–Engels Reader* (New York: Norton, 1978), 174.

6 Friedrich Engels, Letter to Franz Mehring (July 14, 1893), in ibid., 766.

7 Karl Mannheim, *Ideology and Utopia*, trans. Louis Wirth and Edward Shils (New York: Harcourt, Brace, and World, 1936), 82. First published in 1929.

8 Ibid., 81.

9 Mannheim distinguishes idea systems that are outmoded and thus partly dysfunctional for the believer from those that are forward looking and revisionary. An example of the first would be the injunction to live according to a pure ethic of Christian brotherly love in a feudalistic order that requires serfdom. An

example of the second would be the Marxist vision of a classless society.

10 Clifford Geertz, "Ideology as a Cultural System," in *Ideology and Discontent* (New York: Free Press, 1964).

11 Sacvan Bercovitch, "The Problem of Ideology," *Critical Inquiry* 12 (Summer 1986): 631–53 at 636.

12 Ibid., 646.

13 I am indebted to Raymond Boudon for his careful sorting out of what he calls Marx I and Marx II on this issue. See his "Is *Homo Sociologicus* (Always) Irrational?" in *The Analysis of Ideology*.

14 Terry Eagleton, *Ideology* (London: Verso, 1991), includes the best guide to the nuances of Marxist thinking, past and present, about ideology.

15 Engels confessed after Marx's death that polemics had driven them to seem to say something more extreme than their considered opinion: "Marx and I are ourselves partly to blame for the fact that younger people sometimes lay more stress on the economic side than is due to it. We had to emphasise the main principle *vis-à-vis* our adversaries, who denied it, and we had not always the time, the place or the opportunity to allow the other elements involved in the interaction to come into their rights." Letter to Joseph Bloch (September 21–2, 1890), in *Marx-Engels Reader*, 762.

16 H. Stuart Hughes begins his discussion of Sorel in *Consciousness and Society* (New York: Vintage, 1958): "Sometime in the early 1930's, in parallel and almost simultaneous *démarches,* the Russian and Italian ambassadors to France proposed to erect a monument above the grave of Georges Sorel, which, they understood, had fallen into a state of disrepair since his death. Thus had the official representatives of Fascism and Communism chosen to honor in similar fashion the thinker whom they both regarded—with some justice—as an ideological forbear" (61). North, "Eliot, Lukács, and the Politics of Modernism," notes a parallel case in which Sorel appealed almost simultaneously to both Lukács and Eliot (170–1).

17 Georges Sorel, *Reflections on Violence*, trans. T. E. Hulme and J. Roth (Glencoe, Ill.: Free Press, 1950), 57.

18 See Ronald Schuchard, "Eliot and Hulme in 1916: Toward a Revaluation of Eliot's Critical and Spiritual Development" *PMLA* 88 (October 1973): 1083–94.

19 In the essay on Sorel, Hulme registers a connection between Sorel and Maurras via Sorel's affinity to L'Action française:

"The belief that pacifist democracy will lead to no regeneration of society, but rather to its decadence, and the reaction against romanticism in literature is naturally common to many different schools. This is the secret, for example, of the sympathy between Sorel and the group of writers connected with *L'Action française*... His ideology resembles theirs." T. E. Hulme, *Speculations*, ed. Herbert Read (London: Routledge & Kegan Paul, 1924; rpt. 1971), 258.

20 See, e.g., *Criterion* 11 (October 1931): 71, and *Criterion* 12 (April 1933): 473.

21 T. S. Eliot, Letter to Paul Elmer More (March 27, 1936), Princeton University Library.

1. Historical Background

1   George Steiner, "Aspects of Counter-Revolution," in Geoffrey Best, ed., *The Permanent Revolution* (Chicago: University of Chicago Press, 1988), 135.

2   Quoted in Hedva Ben-Israel, *English Historians on the French Revolution* (Cambridge University Press, 1968), 275.

3   Georges Rudé, *Interpretations of the French Revolution*, Historical Association London, General Series, no. 47 (London, 1972), 5.

4   *The Works of Joseph de Maistre*, trans. and intro. by Jack Lively (New York: Macmillan, 1965), 204.

5   Ibid., 192.

6   Ibid., 214.

7   Ibid., 71.

8   Ibid., 69.

9   Ibid., 120.

10 I am indebted in this discussion of Maistre's theory of language to Isaiah Berlin, "Joseph de Maistre and the Origins of Fascism," *New York Review of Books* 37 no. 16 (1990): 56–7.

11 For a short helpful summary of the transformation in Renan's thinking, see Ernst Nolte, *Three Faces of Fascism*, trans. Leila Vennewitz (New York: New American Library, 1969), 67–70.

12 Ernest Renan, *La Réforme intellectuelle et morale de la France* (Cambridge University Press, 1950), 11.

13 Ibid., 46.

14 Ernest Renan, *Oeuvres complètes* (Paris: Calmann-Lévy, n.d.), 170.

15 Renan, *La Réforme intellectuelle*, 52.

16 Rudé, *Interpretations of the French Revolution*, 9.

17 Hippolyte Taine, *The Origins of Contemporary France*, trans. John Durand (Gloucester, Mass.: Peter Smith, 1962), 2: 12.

18 Ibid., 3: 106–7.
19 Ibid., 1: 201.
20 Ibid., 192.
21 Ibid., 202.
22 Hippolyte Taine, *History of English Literature*, trans. H. von Laun (New York: Holt & Williams, 1871), 5.
23 Ibid., 20.
24 Quoted in J. S. McClelland, ed., *The French Right* (New York: Harper & Row, 1970), 95.
25 Quoted in Nolte, *Three Faces of Fascism*, 77.
26 McClelland, ed., *The French Right*, 167–8.
27 Trans. J. S. McClelland, ed., *The French Right*, 244.
28 Charles Maurras, *Romantisme et révolution* (Paris: Nouvelle librairie nationale, 1922), 3.
29 Charles Maurras, *Trois idées politique* (Paris: Librairie ancienne, 1912), 11.
30 Charles Maurras, *Oeuvres capitales* (Paris: Flammarion, 1954), 2: 381.
31 See Maurras, *Romantisme et révolution*, 3, and Charles Maurras, *Anthinea* (Paris: Librairie honoré and Éduoard Champion, 1919), vi–vii, where Maurras is of the opinion that "the brief destiny of that which one calls democracy in the ancient world makes me aware that the characteristic of this regime is only to consume that which the periods of aristocracy have produced."
32 Maurras, *Trois idées politique*, 62.
33 Ibid., 60.
34 Maurras, *Romantisme et révolution*, 3, 4. Maurras borrows this definition of Protestantism from Comte.
35 Ibid., 7. With only minor alterations I have adopted the translation of John Frears in McClelland, ed., *The French Right*, 246.
36 Ibid., 11.
37 Charles Maurras, *Le Conseil de Dante* (Paris: Nouvelle librairie nationale, 1913; rpt. 1920), 29.
38 Ibid., 28.
39 Ibid., 50.
40 Ibid., 43.
41 Ibid., 47.
42 Ibid., 23.
43 Ibid., 80.
44 Ibid., 41.

45 Nolte, *Three Faces of Fascism*, 141.
46 Eugen Weber, *Action française* (Stanford, Calif.: Stanford University Press, 1962), 18–19.
47 Maurras, *L'Avenir de l'intelligence* (Paris: Albert Fontemoing, 1905), 13.
48 Ibid., 16–17.
49 Robert Wohl, *The Generation of 1914* (Cambridge, Mass: Harvard University Press, 1979), 8.
50 Quoted in Weber, *Action française*, 78.
51 Henry Bamford Parkes, *The American Experience* (New York: Vintage, 1959), 266.
52 Thomas R. Nevin, *Irving Babbitt* (Chapel Hill, N.C: University of North Carolina Press, 1984), 91.
53 Pierre Lasserre, *Le Romantisme français* (Paris: Garnier frères, 1919), 15.
54 Ibid., xxii.
55 Ibid., 9.
56 Quoted in Herbert Howarth, *Some Figures Behind T. S. Eliot* (Boston: Houghton Mifflin, 1964), 85.
57 Irving Babbitt, *Literature and the American College* (Boston: Houghton Mifflin, 1908), 47.
58 Ibid., 37.
59 Irving Babbitt, *Rousseau and Romanticism* (Boston: Houghton Mifflin, 1919), 364.
60 Ibid., 300.
61 Babbitt, *Literature and the American College*, 10.
62 Nevin, *Irving Babbitt*, 31.
63 Julien Benda, *The Treason of the Intellectuals*, trans. Richard Aldington (New York: Norton, 1969), 17–23.
64 In 1910 the Vatican had condemned Marc Sagnier's populist Sillon movement for wanting "to make religion accessory to a political party," and Maurras's former teacher Bishop Guillibert of Fréjus sees the same error in Action française: "All tremble before those daring men who with incomparable virtuosity have found the means to set forth the detestable doctrines of the most brutal paganism, or the most subtle modernism, under the immaculate attire of a highly proclaimed confidence in the Catholic Church, as a principle of social order and a necessary ingredient of French unity" (Weber, *Action française*, 65–6). Shortly thereafter Pope Pius X signed the Index Congregation's condemnation of Maurras's books but withheld publication of the finding with the temporizing remark that they were *damn-*

abiles, non damnandus (worthy of condemnation, but not condemned) (Nolte, *Three Faces of Fascism,* 71).

2. The French Connection

1 Peter Ackroyd, *T. S. Eliot: A Life* (New York: Simon & Schuster, 1984), 40.

2 Ibid., 41.

3 For the fullest discusssion to date on the relationship between Eliot and Bergson, see Paul Douglas, *Bergson, Eliot, and American Literature* (Lexington: University of Kentucky Press, 1986).

4 T. S. Eliot, "Mr. Middleton Murry's Synthesis," *Criterion* 6 (October 1927): 346–7.

5. Ackroyd, *T. S. Eliot*, 41, and T. S. Eliot, "A Commentary," *Criterion* 13 (April 1934): 453.

6 T. S. Eliot, "L'Hommage de l'étranger," *Aspects de la France et du Monde* 2 (April 25, 1948): 6.

7 Quoted in Ackroyd, *T. S. Eliot*, 41.

8 T. E. Hulme, *Speculations* (London: Routledge & Kegan Paul, 1924; rpt. 1971), 256. The excerpt is from Hulme's critical introduction to his 1916 translation of Sorel's *Réflexions sur la violence.*

9 Hulme, *Speculations*, 114.

10 Hulme, "A Tory Philosophy" in Alun R. Jones, ed., *The Life and Opinions of T. E. Hulme* (Boston: Beacon, 1960), 187.

11 Ronald Schuchard, "Eliot and Hulme in 1916: Toward a Revaluation of Eliot's Critical and Spiritual Development," *PMLA* 88, no. 5 (1973): 1088–9.

12 Quoted in Schuchard, "Eliot as an Extension Lecturer," *Review of English Studies*, 25 no. 98 (1974): 165–6.

13 T. S. Eliot, "Leibniz's Monads and Bradley's Finite Centers," *Monist* 26 (October 1916): 566–76 at 566.

14 T. S. Eliot, "Mr. Leacock Serious," *New Statesman* (July 29, 1916): 404–5 at 405.

15 Christopher Ricks, *T. S. Eliot and Prejudice* (Berkeley: University of California Press, 1989).

16 Ronald Bush, *T. S. Eliot: A Study in Character and Style* (Oxford: Oxford University Press, 1983), x–xiii; Ackroyd, *T. S. Eliot*, 44–5, 52–3.

17 T. S. Eliot, "Tradition and the Individual Talent," in *The Sacred Wood* (London: Methuen, 1920; rpt. 1960), 58.

18 T. S. Eliot, "Baudelaire," in *Selected Essays* (New York: Harcourt, Brace, 1932), 373.

19 Stephen Spender, *The Destructive Element* (Boston: Houghton Mifflin, 1936), 144.

20 See Bernard Bergonzi, *T. S. Eliot* (New York: Macmillan, 1972), 72; William W. Chace, *The Political Identities of Ezra Pound and T. S. Eliot* (Stanford, Calif.: Stanford University Press, 1973), 131–2; John Peter, "Eliot and the *Criterion*," in Graham Martin, ed., *Eliot in Perspective: A Symposium* (London: Macmillan, 1970), 261–2.

21 T. S. Eliot, "The Metaphysical Poets," *Times Literary Supplement* 1031 (October 20, 1921): 669.

22 Ibid.

23 Ibid., 670.

24 Frank Kermode, *Romantic Image* (New York: Macmillan, 1957), 146.

25 Eliot, "The Metaphysical Poets," 669.

26 T. S. Eliot, "Andrew Marvell," *Times Literary Supplement*, 1002 (March 31, 1921): 201.

27 T. S. Eliot, *Essays Ancient and Modern* (New York: Harcourt, Brace, 1936), 160.

28 Eliot, "The Classics in France – and in England," *Criterion* 2 (October 1923): 104–5. In the same year, more temperately, if not necessarily more believably, Eliot argues that classicism should have the same force in England as it does in the Latin countries: "And I cannot understand why the opposition between Classicism and Romanticism should be profound enough in Latin countries (Mr. Murry says it is) and yet of no significance among ourselves. For if the French are *naturally* classical, why should there be any 'opposition' in France, any more than there is here? And if Classicism is not natural to them, but something acquired, why not acquire it here? Were the French in the year 1600 classical, and the English in the same year romantic? A more important difference, to my mind, is that the French in the year 1600 *had already a more mature prose*" ("The Function of Criticism," in *Selected Essays*, 17).

29 Eliot, "A Commentary," *Criterion* 2 (April 1924): 231.

30 Ibid., 232.

31 Wellek remarks on Eliot's ideological abhorrence of Shelley in "The Criticism of T. S. Eliot," *Sewanee Review* 64 (1956): 434–5. See esp. T. S. Eliot, "Shelley and Keats," in *The Use of Poetry and the Use of Criticism* (London: Faber & Faber, 1933; rpt. 1980), pp. 87–102.

32 Eliot, *The Sacred Wood*, 157.

33 T. S. Eliot, "Byron," in *On Poetry and Poets* (London: Faber & Faber, 1957), 196.

34 Eliot, *Sacred Wood,* 157–8.

35 Ibid., 157.

36 Eliot, *On Poetry and Poets,* 194–5.

37 Wellek, "The Criticism of T. S. Eliot," 432.

38 Ackroyd recounts the following exhange between Eliot and Robert Frost: "Somehow the conversation turned to Scottish poetry, and Eliot declared that no good poetry had been written in Scotland except William Dunbar's 'Lament for the Makaris.' Frost asked if an exception might be made for Robert Burns. No, Eliot replied. But was he not at least a good song-writer? 'One might grant,' he said, 'that modest claim' " (Ackroyd, *T. S. Eliot,* 194).

39 Terry Eagleton, *Literary Theory* (Minneapolis: University of Minnesota Press, 1983), 46–51.

40 Eliot, "The Idea of a Literary Review," *Criterion* 4 (January, 1926): 5.

41 Rene Wellek, "The Criticism of T. S. Eliot," 432–3.

42 Spender writes: "This is a work that trembles on the verge of many things, not least that of Shelleyan romanticism. We are not far from the stars in Shelley's 'Ode to a Skylark.' " See Stephen Spender, *T. S. Eliot* (New York: Viking, 1976), 125.

43 Eliot, "A Commentary," *Criterion* 5 (June 1927): 284–5.

44 One of the earliest of these critical works was C. K. Stead, *New Poetic: Yeats to Eliot* (London: Hutchinson, 1964), in which the author argues that Eliot's theory of poetry with its emphasis on unconscious processes is essentially Romantic. The fullest account of Eliot as part of the Romantic tradition in criticism is Edward Lobb, *T. S. Eliot and the Romantic Critical Tradition* (London: Routledge & Kegan Paul, 1981), esp. "Romantic Criticism and the Golden Age," 60–92. A. D. Moody, *Thomas Stearns Eliot: Poet* (Cambridge University Press, 1979), devotes a chapter to the romanticism of the early poetry: "Prufrock Observed," 17–40. And Frank Kermode's well-known *The Romantic Image* (London: Routledge & Kegan Paul, 1957) places Eliot squarely in the Romantic–symbolist tradition of the isolated artist, outcast but superior to his society.

45 Quoted in Eugen Weber, *Action française* (Stanford, Calif.: Stanford University Press, 1962), 8.

46 T. S. Eliot, *For Lancelot Andrewes* (Garden City, N.Y.: Doubleday Doran, 1929), 57.

47 Ibid., 53.
48 Ibid.
49 Ibid., 55.
50 Eliot, "A Commentary," *Criterion* 5 (June 1927): 283.
51 T. S. Eliot, A review of *A Defense of Conservatism* by Anthony M. Ludovici, *Criterion* 6 (July 1927): 70.
52 Eliot, "The *Action Française*, M. Maurras, and Mr. Ward," *Criterion* 7 (March 1928): 202.
53 Ibid., 196.
54 Ibid., 197.
55 Leo Ward, "L'Action Française," *Criterion* 7 (June 1928): 364–72, at 372.
56 Eliot, "A Reply to Mr. Ward," *Criterion* 7 (June 1928): 375.
57 Eliot, "Mr. Barnes and Mr. Rowse," *Criterion* 8 (July 1929): 690–1.
58 Eliot, "The Literature of Fascism," *Criterion* 8 (December 1928): 288.
59 Eliot, "Second Thoughts about Humanism," in *Selected Essays*, 433.

3. Orthodoxy and Heresy

1 T. S. Eliot, "Ulysses, Order, and Myth," *Dial* 75 (November 1923): 483.
2 In his dissertation Eliot offers the following example of what Bradley intended by "immediate experience": "We stand before a beautiful painting, and if we are sufficiently carried away, our feeling is a whole which is not, in a sense, *our* feeling, since the painting, which is an object independent of us, is quite as truly a constituent as our consciousness or our soul. The feeling is neither here nor anywhere: the painting is in the room, and my 'feelings' about the picture are in my 'mind.' " T. S. Eliot, *Knowledge and Experience in the Philosophy of F. H. Bradley* (New York: Columbia University Press, 1964): 20.
3 F. H. Bradley, *Appearance and Reality* (1893; rpt., Oxford: Clarendon Press, 1962), 472.
4 T. S. Eliot, "Leibniz's Monads and Bradley's Finite Centers," *Monist* 26 (October 1916): 570. The most extensive treatment of Eliot's relationship to Bradley is Richard Wollheim, "Eliot and F. H. Bradley: An Account," in C. G. Martin, ed., *Eliot in Perspective: A Symposium* (London: Macmillan, 1970). Also helpful in this regard are James Longenbach, *Modernist Poetics of*

History (Princeton, N.J.: Princeton University Press, 1987); Louis Menand, *Discovering Modernism* (Oxford: Oxford University Press, 1987), 42–53; and Michael Levenson, *A Genealogy of Modernism* (Cambridge University Press, 1984), 176–193.

5 Bradley, *Appearance and Reality,* 173.

6 Adrian Cunningham, "Continuity and Coherence in Eliot's Religious Thought," in Martin, ed., *Eliot in Perspective,* 220.

7 T. S. Eliot, "Tradition and the Individual Talent," in *Selected Essays* (New York: Harcourt, Brace, 1932), 5.

8 Letter to Austin Warren, August 11, 1929, quoted in Arthur Hazard Dakin, *Paul Elmer More* (Princeton, N.J.: Princeton University Press, 1960), 269n.

9 Eliot, "The Literature of Fascism," *Criterion* 8 (December 1928): 282.

10 Eliot, "A Commentary," *Criterion* 8 (December 1928): 188.

11 Eliot, "A Commentary," *Criterion* 12 (July 1933): 644.

12 Eliot, "A Commentary," *Criterion* 11 (October 1931): 71.

13 Eliot, "A Commentary," *Criterion* 12 (April 1933): 473.

14 T. S. Eliot, "Clark Lectures on Metaphysical Poetry," no. 3, 10–11, John Hayward Collection, King's College, Cambridge.

15 Ibid., 7.

16 T. S. Eliot, *After Strange Gods: A Primer of Modern Heresy* (London: Faber & Faber, 1934), 26.

17 Ibid., 27–8.

18 Ibid., 22.

19 Ibid., 13.

20 Ibid., 11–12.

21 *I'll Take My Stand — The South and the Agrarian Tradition,* by Twelve Southerners (New York: Harper, 1962), 14.

22 Ibid., 3.

23 Eliot, *Gods,* 16.

24 Ibid., 20.

25 I. A. Richards, *Principles of Literary Criticism* (1925; rpt., New York: Harcourt, Brace, 1949), 267.

26 I. A. Richards, *Science and Poetry* (London: K. Paul, Trench, Trubner, 1926), 96.

27 Ibid., 95.

28 T. S. Eliot, "Literature, Science, and Dogma," *Dial* 82 (March 1927): 243.

29 Eliot, "Shakespeare and the Stoicism of Seneca," in *Selected Essays,* 116.

30 Ibid., 116–17.

31   Eliot, "Dante," in *Selected Essays,* 218.

32   Ibid., 230.

33   Ibid., 231.

34   T. S. Eliot, "Poetry and Propaganda," *Bookman,* 70 no. 6 (1930): 599.

35   Ibid., 599.

36   René Welleck "The Criticism of T. S. Eliot," *Sewanee Review* 64 no. 3 (1956): 417.

37   T. S. Eliot, *The Use of Poetry and the Use of Criticism* (London: Faber & Faber, 1933; rpt. 1980), 96.

38   Eliot, "Poetry and Propaganda," 601.

39   Eliot, "Modern Education and the Classics," in *Selected Essays,* 459.

40   T. S. Eliot, *Essays Ancient and Modern* (London: Faber & Faber, 1936), 110.

41   Ibid., 93.

42   T. S. Eliot, A review of *Son of Woman: The Story of D. H. Lawrence* by Middleton Murry, *Criterion* 10 (July 1931): 771.

43   Ibid., 769.

44   Eliot, *After Strange Gods,* 28.

45   Ronald Bush, *T. S. Eliot* (Oxford: Oxford University Press, 1983), 108.

46   Eliot, "Dante," 200–1.

47   Bush, *T. S. Eliot,* 108–9.

48   Eliot, *The Use of Poetry,* 152–3.

49   Eliot, "A Commentary," *Criterion* 11 (July 1932): 680.

50   The most biting and informed criticism along these lines came in G. M. Turnell's essay "Tradition and T. S. Eliot" in the Catholic journal *Colosseum* (1 [June 1934]: 44–54): "Mr. Eliot does not belong to the European tradition. He is neither possessed of a European consciousness nor does he feel as a European. This means that in his hands the principles underlying Tradition become mere counters completely divorced from the spiritual life which produced them (50) . . . When Mr. Eliot speaks of dogmatic theology, he means the dogmatic theology of the English not of the Catholic Church. It seems to me that theological differences are ultimately responsible for most of the differences between the two traditions" (53). Adrian Cunningham, in a cogent account of Eliot's religious career, presents his difficulty in fitting England and its church into the European tradition as part of the larger Bradleyan problem of relating the particular to the universal. See Adrian Cunningham,

"Continuity and Coherence in Eliot's Religious Thought," in Martin, ed., *Eliot in Perspective,* 211–31.

51 Francis Fergusson, "*Murder in the Cathedral*: The Theological Scene," in David R. Clark, ed., *Twentieth Century Interpretations of Murder in the Cathedral* (Englewood Cliffs, N.J.: Prentice-Hall, 1971), 27–8.

52 Katherine Worth, "Eliot and the Living Theatre," in Martin, ed., *Eliot in Perspective,* 156. Her opinion is echoed by, among others, Francis Fergusson: "The dramatis personae are as discontinuous from each other and from any common world as the parts of a machine" (see Ferguson, *Murder in the Cathedral,* 33).

4. Architect of a Christian Order

1 T. S. Eliot, "Thoughts after Lambeth," in *Selected Essays,* 342.

2 Roger Kojecky, *T. S. Eliot's Social Criticism* (London: Faber & Faber, 1971), 159–70.

3 It might seem strange that Löwe and Mannheim, both Jewish, should have found themselves in a group dedicated to promoting Christian ideals. Their understanding of "Christian," unlike that of the doctrinally committed, was, however, little more than a synonym for the old international European order, something infinitely preferable to the then current situation.

4 Quoted in Kojecky, *Eliot's Social Criticism,* 164.

5 From the *Christian News-Letter* (the Moot's publication) (August 1940), quoted in ibid., 179.

6 Quoted in John D. Margolis, *T. S. Eliot's Intellectual Development* (Chicago: University of Chicago Press, 1972), p. 177. See the whole of chap. 6 in Margolis's excellent book for a thorough account of the last days of the *Criterion*.

7 Eliot, "A Commentary," *Criterion* 16 (April 1937): 474.

8 Eliot, "A Commentary," *Criterion* 18 (January 1937): 290.

9 Eliot, "Last Words," *Criterion* 18 (January 1939): 271.

10 T. S. Eliot, *After Strange Gods: A Primer of Modern Heresy* (London: Faber & Faber, 1934), 26.

11 T. S. Eliot, *The Use of Poetry and the Use of Criticism* (London: Faber & Faber, 1933; rpt. 1980), 99. When Eliot had argued earlier for a seamless classicism of discursive prose and poetry, he was taken to task for not being able to put the two together. Now, ironically, when he concedes the rupture, his own work is most of a piece.

12 T. S. Eliot, *The Idea of a Christian Society* (London: Faber & Faber, 1939) reprinted in *Christianity and Culture* (New York: Harcourt, Brace, Jovanovich, 1968), 6.

13 Ibid., 12.

14 Ibid., 50.

15 Ibid., 8–9.

16 See "A Christian Elite" in Kojecky, *T. S. Eliot's Social Criticism.*

17 Eliot, *Idea,* 21.

18 Ibid., 29.

19 Ibid., 23.

20 Ibid.

21 E. J. Hobsbawm, *The Age of Empire: 1875–1914* (New York: Pantheon, 1987), 85.

22 Eliot, *Idea,* 59–60.

23 Ibid., 61.

24 Ibid., 30.

25 Samuel Taylor Coleridge, *On the Constitution of Church and State,* in John Colmar, ed., *Collected Works* (Princeton, N.J.: Princeton University Press, 1976), 43.

26 Ibid., 42. Raymond Williams, *Culture and Society: 1780–1950* (New York: Columbia University Press, 1983), has some valuable insights on Coleridge's contribution to the concept of culture. See esp. pp. 49–70.

27 Eliot, *Idea,* 28.

28 Ibid., 30.

29 Ibid., 27.

30 T. S. Eliot, *Notes Towards the Definition of Culture* (London: Faber & Faber, 1948), reprinted in *Christianity and Culture* (New York: Harcourt, Brace, Jovanovich, 1968), 88–9. This passage has a well-deserved history of offending readers. See, e.g., Williams, *Culture & Society: 1780–1950,* 231–2; and Terry Eagleton, "Eliot and Common Culture," in Graham Martin, ed., *Eliot in Perspective: A Symposium* (London: Macmillan, 1970).

31 Eliot, *Notes,* 101.

32 Ibid., 104.

33 Ibid., 92.

34 Ibid., 121. This idea receives its clearest expression, in the work of Coleridge, in "On Poesy or Art." See David Perkins, ed., *English Romantic Writers* (New York: Harcourt, Brace & World, 1967), 491–9. The German idealist tradition, particularly in its Hegelian form, would, of course, have been familiar to Eliot from his study of F. H. Bradley.

35 Ibid., 184.
36 Ibid., 103.
37 Ibid., 122.
38 Eagleton, "Eliot and Common Culture," 285.
39 Eliot, *Notes,* 77.
40 Ibid., 159. The idea of the aristocrat drawn away from more
    congenial pursuits to the exercise of rule is discussed in Plato's
    Republic, which may suggest one more debt of Eliot's.
41 Williams, *Culture & Society: 1780–1950,* 242.
42 Staffan Bergsten, *Time and Eternity: A Study in the Structure and
    Symbolism of T. S. Eliot's Four Quartets* (Stockholm: Svenska, 1960),
    164–7.
43 J. M. Bradbury, "*Four Quartets:* The Structural Symbolism," *Saw-
    nee Review* 59 (1951), 268.
44 See Bergstan, *Time and Eternity,* 104–12.
45 S. E. Lemberg, introduction to Thomas Elyot, *The Book Named
    the Governour* (London: Dent, 1962), vii.
46 Elyot, *The Book Named the Governour,* 3–4.
47 Harry Blamires, *Word Unheard: A Guide Through Eliot's Four Quar-
    tets* (London: Methuen, 1969), 46.
48 Helen Gardner, *The Art of T. S. Eliot* (London: Dutton, 1950),
    44–5.
49 Ibid., 44.
50 See Blamires, *Word Unheard,* 124.
51 Northrop Frye, *T. S. Eliot* (Chicago: University of Chicago Press,
    1963; rpt. 1981), 72–99.
52 T. S. Eliot, *On Poetry and Poets* (London: Faber & Faber, 1957),
    148.
53 Almost all commentary on this passage points out in passing
    that the prototype for this encounter is that of Dante the pil-
    grim and the ghost of Brunetto Latini, one of his acknowledged
    masters (*Inferno,* XV). What goes unremarked, however, is what
    Brunetto actually says to Dante. If we bother to read the original
    carefully, we find that at some length (ll. 55–78), Brunetto dis-
    closes to the respectfully attentive Dante how he will become
    the victim of political hatreds, information that the pilgrim says
    he intends to refer to Beatrice for her (higher) perspective. As
    it turns out it is not Beatrice but Dante's ancestor Cacciaguida
    who advises him (*Paradiso,* XVII) to rise above political discord
    for the not entirely charitable reason that "your future stretches
    / far beyond the reach of what they do / and far beyond the
    punishment of wretches." With the full allusiveness of Dante in

mind, and it would be arrogant to assume that Eliot hadn't read at least this closely, we can get a clearer notion of the political matrix of the reference.

54 Blamires, *Word Unheard,* 172.
55 J. S. McClelland, ed., *The French Right* (New York: Harper & Row, 1970), 248.

5. *Visions and Revisions*

1 Quoted in Peter Ackroyd, *T. S. Eliot: A Life* (New York: Simon & Schuster, 1984), 290.
2 T. S. Eliot, *The Use of Poetry and the Use of Criticism* (London: Faber & Faber, 1933; rpt. 1980), 154.
3 Ackroyd, *T. S. Eliot,* 317.
4 David Lewin, "Beautiful – But What's the Meaning?" *Daily Express,* August 23, 1949: 3.
5 Martin Esslin, *The Theatre of the Absurd* (New York: Penguin, 1983), 19–21.
6 T. S. Eliot, "Poetry and Drama," in *On Poetry and Poets* (London: Faber & Faber, 1957), 85.
7 T. S. Eliot, *The Idea of a Christian Society,* in *Christianity and Culture* (New York: Harcourt, Brace, Jovanovich, 1968), 10.
8 Ibid.
9 Ibid., 34.
10 Hannah Arendt, *The Life of the Mind,* vol. 2, *Willing* (New York: Harcourt, Brace, Jovanovich, 1978), 102–10.
11 Quoted in ibid, 122.
12 Ibid., 116.
13 I am indebted for this and the following examples to William Arrowsmith's valuable early commentary on the play "English Verse Drama (II): *The Cocktail Party,*" in *Hudson Review* 3 (Autumn 1950): 411–29.
14 Ackroyd, *T. S. Eliot,* 52.
15 In a letter to Paul Elmer More dated Shrove Tuesday, 1928, Eliot tries to account for these impulses that he detects in himself: "They [those with no religious instincts] may be very good, or very happy; they simply seem to miss nothing, to be unconscious of any void – the void that I find in the middle of all human happiness and all human relations, and which there is only one thing to fill. I am one whom this sense of void tends to drive towards asceticism or sensuality, and only Christianity

helps to reconcile me to life, which is otherwise disgusting."
Princeton University Library.

16 I am indebted to William Arrowsmith for pointing out that Reil-
ly's song "is Eliot's variant upon a well-known and thoroughly
obscene RAF song," which explains Julia's outrage when he
sings it to her. See Arrowsmith, "English Verse Drama," 413
and 421.

17 Lesley Chamberlain, "Through a Cocktail Glass Darkly," *Modern Drama* 31 no. 4 (1988), 516.

18 T. S. Eliot, *On Poetry and Poets* (London: Faber and Faber, 1957),
138.

19 Ibid., 144.

20 In the 1961 essay "To Criticize the Critic," Eliot, reflecting on
his critical corpus, claimed that "Milton II" was not actually
intended as a recantation although it had been read in that
way. He had only meant, he said, to offer a "development" of
his earlier opinion. While this is actually a fairer description of
what Eliot accomplished in the essay, it is not what he seems to
announce in the contrite opening paragraph: "Some of the er-
rors and prejudices [with regard to Milton] have been associated with my own name, and of these in particular I shall find
myself impelled to speak; it will I hope, be attributed to me for
modesty rather than for conceit if I maintain that no one can
correct an error with better authority than the person who has
been held responsible for it."

21 Eliot, *On Poetry and Poets,* 148.

22 J. S. McClelland, ed., *The French Right* (New York: Harper & Row,
1970), 248.

23 Eliot, *The Use of Poetry and the Use of Criticism,* 99.

24 Eliot, *On Poetry and Poets,* 67.

25 Ronald Duncan, *How to Make Enemies* (London: Rupert Hart-
Davis, 1968), 384.

26 Eliot, *The Use of Poetry and the Use of Criticism,* 89–96.

27 Eliot, "What Dante Means to Me," in *To Criticize the Critic* (New
York: Farrar, Straus & Giroux, 1965), 132.

28 Eliot, "To Criticize the Critic," in *To Criticize the Critic,* 19–20.

29 Ibid., 17.

30 Ibid., 25.

31 Ibid., 20.

32 T. S. Eliot, *The Sacred Wood* (London: Methuen, 1920; rpt.
1960), 14–15.

33 See esp. "The Music of Poetry," in Eliot, *On Poetry and Poets,* 30-

1: "A poem may appear to mean very different things to different readers, and all of these meanings may be different from what the author thought he meant. For instance, the author may have been writing some peculiar personal experience, which he saw quite unrelated to anything outside; yet for the reader the poem may become the expression of a general situation, as well as of some private experience of his own. The reader's interpretation may differ from the author's and be equally valid – it may even be better. There may be much more in a poem than the author was aware of. The different interpretations may all be partial formulations of one thing; the ambiguities may be due to the fact that the poem means more, not less, than ordinary speech can communicate."

34   Eliot, "The Function of Criticism," in *Selected Essays*, 13.

35   T. S. Eliot, "The Metaphysical Poets," *Times Literary Supplement*, 1031 (October 20, 1921): 669; T. S. Eliot, "The Metaphysical Poets," in *Selected Essays* (New York: Harcourt, Brace, 1932), 247; T. S. Eliot, "Milton II," in *On Poetry and Poets*, 152–3.

36   All quotations from Eliot's piece are from "L'Hommage de l'étranger," *Aspects de la France et du Monde* 2 (April 25, 1948): 6.

37   T. S. Eliot, "The Literature of Politics," in *To Criticize the Critic*, 142–3.

6. Eliot and the New Criticism

1   T. S. Eliot, *On Poetry and Poets* (London: Faber & Faber, 1957), 113, 106.

2   See John Crowe Ransom, "T. S. Eliot: The Historical Critic" in *The New Criticism* (Norfolk, Conn.: New Directions, 1941), esp. 135–45.

3   Yvor Winters, *In Defense of Reason* (Denver: Swallow, 1947), 460.

4   William Wimsatt, *Day of the Leopards* (New Haven, Conn.: Yale University Press, 1976), 14–15.

5   John Crowe Ransom claims: "Discussion of the new criticism must start with Mr. Richards. The new criticism very nearly began with him." *The New Criticism*, 3.

6   T. S. Eliot, "Literature, Science, and Dogma," *Dial* 32 (March 1927): 243.

7   *Paris Review* interview, reprinted in *Robert Penn Warren Talking: Interviews 1950–1978*. Quoted in René Wellek, *A History of Modern Criticism: 1750–1950*, vol. 6 (New Haven, Conn.: Yale University Press, 1986), 214.

8   Edmund Wilson, *Axel's Castle* (New York: Scribner, 1931; rpt. Norton, 1959), 119.

9   See John Ellis, *Against Deconstruction* (Princeton, N.J.: Princeton University Press, 1989), esp. chap. 3, "Deconstruction and the Theory and Practice of Criticism."

10 I. A. Richards, *The Philosophy of Rhetoric* (London: Oxford University Press, 1936; rpt. 1950), 53, 55.

11 For the best discussion of this line of attack on the New Criticism, see Gerald Graff, "What was New Criticism? Literary Interpretation and Scientific Objectivity," *Salmagundi* 27 (1974): 72–93. I am indebted to his article in this section of my presentation.

12 Richard Palmer, *Hermeneutics: Interpretation Theory in Schleiermacher, Dilthey, Heidegger, and Gadamer* (Evanston, Ill.: Northwestern University Press, 1969), 247.

13 Wellek, *A History of Modern Criticism*, 6: 146.

14 Allen Tate, "Miss Emily and the Biographer," originally delivered as a lecture at Princeton University, April 10, 1941. Printed in Tate, *Essays of Four Decades* (Chicago: Swallow, 1968), 150.

15 See his essay "Reconstructed but Unregenerate" in the collection of essays dedicated to the virtues of southern agrarian life, *I'll Take My Stand* (1930; rpt. New York: Harper, 1962).

16 John Crowe Ransom, *The World's Body* (New York: Scribner, 1938), 41–2.

17 Ibid., 33.

18 For the best account of the conservative political implications of the New Criticism, see Robert Weimann, *"New Criticism" und die Entwicklung bürgerliche Literaturwissenschaft* (München: Verlag Ch. H. Beck, 1974).

19 Ransom, "Reconstructed but Unregenerate," 173.

20 Ibid., 14

21 Ibid., 6.

22 T. S. Eliot, *Notes Towards the Definition of Culture* (London: Faber & Faber, 1948), reprinted in *Christianity and Culture* (New York: Harcourt, Brace, Jovanovich, 1968), 125.

23 Ransom, "Reconstructed but Unregenerate," 175.

24 Eliot, *Notes Towards the Definition of Culture*, 126.

25 Frederick Copleston, for example, devotes three sentences to Bramhall in a fifty-one-page section on Hobbes in his *History of Philosophy*.

26 T. S. Eliot, "John Bramhall," *Selected Essays* (New York: Harcourt, Brace, 1932), 312.

27 Ibid., 313.

28 Ransom also detects the pernicious influence of Hobbes, although he sees him as an extension of Bacon. See Ransom, *The World's Body,* 134–5, quoted at length later in my text.

29 Cleanth Brooks, *Modern Poetry and the Tradition* (Chapel Hill, N.C.: University of North Carolina Press, 1939), 52.

30 Wimsatt, *Day of the Leopards,* 160–1.

31 Eliot, *On Poetry and Poets,* 170.

32 The lack Eliot detected in the Victorians figures prominently in his criticism of Tennyson: "And I do not believe for a moment that Tennyson was a man of mild feelings or weak passions. There is no evidence in his poetry that he knew the experience of violent passion for a woman; but there is plenty of evidence of emotional intensity and violence – but of emotion so deeply suppressed, even from himself, as to tend rather towards the blackest melancholia than towards dramatic action. And it is emotion which, so far as my reading of the poems can discover, attained no ultimate clear purgation." ("In Memoriam," in *Selected Essays,* 290)

33 Yvor Winters, *Forms of Discovery* (n.p.: Alan Swallow, 1967), 147.

34 Ibid., 148.

35 Eliot, *On Poetry and Poets,* 55.

36 Ibid., 60.

37 Ransom, "T. S. Eliot," 139.

38 Ransom, *The World's Body,* 134–5.

39 Brooks distinguishes among the three terms in the following way: "1) wit, as an awareness of the multiplicity of possible attitudes to be taken toward a given situation . . . 2) paradox, as a device for contrasting the conventional views of a situation, or the limited and special view of it such as those taken in practical and scientific discourse, with a more inclusive view . . . 3) irony, as a device for definition of attitudes by qualification." *The Well Wrought Urn* (New York: Harcourt, Brace & World, 1947; rpt. 1975), 257.

40 Cleanth Brooks, *Modern Poetry and the Tradition* (Chapel Hill, N.C.: University of North Carolina Press, 1939), 235.

41 Ibid., 237.

42 Brooks tries to rescue the "Intimations" ode for New Criticism but can do so only by positing a Wordsworth so dimly aware of his craft that the poem seems to have emerged despite the author. In fact, Brooks briefly advances the idea that whatever is

valuable in the poem may have bubbled up from "the dark side" of Wordsworth's mind. This explanation is quickly dropped, however, as Brooks realizes full well it constitutes the Romantic-biographical theory of poetry that the New Criticism is dedicated to replacing. See *The Well Wrought Urn*, 125–6.

43 Winters, *Forms of Discovery*, 167.

44 Winters, *In Defense of Reason*, 62.

45 Ransom, "T. S. Eliot," 302.

46 See Murray Krieger's fine chapter "The Transformation of Richards," in *The New Apologists for Poetry* (Minneapolis: University of Minnesota Press, 1956), 123–39.

47 Allen Tate, *Essays of Four Decades* (Chicago: Swallow, 1968), 64.

48 Ransom, *The World's Body*, 59.

49 Brooks, *The Well Wrought Urn*, 256–7.

50 David Daiches, *Critical Approaches to Literature* (Englewood Cliffs, N.J.: Prentice-Hall, 1956), 302. Also, see Krieger, *The New Apologists for Poetry*, 134.

51 R. S. Crane, *The Languages of Criticism and the Structure of Poetry* (Toronto: University of Toronto Press, 1953), 105.

52 R. S. Crane, "The Critical Monism of Cleanth Brooks," in R. S. Crane, ed., *Critics and Criticism* (Chicago: University of Chicago Press, 1952), 95.

53 T. S. Eliot, Clark Lectures on Metaphysical Poetry, no. 3, 15. John Hayward Collection, King's College, Cambridge.

54 Ibid., no. 4, 17.

55 Ransom, *The World's Body*, 111.

56 Ibid., 122.

57 Ibid., 116.

58 Ibid., 128.

59 Wellek, *A History of Modern Criticism*, 6: 161.

60 Ransom, *The World's Body*, 124.

61 In this regard Ransom's *Dinglichkeit* resembles Rilke's similar notion in the *Duino Elegies* (see later this note), although Ransom reported to René Wellek (*History of Modern Criticism*, 6: 160) that he had no specific German source in mind when he used the term: "Even for our grandparents a 'House,' a 'Well,' a familiar tower, their very dress, their cloak, was infinitely more, infinitely more intimate: almost everything a vessel in which they found and stored humanity. Now there come crowding over from America empty, indifferent things, pseudo-things [*Scheindinge*], DUMMY-LIFE . . . A house, in the American understanding, an American apple or vine, has NOTHING in com-

mon with the house, the fruit, the grape into which the hope and meditation of our forefathers had entered . . . The animated, experienced things that SHARE OUR LIVES are coming to an end and cannot be replaced. WE ARE PERHAPS THE LAST TO HAVE KNOWN SUCH THINGS. On us rests the responsibility of preserving, not merely their memory (that would be little and unreliable), but their human and laral worth" (from a letter of Rilke to Withold von Hulewicz dated November 13, 1925, quoted in Rainer Maria Rilke, *Duino Elegies,* trans. J. B. Leishman and Stephen Spender [New York: Norton, 1963], app. 4, 129).

62 Ransom, *The World's Body,* 120.

63 Ibid., 139.

64 Ibid., 136.

65 Ibid., 140.

66 Ibid.

67 Quoted without reference in Ransom, *The New Criticism,* 288.

68 Ibid., 289.

69 William Wimsatt, *The Verbal Icon* (Lexington: University of Kentucky Press, 1954), x.

70 Eliseo Vivas discussed briefly but pointedly some of the difficulties of both the lesser and greater claims in a review essay of Wimsatt's book reprinted in Vivas, *The Artistic Transaction* (Columbus: Ohio State University Press, 1963), pp. 232–40.

71 Wimsatt, *The Verbal Icon,* 241.

72 Ibid., 268–9.

73 Ibid., 270.

74 Wellek, *A History of Modern Criticism,* 6: 285.

75 William K. Wimsatt, Jr., and Cleanth Brooks, *Literary Criticism: A Short History* (New York: Knopf, 1959), 746.

76 See Tate, *Essays of Four Decades,* 4–5, 410.

77 Eliot, *On Poetry and Poets,* 98.

78 As far as I know, Gerald Graff is the only one to draw the connection between Eliot and the New Critics on the basis of the doctrine of Original Sin. He traces it back to Hulme but does not mention the French sources. See Graff, "What was New Criticism?"

Conclusion

1 The article referred to here is Paul Elmer More, "The Cleft Eliot," discussed by Ronald Bush in "But Is It Modern?: T. S. Eliot in 1988," *Yale Review* 77 (Winter 1988): 193–206. More's

piece appeared originally in *Saturday Review of Literature* (November 12, 1932).

2   T. S. Eliot, *After Strange Gods: A Primer of Modern Heresy* (London: Faber & Faber, 1934), 28.

3   When I say that Eliot's theory justifies itself on almost purely emotional grounds, I am thinking specifically of his claims that 1) art is distinguished from nonart by its emotional effect on the observer and 2) the true critic of poetry (very few of its readers) can tell when a significant emotion is in the work of art. Confirmation of the tremendous emotional tension involved in the creation of poetry is more openly offered in Eliot's later description in "The Three Voices of Poetry": "He [the poet] is oppressed by a burden which he must bring to birth in order to obtain relief. Or, to change the figure of speech, he is haunted by a demon, a demon against which he feels powerless, because in its first manifestation it has no face, no name, nothing; and the words, the poem he makes, are a kind of form of exorcism of this demon" (98).

4   Denis Donoghue, "The Idea of a Christian Society," *Yale Review* 78 (Winter 1989): 218–34, at 234.

INDEX

Action française, 28–30, 34, 45, 53,
  56, 63, 87, 89, 92, 169n19
Anesaki, Masaharu, 2
anti-Semitism, 17, 20, 140
Arendt, Hannah, 116
Aristotle, 27, 30–2, 116, 132;
  Nichomachean Ethics, 31
Arnold, Matthew, 2, 41, 50, 68,
  153
Athenaeum, 39
Atlantic Monthly, 33
Aspects de la France du Monde, 130
Augustine, St., 15, 44, 116, 121

Babbitt, Irving, 30–3, 35, 36, 37,
  53, 56, 58–60, 63, 113, 161;
  Democracy and Leadership, 53
Barrès, Maurice, 21–2, 33
Baudelaire, Charles, 2, 41
Becket, Thomas à, 80–4
Beckett, Samuel, 111, 114, 142;
  Waiting for Godot, 111, 142; Watt,
  142
Benda, Julian, 33, 53; La Trahison
  des Clercs, 33; Belphégor, 53
Bercovitch, Sacvan, 5
Bergson, Henri, 32, 35–6;
  L'Évolution créatrice, 35
Berl, Emmanuel, 55
Berman, Russell: The Rise of the
  Modern German Novel, 10
Billy, André, 57
Blackmur, R. P., 134
Blake, William, 48–50, 71–2, 125,
  145; "London," 145

Bradley, F. H., 60–2, 160, 176n2;
  Appearance and Reality, 60; Ethical
  Studies, 61; Principles of Logic, 61
Bramhall, John (Bishop of Derry),
  141
Brooks, Cleanth, 42, 134, 141–2,
  144–50, 152, 155; The Well
  Wrought Urn, 147
Buddhism, 2
Burke, Edmund, 94
Bush, Ronald, 11, 77
Byron, George Gordon, Lord, 49,
  50

Calendur, 53
Camelots du roi, 29, 36
capitalism, 17, 20–1, 24, 30, 67, 88,
  137, 150, 160–1
Carlyle, Thomas, 18
Chace, William: The Political Identities
  of Ezra Pound and T. S. Eliot, 10
Chapman, George, 47
Charles I, 97, 99, 104, 141
Charles II, 141
Chateaubriand, Vicomte François
  Réne de, 22, 26, 30
Chaucer, Geoffrey, 49, 115
Christian Community, 90, 94, 111,
  162
classicism, 30–2, 37, 59, 85, 95,
  150; Eliot's support of, 8–10, 15,
  28, 33–4, 37–41, 48, 56, 60, 65–
  6, 73, 96, 105–6, 127–30, 153,
  158, 161–3; French conservative
  use of term, 8, 19, 23–8, 62

clerisy, 92, 114
Coleridge, Samuel Taylor, 49, 92, 95, 114, 150
Community of Christians, 91–2, 94, 114–15
Comte, Auguste, 19
Crane, R. S., 148–50
Criterion, 7–8, 10, 45, 48, 52, 54, 55–7, 64, 67, 86–7, 127, 133, 139, 157, 161

Daiches, David, 148
Daily Express (Edinburgh), 110
Dante, 2, 19, 25–7, 41–3, 59, 65, 69–73, 77, 98, 100, 106, 126, 130, 144, 149; *Divine Comedy*, 25, 27, 126, 181n53; *Inferno*, 27, 42, 77
Dawson, Christopher, 85
deconstruction, 1
democracy, 8, 15, 21, 24, 31–2, 41, 53, 88, 137, 161
Dernier Jour, 55
Descartes, René, 19, 39, 156
Dickens, Charles, 78
dissociation of sensibility, 46, 87, 127, 129, 141–6, 149, 156
Donne, John, 2, 46, 98, 127, 129, 149, 152; "The Ecstasy," 149
Donoghue, Denis, 164
Douglas, Major C. H., 79
Drieu La Rochelle, Pierre, 55
Drumont, Edouard: *La France juive*, 20
Dryden, John, 2, 129–30, 145, 151–2
Duncan, Ronald, 126

Eagleton, Terry, 52
Eckhardt, Meister, 65
Egoist, 39
Elgar, Sir Edward, 93
Eliot, George, 66, 69
Eliot, T. S., works by:
    After Strange Gods: A Primer of Modern Heresy, 65, 75, 89, 164,

139; "Animula," 75; "Andrew Marvell," 47–8; *Ash Wednesday*, 1; "Baudelaire," 2, 41; "Burbank With a Baedecker: Bleistein With a Cigar," 40; "Burnt Norton," 98–9; *Clark Lectures on Metaphysical Poetry*, 65, 149–50; *The Cocktail Party*, 9, 10, 110–22, 162; "The Dry Salvages," 99–100; "East Coker," 101, 104, 107; *For Lancelot Andrewes*, 56, 58; *Four Quartets*, 9, 10, 97–108, 109, 124, 162; "The Frontiers of Criticism," 110; "Goethe as the Sage," 125–6; "Hamlet," 2, 127; *The Hollow Men*, 53, 75; "Hommage a Charles Maurras," 130–1; *The Idea of a Christian Society*, 10, 45, 87–93, 101, 111, 113, 114, 163; "John Bramhall," 141; "Journey of the Magi," 75–6; "King Bolo and His Great Black Queen," 121; "Little Gidding," 97–8, 99–100, 104–7; "Leibnitz's Monads and Bradley's Finite Centers, 39, 61, 62; *The Love Song of J. Alfred Prufrock*, 35, 75; "Love Song of St. Sebastian," 121; "The Metaphysical Poets," 46–7; "Milton I," 123–4; "Milton II," 124–5, 183n20; *Murder in the Cathedral*, 9, 80–3, 90, 113, 121; *Notes Towards the Definition of Culture*, 10, 45, 93–7, 110, 111, 140, 163; "Poetry and Propaganda," 71–3; *Preludes*, 76; "Religion and Literature," 74; *The Rock*, 78–81; *The Sacred Wood*, 129; "Second Thoughts about Humanism," 58; "A Song For Simeon," 77; "Sweeney Among the Nightingales," 40; "Sweeney Erect," 40; *Syllabus of a Course of Six Lectures on Modern French*

Literature, 37–9; *To Criticize the Critic,* 127, 130; "Tradition and the Individual Talent," 62, 106, 134, 163; *The Use of Poetry and the Use of Criticism,* 110; "What is a Classic?" 125–6; "William Blake," 48–50; *The Waste Land,* 9, 10, 52, 41–4, 60, 62, 102, 109, 121, 160, 162;
elitism, 28, 78; Eliot's faith in, 7, 82, 85–6, 89–97, 107, 114–21
Elyot, Thomas, 101–3; *The Governour,* 102
Emerson, Ralph Waldo, 5
Empedocles, 103
Engels, Friedrich, 3, 4, 6, 169*n*15
English Civil War, 105, 124, 130, 157, 158
enlightenment, 12–15, 21, 22, 163
Epicurus, 72

fascism, 45, 58, 85, 86, 88
Feuerbach, Ludwig, 17
Fichte, Johann Gottlieb, 21, 95; *Reden an die deutsche Nation,* 21
Foucault, Michel, 6–7
Franco, Francisco, 11, 16, 86
Frankfurt School, 91
Frazer, Sir James, 60
French Revolution, 8, 11–12, 14–19, 22, 128, 158, 161, 163
Freud, Sigmund, 43, 68, 117
Frost, Robert, 175*n*38
Frye, Northrop, 105
Furet, François, *Interpreting the French Revolution,* 11

Galileo, 147
Gardner, Helen, 103
Geertz, Clifford, 4
George Eliot, *see* Eliot, George
Gide, André: *La porte étroite,* 122
Goethe, Johann Wolfgang von, 71–2, 125–6, 144

Gourmont, Rémy de, 129
Grierson, Sir Herbert, 46

Hardy, Thomas, 66
Harrison, John: *The Reactionaries,* 10
Hartley, David, 144
Hegel, Georg Wilhelm Friedrich, 19, 82
Heidegger, Martin, 151
Herbert, Edward Lord Cherbury 46
heresy, 10, 54, 60–6, 84, 88, 100, 123, 162
Herf, Jeffrey: *Reactionary Modernism,* 10
Hinduism, 99
historical materialism, 6
Hitler, Adolf, 11, 68, 85, 88
Hobbes, Thomas, 141–5, 158
Hobsbawm, Eric, 90
Hopkins, Charles Manley, 155
Hulme, T. E., 7, 36–7, 48, 53, 122, 161; *Speculations,* 7, 36–7, 53
Hume, David, 144
Husserl, Edmund, 70
Huxley, Aldous, 74

icon, 153–5, 159
ideology, 36, 49, 51–2, 88, 93, 143, 163; history of term, 3–10
I'll Take My Stand, 139
individualism, 6, 23–4, 29, 33, 66, 108, 139, 161; associated with Rousseau, 9, 15, 17, 22
International Journal of Ethics, 39

Jacobins, 18
James I, 102
Jesus (Christ), 16, 17, 24, 27
Johnson, Samuel, 48, 123, 142–3, 149, 151–2; *Rasselas,* 42
Joyce, James, 1, 40, 60, 155; *Ulysses,* 40, 60, 63
Jünger, Ernst, 7

Keats, John, 49, 125
Knight, Wilson, 127

Kojecky, Roger, 86
Krieger, Murray, 148

La Bruyère, Jean de, 125
Laforque, Jules, 2
La Rochefoucauld, Duc François de, 19, 125
Lasserre, Pierre, 20, 30–1, 37; *Le Romantisme français*, 30
Latini, Brunetto, 27
La Tour du Pin, Rene de, 20
Lawrence, D. H., 48, 65–6, 74–5, 102, 115, 138, 163–4
Leavis, F. R., 134
Lebensphilosophie, 163
Leibnitz, Gottfried Wilhelm von, 39, 61, 62
Lenin, V. I., 7
Levenson, Michael: *A Genealogy of Modernism*, 10
Lewis, Wyndham, 1
liberalism, 16–18, 21, 45, 53, 61, 64, 66, 88, 101
Locke, John, 143
Longenbach, James: *The Modernist Poetics of History*, 10
Louis XIV, 19, 24
Louis XVI, 16
Löwe, Adolf, 85, 179n3
Lucretius, 26, 71–3; *De rerum naturae*, 26
Ludovici, Anthony, 55, 56; *A Defense of Conservatism*, 55
Lukács, Georg, 150–1
Luther, Martin, 21, 24, 54

Machiavelli, Niccolo, 27, 43, 54–5, 92, 164
Maistre, Joseph de 10, 12–18, 21, 22, 25–6, 34, 57, 94, 161, 163
Mannheim, Karl, 3–6, 85, 96, 115, 168–9n9, 179n3; *Ideology and Utopia*, 4
Maritain, Jacques, 53–4, 57, 85, 114, 117, 155; *Réflexions sur l'intelligence*, 53; *Une opinion sur*

Charles Maurras et le devoir des catholiques, 54
Marvell, Andrew, 43, 47–8
Marx, Karl, 3–6, 17, 25, 64, 93, 118
Marxism, 4, 11
Massis, Henri, 29
Maurras, Charles, 10, 11, 17–18, 84, 95, 96; condemnation by Vatican, 9, 53–9, 161, 172–3n64; Eliot's estimation of, 36, 56–8, 130–2; evolution of thought, 21–30; influence on Eliot, 3, 7–9, 15, 20, 26, 28, 34, 36–7, 43, 52, 56–9, 60–4, 68, 75, 85, 89, 92, 107–8, 116, 122, 127–30, 138, 140, 161–2; influence on Babbitt, 30–4; and New Criticism, 146, 157–9; works by: *L'Avenir de l'intelligence*, 28, 36, 53, 127; *Enquête sur la monarchie*, 28, see also *Action française*
Menand, Louis: *Discovering Modernism*, 10
metaphysical poetry, 2, 46–8, 51, 65, 127, 141–3, 145, 149, 152–3
Mill, John Stewart, 61
Milton, John, 2, 48, 50, 72, 105, 123–7, 129–30; *Paradise Lost*, 123
Monist, 39, 61
Moot, The, 85–6, 89
More, Paul Elmer, 8, 63, 160
Morris, Charles: *Encyclopedia of Unified Science*, 153
multiculturalism, 1
Murry, Middleton, 74
Mussolini, 11, 57
myth, 7–8, 42–3, 60, 64, 80, 90–2, 118, 153

Nation, 33
New Criticism, 1, 10, 51–2, 67, 133–59, 160, 162

New Statesman, 39
Nietzsche, Friedrich, 6, 13, 69, 86, 163
Nolte, Ernst, 28
North, Michael: *The Political Aesthetic of Yeats, Eliot and Pound*, 10
Nouvelle Revue Française, 3, 36

objective correlative, 2, 127, 157
Original Sin, 7, 12, 16, 36–8, 42–4, 54, 122, 158, 161
orthodoxy, 10, 12, 60, 64–6, 68, 72, 75–6, 80–4, 89–92, 127, 162
Orwell, George, 164

Palmer, Richard, 136
Paris Commune, 16
Perl, Jeffrey, 167–8n3
Plato, 5, 23, 90, 115, 132, 150, 181n40; *Theaetetus*, 5
Pope, Alexander, 17, 48, 143, 151; *Essay on Man*, 143
postmodernism, 1
Pound, Ezra, 1, 10, 36, 109, 124, 160
Praz, Mario, 50
propaganda, 69–73, 79, 92
Protestantism, 9, 66, 139, 145; Eliot's opposition to, 44, 56, 72, 79, 116, 122; French conservative opposition to, 8, 14, 92 5, 161
Puritans, 79, 99, 105, 124

Racine, Jean Baptiste, 19, 77
Ransom, John Crowe, 67, 133, 137–40, 144–7, 150–5; *The New Criticism*, 133; *The World's Body*, 150, 153
regionalism, 140
Renan, Ernest, 16–21, 27; *La Vie de Jésus*, 15
Richards, I. A., 43, 68–70, 73, 134, 136, 146–8, 153; *Science and Poetry*, 69

Ricks, Christopher: *T. S. Eliot and Prejudice*, 41
Rilke, Rainer Maria, 187–8n61
ritual, 25, 42–4, 52, 78, 107, 109, 138
romanticism, 10, 18, 30–3, 65–6, 95, 128, 145–6, 163; Eliot's opposition to, 37–8, 49–52, 139, 161–2
Rousseau, Jean-Jacques, 30–3, 86; Eliot's opposition to, 37–9, 48, 127; French conservative opposition to, 9, 14–24, 163; *Confessions*, 25; *Héloïse*, 25
Russian Revolution, 45

St. Victor, Richard of, 65
Santayana, George, 31
Sartre, Jean Paul, 111, 114; *No Exit*, 111
Schelling, Friedrich Wilhelm Josef von, 95
Schwartz, Sanford: *The Matrix of Modernism*, 10
science, 16, 38, 49, 69, 136–9, 142, 145, 147, 153, 156
Shaftesbury, First Earl of, 143–4
Shakespeare, William, 2, 19, 48, 69, 71, 77, 126–7; *Antony and Cleopatra*, 127; *Coriolanus*, 127; *Hamlet*, 2, 127; *Timon*, 127
Shaw, George Bernard: *Heartbreak House*, 119
Shelley, Percy Bysshe, 49–50, 53, 71–2, 87, 125–7, 145; *The Triumph of Life*, 126
Smith, Adam, 91
Sophocles: *Antigone*, 82
Sorel, Georges, 7–8, 36, 53, 64; *Reflections on Violence*, 7, 52–3, 64, 111, 169n16, 169–70n19
Spanish Civil War, 86
Spender, Stephen, 42, 53
Spinoza, Benedict (Baruch), 39
Staël, Madame de, 21, 30
Stalin, Joseph, 88

Stevens, Wallace: "Sea Surface Full of Clouds," 147
Swift, Jonathan, 48, 148

Tacitus, 21
Taine, Hippolyte, 11, 18–22; *Histoire de la littérature anglaise,* 20
Tate, Allen, 67, 134, 137, 139–40, 144, 147, 150, 155–6
Tennyson, Alfred, 46, 157
Theresa, St., 65
Thomas Aquinas, St., 70, 80, 81, 82, 83, 101, 102, 141
Tillyard, E. M. W., 130
Times Literary Supplement, 46

Vatican, The, 8, 9, 34, 45, 53, 56, 65, 128, 131, 161
Vauvenargues, Marquis de, 125–6
Vichy Government, 11, 84
Virgil, 27, 36, 42, 44, 100, 130; *Aeneid,* 27
Voltaire: *Candide,* 39

Ward, Leo, 56–7
Warren, Robert Penn, 67, 134–5, 139
Wellek, René, 51, 72, 155
Weston, Jesse, 42, 60; *From Ritual to Romance,* 42
Whitehead, Alfred North, 71
Whitman, Walt, 5, 146
Williams, Raymond, 97
Wilson, Edmund, 135
Wimsatt, William, 9, 134, 136, 142–4, 154–5, 158; "The Affective Fallacy," 9, 136, 154, 158; "The Intentional Fallacy," 136, 157; *Literary Criticism,* 155; *The Verbal Icon,* 154
Winters, Yvor, 133–4, 141, 143–6, 148, 156, 157, 158
Woods, James Haughton, 2
Woolf, Virginia, 1
Wordsworth, William, 49, 51, 71, 146, 186–7n42
Worth, Katherine, 81

Continued from the front of the book

65. Thomas Strychacz, *Modernism, Mass Culture, and Professionalism*
64. Elisa New, *The Regenerate Lyric: Theology and Innovation in American Poetry*
63. Edwin S. Redkey, *A Grand Army of Black Men: Letters from African-American Soldiers in the Union Army, 1861–1865*
62. Victoria Harrison, *Elizabeth Bishop's Poetics of Intimacy*
61. Edwin Sill Fussell, *The Catholic Side of Henry James*
60. Thomas Gustafson, *Representative Words: Politics, Literature, and the American Language, 1776–1865*
59. Peter Quartermain, *Disjunctive Poetics: From Gertrude Stein and Louis Zukovsky to Susan Howe*
58. Paul Giles, *American Catholic Arts and Fictions: Culture, Ideology, Aesthetics*
57. Ann-Janine Morey, *Religion and Sexuality in American Literature*
56. Philip M. Weinstein, *Faulkner's Subject: A Cosmos No One Owns*
55. Stephen Fender, *Sea Changes: British Emigration and American Literature*
54. Peter Stoneley, *Mark Twain and the Feminine Aesthetic*
53. Joel Porte, *In Respect to Egotism: Studies in American Romantic Writing*
52. Charles Swann, *Nathaniel Hawthorne: Tradition and Revolution*
51. Ronald Bush (ed.), *T. S. Eliot: The Modernist in History*
50. Russell Goodman, *American Philosophy and the Romantic Tradition*
49. Eric J. Sundquist (ed.), *Frederick Douglass: New Literary and Historical Essays*
48. Susan Stanford Friedman, *Penelope's Web: Gender, Modernity, H.D.'s Fiction*
47. Timothy Redman, *Ezra Pound and Italian Fascism*
46. Ezra Greenspan, *Walt Whitman and the American Reader*
45. Michael Oriard, *Sporting with the Gods: The Rhetoric of Play and Game in American Culture*
44. Stephen Fredman, *Poet's Prose: The Crisis in American Verse, Second Edition*
43. David C. Miller, *Dark Eden: The Swamp in Nineteenth-Century American Culture*
42. Susan K. Harris, *19th-Century American Women's Novels: Interpretive Strategies*
41. Susan Manning, *The Puritan Provincial Vision: Scottish and American Literature in the Nineteenth Century*
40. Richard Godden, *Fictions of Capital: Essays on the American Novel from James to Mailer*
39. John Limon, *The Place of Fiction in the Time of Science: A Disciplinary History of American Writing*
38. Douglas Anderson, *A House Undivided: Domesticity and Community in American Literature*
37. Charles Altieri, *Painterly Abstraction in Modernist American Poetry*
36. John P. McWilliams, Jr., *The American Epic: Transforming a Genre, 1770–1860*
35. Michael Davidson, *The San Francisco Renaissance: Poetics and Community at Mid-Century*
34. Eric Sigg, *The American T. S. Eliot: A Study of the Early Writings*

33. Robert S. Levine, *Conspiracy and Romance: Studies in Brockden Brown, Cooper, Hawthorne, and Melville*
32. Alfred Habegger, *Henry James and the "Woman Business"*
31. Tony Tanner, *Scenes of Nature, Signs of Man*
30. David Halliburton, *The Color of the Sky: A Study of Stephen Crane*
29. Steven Gould Axelrod and Helen Deese (eds.), *Robert Lowell: Essays on the Poetry*
28. Robert Lawson-Peebles, *Landscape and Written Expression in Revolutionary America: The World Turned Upside Down*
27. Warren Motley, *The American Abraham: James Fenimore Cooper and the Frontier Patriarch*
26. Lynn Keller, *Re-making it New: Contemporary American Poetry and the Modernist Tradition*
25. Margaret Holley, *The Poetry of Marianne Moore: A Study in Voice and Value*
24. Lothar Hönnighausen, *William Faulkner: The Art of Stylization in His Early Graphic and Literary Work*
23. George Dekker, *The American Historical Romance*
22. Brenda Murphy, *American Realism and American Drama, 1880–1940*
21. Brook Thomas, *Cross-examinations of Law and Literature: Cooper, Hawthorne and Melville*
20. Jerome Loving, *Emily Dickinson: The Poet on the Second Story*
19. Richard Gray, *Writing the South; Ideas of an American Region*
18. Karen E. Rowe, *Saint and Singer: Edward Taylor's Typology and the Poetics of Meditation*
17. Ann Kibbey, *The Interpretation of Material Shapes in Puritanism: A Study of Rhetoric, Prejudice, and Violence*
16. Sacvan Bercovitch and Myra Jehlen (eds.), *Ideology and Classic American Literature*
15. Lawrence Buell, *New England Literary Culture: From Revolution through Renaissance*
14. Paul Giles, *Hart Crane: The Contexts of "The Bridge"*
13. Albert Gelpi (ed.), *Wallace Stevens: The Poetics of Modernism*
12. Albert J. von Frank, *The Sacred Game: Provincialism and Frontier Consciousness in American Literature, 1630–1860*
11. David Wyatt, *The Fall into Eden: Landscape and Imagination in California*
10. Elizabeth McKinsey, *Niagara Falls: Icon of the American Sublime*
9. Barton Levi St. Armand, *Emily Dickinson and Her Culture: The Soul's Society*
8. Mitchell Breitwieser, *Cotton Mather and Benjamin Franklin: The Price of Representative Personality*
7. Peter Conn, *The Divided Mind: Ideology and Imagination in America, 1898–1917*
6. Marjorie Perloff, *The Dance of the Intellect: Studies in Poetry of the Pound Tradition*

The following titles are out of print

5. Stephen Fredman, *Poet's Prose: The Crisis in American Verse*, first edition
4. Patricia Caldwell, *The Puritan Conversion Narrative: The Beginnings of American Expression*

3. John McWilliams, Jr., *Hawthorne, Melville, and the American Character: A Looking-Glass Business*
2. Charles Altieri, *Self and Sensibility in Contemporary American Poetry*
1. Robert Zaller, *The Cliffs of Solitude: A Reading of Robinson Jeffers*